oring Series

A FalconGuide® to California's Missions and Presidios

A Guide to Exploring California's Spanish and Mexican Legacy

Tracy Salcedo-Chourré

FALCON GUIDES®

GUILFORD, CONNECTICUT
HELENA, MONTANA

AN IMPRINT OF THE GLOBE PEQUOT PRESS

FALCONGUIDES®

Copyright © 2005 Morris Book Publishing, LLC

FalconGuides is an imprint of The Globe Pequot Press.
Falcon and FalconGuides are registered trademarks of Morris Book Publishing, LLC.

Maps by Stephen Stringall © Morris Book Publishing, LLC
See page 231 for a list of photo credits.

Library of Congress Cataloging-in-Publication Data
Salcedo-Chourré, Tracy.
  A Falcon guide to California's missions and presidios : a guide to exploring California's Spanish and Mexican legacy / Tracy Salcedo-Chourré.
    p. cm. – (Exploring series)
  Includes bibliographical references and index.
  ISBN 978-0-7627-2793-3
    1. Spanish mission buildings—California—Guidebooks. 2. Fortification—California—Guidebooks. 3. Historic buildings—California—Guidebooks. 4. Historic sites—California—Guidebooks. 5. California—Guidebooks. 6. California—History, Local. 7. California—History—To 1846. I. Title. II. Series.

F862.S216 2004
979.4'01—dc22

2004054156

Manufactured in the United States of America
First Edition/Second Printing

For Jesse and Cruz, who studied "Mission San Luis Archipelago"
and Mission San "It starts with a C, and it's got a really long name"
while I was researching this book.
And for my Nana, the most devout Catholic I have known.

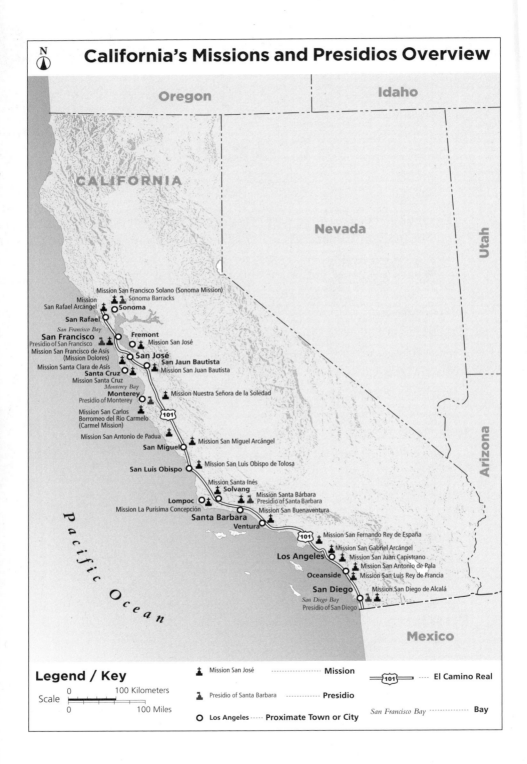

California's Missions and Presidios Overview

N

Oregon   Idaho

CALIFORNIA

Nevada

Utah

Arizona

Mission San Francisco Solano (Sonoma Mission)
Sonoma Barracks
Mission San Rafael Arcángel
San Rafael
San Francisco Bay
San Francisco
Presidio of San Francisco
Mission San Francisco de Asís (Mission Dolores)
Mission Santa Clara de Asís
Santa Cruz
Mission Santa Cruz
Fremont
Mission San José
San José
San Jaun Bautista
Mission San Juan Bautista
Monterey Bay
Monterey
Presidio of Monterey
Mission Nuestra Señora de la Soledad
Mission San Carlos Borromeo del Río Carmelo (Carmel Mission)
Mission San Antonio de Padua
101
San Miguel
Mission San Miguel Arcángel
San Luis Obispo
Mission San Luis Obispo de Tolosa
Mission Santa Inés
Solvang
Lompoc
Mission Santa Bárbara
Presidio of Santa Barbara
Mission La Purísima Concepción
Santa Barbara
Mission San Buenaventura
Ventura
101
Mission San Fernando Rey de España
Mission San Gabriel Arcángel
Los Angeles
Mission San Juan Capistrano
Mission San Antonio de Pala
Oceanside
Mission San Luis Rey de Francia
San Diego
Mission San Diego de Alcalá
San Diego Bay
Presidio of San Diego

Pacific Ocean

Mexico

Legend / Key

Scale
0   100 Kilometers
0   100 Miles

Mission San José ····· **Mission**

Presidio of Santa Barbara ····· **Presidio**

Los Angeles ····· **Proximate Town or City**

101 ····· **El Camino Real**

San Francisco Bay ····· **Bay**

Contents

Acknowledgments

I have culled historical information about California's missions and presidios from a cornucopia of books, articles, pamphlets, and Web sites (many listed in the appendix of this guide), and I am indebted to the authors of these resources.

I'm most appreciative of the information imparted by California State Parks employees and docents at those missions and presidios managed by the parks department. Likewise, there were many historians and local experts whom I consulted or who consented to check information for accuracy, among them Janet Bartel, Alfred Sanchez, Robert Shafer, Barbara Baker, Monsignor Weber at Mission San Fernando Rey de España, Father Virgil Cordano of Mission Santa Bárbara, Father John Gini at Mission San Antonio de Padua, Dan Weber, Nick Bianchi, Richard Menn, Charlie White, Monsignor O'Brien at Mission San Buenaventura, Friar Bill Short at Mission San Miguel Arcángel, Father Fitz-Henry at Mission San Juan Bautista, Karma Graham, Dolores Firenz, Andrew Galvan, Paul Coddington, Jim Danaher, Jim Conway, and Will Elder.

Thanks to Kelly, Peter, Dylan, and Ellen Knappe for opening the doors of their home (okay, their motor home) to me during my stay in Santa Barbara; likewise Sandy, Greg, and Emily Mattson, and my niece Rebecca Chourré and her husband, Justin.

Finally, and forever, I am grateful to my family, especially my sons, Jesse, Cruz, and Penn, who are always willing to adventure with me, and to my impossibly patient husband, Martin.

Map Legend

TRANSPORTATION

680	Interstate Freeway
101	Interstate Freeway
	Freeway Interchange
84	State Highway
J2	Other Paved Routes
	Main City Street
	Other City Street
	Trails and Private Roads
	Railroad/Light Rail

HYDROLOGY

O'Neil Lake	Lakes/Reservoirs
	Ocean
	Stream
	Wetlands

FILLS

Palomar Mountain State Park	Park
Air Force Base	Military Base

ORIENTATION / SCALE

N

0   5   10km

5   10 mi.

SYMBOLOGY

(Featured Items)

⚓	⚓	Mission/Featured Mission
⚒	⚒	Presidio/Featured Presidio

(Other Symbols)

✈	Airport
⚲	Beach
🚌	Bus Stop
△	Campground
♠	Church
🏫	College/University
⚖	Courthouse
◎ Fallbrook	City/Town
⛳	Golf Course
⚔	Historic Site (Military)
✛	Hospital
❷	Information Center
⚓	Marina/Port
🏛	Museum
Sugarloaf Peak ▲	Peak/Mountain
✳	Playground
▪	Point of Interest
🅿	Recreation Area Parking
⚑	School
◯	Sports Field/Stadium
⚑	State Park
⌒	Tunnel
👁	Vista/Scenic View
✦	Wildlife Area

Introduction

Father Junípero Serra presides over an undeveloped stretch of Interstate 280 just south of San Francisco. In the form of a huge, rather cheesy statue, the Franciscan friar credited with establishing California's mission system bestows a stony blessing on all who speed by. Every time I headed south from my Sonoma home to another mission town, I'd pass under his upraised hand and be reminded of another Serra, one that has disappeared from the landscape, which my family would pass each time we left our little tract home in Daly City to head into San Francisco. That statue was slender and white, holy and lofty, and it is in my memory of this that I see most clearly the man who walked the coast of California on a mission.

When I grew older, I was briefly fascinated with Serra and the missions he established on the California frontier—a fascination very selfish in that it grew from the knowledge that I'd been baptized in Mission Dolores. No ordinary Catholic church for me, and no ordinary hero, either. Mine was the priest who, according to legend, walked in the wilderness saving wayward Indians and their poor children, spreading peace and prosperity wherever he went.

As I grew older, I moved on to more prosaic fascinations—teen rock idols, scary movies, surfers—but the story of Serra and the missions, like that of the Gold Rush, the San Francisco Earthquake, Ishi the last wild Indian in California, and John Muir's Yosemite, remained a part of me, an element of identity, part of a history unique to those of us born in the Golden State.

The legacy of the missions, which as a girl I thought was unsullied, is bloodied by the understanding that the Franciscan friars didn't, in fact, save California's Indians—they helped obliterate them. The missionaries, like other religious, philosophical, and political zealots, believed they could improve the lives of the Natives by forcing their conversion, blinded to the sovereignty of the others by righteousness. The process destroyed something of great value. It's a process I regret and dislike, but one that persists into modern times.

I may hate the destruction wreaked on indigenous populations by Catholicism, but I can't help but be moved by the ceremonies and faith that inspire good Christians. On the day I toured Mission Dolores, a pretty little girl with thick black curls and huge brown eyes was being baptized, held securely in the arms of her godfather, her white dress spilling over the sleeve of his dark dress suit, and her little feet in white patent leather dangling by his side. Decades before, I had been that child . . .

In Mission San Antonio de Pala, the congregation assembled for a Sunday Mass spilled out onto the veranda, a gaily dressed population of Spanish-speaking worshipers responding to ritual with hands upraised. In Mission Santa Clara de Asís, the church was decorated with white ribbons and white flowers, both for Easter and for a wedding. As I wandered up and down the nave, making notes and snapping pictures, the pews filled with the families of the betrothed, impatient eyes turned toward the heavy doors at the back of the church where the bride would soon appear. At Mission San Buenaventura it was a funeral, the voice of a daughter high-pitched and disorganized as she eulogized her mother.

But I was most moved when the churches were empty and echoing. It was then that I most powerfully felt the magic of the religion that built them and sustained them for more than two centuries. It was in the empty churches that I fell back into practices I'd not performed in all my adult life: blessing myself with holy water, crossing myself before sitting in a pew, lighting votives for those in my life I knew needed prayers. I will never wholeheartedly embrace the church into which I was baptized, but in exploring these missions, I came to understand a little better the beauty and power of Catholicism.

I am not a historian, nor am I a practicing Catholic. My interpretations of these two much larger studies are simply that—my own, offered humbly and with the greatest respect to those whose knowledge and faith far exceed my own.

California's Missions and Presidios describes what can be found on the ground at the twenty-one historic missions and four presidios built in California beginning in 1769, as well as exploring their history in brief. It also covers the practical aspects of visiting California's missions and presidios, from driving directions to schedules of Masses and special events. The entries are listed geographically, from south to north.

Historical Information

Though this is a guidebook, not a history, I would have been remiss to write about the sites without including a historical perspective. What I include has been gleaned from literature provided at the missions themselves and from more thorough histories listed in the bibliography.

Religious Interpretation

My short and youthful journey through the mysteries of Catholicism endowed me with a residual reverence for all that is Catholic about the missions, but left me with only the crudest understanding of the practical and ritual workings of a modern church, much less a historic one. Again, I have relied upon materials provided by the missions and within historical sources to flesh out ecumenical references.

Maps

In addition to written driving directions included in each site description, the maps that have been provided should ensure that you reach each mission and presidio with relative ease.

Other Mission-Era Historic Sites

In addition to what might be called the core missions and presidios, I've included brief descriptions of a few other sites—the *asistencias* (auxiliary missions) at Rancho San Bernardino in Redlands and in the small town of Pala, San Carlos Cathedral in Monterey, San Juan Bautista State Park, and the Sonoma Barracks—either because of their proximity to one of the star sites, or because they illustrate an integral aspect of mission-era life. You will find other mission-era sites—California is littered with ranchos, adobes, casas, *asistencias*, and battle sites—listed in the sections titled Nearby Points of Interest, which follow some mission and presidio descriptions.

Names and Dates

The names of some of the explorers, missionaries, and other persons and places integral to the mission story appear in various texts with different spellings. The spellings included here are those that appear most consistently in the various sources.

Dates of significant events also, on rare occasion, vary according to the source. When that has occurred, I've used the date common to the most sources.

You'll find a glossary at the back of this book defining some of the more common mission- and presidio-related terms used, both Spanish and English.

California's Spanish and Mexican Legacy

These days California is a trendsetter, a place where things happen first, the place to be. But in the Age of Exploration, when European kingdoms were colonizing new and exotic lands, California was swathed in obscurity, overshadowed by flashy cultures to the south that were rich in currencies the conquerors understood: slaves and gold.

It was, of course, only a matter of time before California would come into its own—especially in terms of gold. But for more than two centuries after Juan Rodriguez Cabrillo claimed it for Spain in 1542, California was neglected. Sebastian Vizcaino sailed north along the coast in 1602, bestowing names on landmarks that have endured into modern times, but Spain didn't bother to secure its claims to California in any more substantial way during those long years. It focused, instead, on explorations in Florida and along the coast of the Gulf of Mexico, in the American Southwest, and in Mexico. But such riches as were found by Hernán Cortés among the Aztecs of central Mexico and by Francisco Pizarro in the Peruvian cities of the Incas were not forthcoming along the northern boundaries of New Spain (Mexico).

There were no rumors of fountains of youth or cities of gold to lure the Spanish into California, and thus, according to historian David J. Weber, California was deemed too costly to settle, with an uncertain return on Spanish investment. Still, the region did possess desirable attributes. Key among them was the fact that harbors on the coast, such as those at San Diego, Monterey, and San Francisco, could serve as sites where Spanish galleons with holds full of treasure from the Philippines and other eastern ports could reprovision. And there was a population of indigenous people to be saved and exploited.

It wasn't until the Russians began to expand their fur trade south down the Pacific coast from strongholds in Alaska, eventually establishing Fort Ross an unsettling 50 miles northwest of Sonoma, that the Spanish were spurred to action in California. Spanish claims to the region would withstand a number of challenges. Englishman Francis Drake, for instance, landed his *Golden Hind* in a California bay (the exact location is a matter of some controversy) in 1579 and then claimed both bay and surroundings for England. Later the Americans supplanted the English threat to Spanish holdings in what would become the southeastern United States, then pushed relentlessly westward over a continent that Manifest Destiny told them was theirs.

Carlos III of Spain dispatched the first expedition into Alta California in 1769, initiating a relatively short-lived Spanish domination of the region that would have long-lived effects. At that time the area roughly encompassing today's modern state of California was known as Alta (or Upper) California. This name distinguished it from Baja (or Lower) California, which is currently part of modern-day Mexico. Visitador-General José de Galvez, agent for the king in the viceroyalty of New Spain, was the political force behind the colonization effort; Gaspar de Portolá, who would later discover San Francisco Bay, and Junípero Serra, the zealous Franciscan friar who would later be beatified for his missionary efforts in California, were the expedition's leaders. By land and by sea the Spaniards came. The *San Carlos* and the *San Antonio* dropped anchor in San Diego Bay in the spring of 1769, and the two overland contingents—one led by Fernando de Rivera y Moncada and the second by Portolá and Serra—arrived in the summer of that same year. The California Indian was no longer alone in the future Golden State; the Spanish era was under way.

Military might had previously dominated Spanish imperial success in the New World, exemplified by the bloody conquests of Cortés and Pizarro. But in the northern reaches of New Spain, holy men would wage an equally successful coup—not bloodless, but arguably less violent.

The intent of the small army of Franciscan missionaries who, over the next fifty years or so, built the missions that line California's coast was to manage those missions for ten years, converting to Catholicism the Natives who lived in neighboring *rancherias* and teaching them "civilized" ways to live, then return the missions and their holdings to the indigenous people. This secularization process never occurred. The missions remained in the hands of invaders—soldier, friar, settler; Spanish, Mexican, American—into modern times. And though the missionaries and those who followed them claimed the Indians were never ready to resume managing their own lives, it's clear that the land they had lived on for centuries had become too valuable to be returned.

The Missions

California's missions are amazingly diverse, which is remarkable given that they grew out of a fairly regimented design. What remains on the landscape today, with but a few exceptions, doesn't clearly demonstrate that uniformity; instead, each mission's modern setting gives it an individuality further augmented by subtle differences in original decoration and design. Still, the underlying pattern is obvious to those who visit the missions, stand in their long, narrow naves, and study historical drawings and models.

Though missions throughout New Spain often covered large tracts of land, their core components, for the most part, were laid out as quadrangles. Within

Mission San Luis Rey de Francia was one of the most productive and beautiful missions erected in Alta California.

these quads, or within close proximity to them, an ultimately self-sufficient village was created, with all the facilities needed to sustain the temporal and spiritual needs of those who lived within.

The church served as the cornerstone of the mission quadrangle, the loftiest structure within the plan. The *convento* (padres' quarters)—often fronted by an arcade—stretched off to one side. The low structures that made up the remaining sides of the quadrangle housed workshops (weaving rooms, kitchens, carpenter's shops, and the like), storerooms, dormitories (with separate quarters for unmarried Indian women), quarters for the *mayordomo*, and soldiers' barracks. Tanneries, soap- and candle-making facilities, blacksmith's shops, and infirmaries might also have been housed within the wings of the quad or in separate structures built outside it. The *camposanto* (cemetery) was usually laid out along the outside wall of the church.

Farther flung from the quad, missionaries and their Indian laborers established and maintained croplands, orchards, and vineyards, and built springhouses, reservoirs, aqueducts, and *lavanderias* (laundries). Mission sites were selected based on the accessibility of a good water supply, the fertility of the land, and proximity to a population of Natives who could be converted to Catholicism and incorporated into the mission workforce. Thus, Indian villages, or *rancherias*, often fell within the larger boundaries of the missions, and sometimes were constructed right outside the walls of the quadrangle.

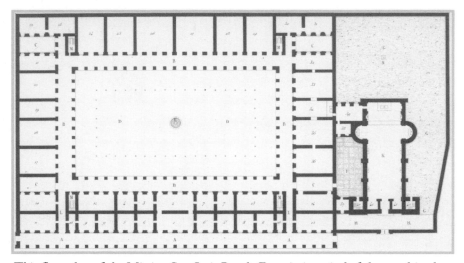

This floor plan of the Mission San Luis Rey de Francia is typical of that used in the creation of nearly every California mission, with the church anchoring one side of a large quadrangle in which dormitories, kitchens, and workrooms were housed.

As a rule, a newly established mission began as a simple construction of wood and mud. Often these chapels and enclosures succumbed to flood or fire; regardless, they were invariably replaced by more permanent adobe structures. The adobe bricks used in their construction were composed of clay, straw, and manure, which barefoot neophytes mixed with their feet, and which were cured in the sun. The forms used for these tiles can be seen in several mission museums, as can the familiar curved roof tiles and the forms used to make them.

Using adobes, tiles, and sometimes fired brick, neophytes under the direction of the padres constructed long, narrow churches and chapels, with towering ceilings and small windows perched high in the thick walls. Often the width of the church's nave was determined by the length of the timbers harvested from local forests to support the lofty roofs. The sanctuary was usually elevated and separated from the nave by a communion rail. Pulpits mounted on the walls of some churches and chapels further elevated the priest from his congregation; one mission docent noted that these pulpits raised the celebrant above the dust and flies that sometimes swarmed among the congregants.

The mission bells, the stuff of legend and song, were usually hung in *campanarios*—walls punched with arches in which the bells were hung—or in campaniles (bell towers). The *campanarios* housed as many as six bells, most cast in Spain or Mexico and shipped to the missions of Alta California; the campaniles held as many as nine bells. In historical times the bells rang for Masses and meals, to warn of danger, for fiestas and siestas, for weddings and baptisms and funerals.

Nary a mission quadrangle has survived intact into modern times, but at a few of the missions—notably San Antonio de Padua and La Purísima Concepción—visitors can get a feel for what such an enclosure encompassed and fostered.

The Presidios

The soldiers who built and manned Alta California's four royal Spanish presidios play second fiddle to missionaries in the minds of most casual mission-era enthusiasts, but they were as integral to shaping the region's cultural and political landscape at the time as were the padres. They were Spain's first line of defense against threats posed by other imperial powers—England, France, and Russia—and against the indigenous populations of the lands to which the Spaniards laid claim.

The primary task of the Spanish soldiers was to establish a political and military presence in Alta California, a duty they executed successfully, if rather haphazardly. During more than fifty years of Spanish oversight, they built the presidios and from them engaged in a handful of battles against both Indian insurgencies and foreign invaders. Their performances weren't stellar—they failed to protect the fledgling Mission San Diego de Alcalá from destruction in 1775, and abandoned the Presidio of Monterey to the ravages of privateer Hippolyte Bouchard in 1818. Still, the *soldados de cuera*—called leatherjackets because they wore armor composed of many layers of deerskin to repel Indian arrows—performed well enough to keep the Indian population from ousting the colonials. In *The California Missions*, a popular pictorial guide published by Sunset, the authors write, "That the mission guard was effective is certainly proven by the fact that a mere 300 soldiers, dispersed over 650 miles, were able to keep in check an Indian population of 100,000."

Spanish *soldados* were a flexible bunch. In addition to providing protection for residents of the missions and presidios, they served as explorers, escorts, and mail carriers; helped establish the pueblos at San José (1777) and Los Angeles (1781); and worked as vaqueros (cowboys), farmers, tanners, smiths, potters, and carpenters. They also were enlisted to teach neophytes these various trades.

Relations between the missionaries and the military were strained during most of the mission era. Power, of course, was the source of the conflict—power to control the Native population, power to control the fruits teased from the fertile earth. On occasion the conflicts proved insurmountable: When soldiers were discovered abusing neophyte women, thus incurring the wrath of the Franciscans, the padres moved their missions—San Diego de Alcalá and San Carlos Borromeo—away from the presidios they'd been established in conjunction with. The reluctance of Spanish governors to expand the mission chain

Louis Choris created this view of the Presidio of San Francisco with soldiers on horseback as it appeared in 1815.

was another source of conflict: When Governor Pedro Fages held up the process, Junípero Serra traveled to Mexico City to appeal to the viceroy for intercession.

Whereas the missions were eventually to be handed over to the Indian population, the presidios were permanent Spanish settlements, and each would form the nucleus of a pueblo that would eventually subsume it. Presidio compounds were intended to be uniform, built in a square around a parade ground at least a mile from shore and "out of cannonball range from any hostile foreign ship," according to historian Sonia Honig. Barracks, a chapel, a residence for the *comandante*, an armory, kitchens, and other facilities were to be built within a defensive perimeter wall. But that uniformity was executed to varying degrees, variations no doubt attributable to the supplies on hand, levels of manpower, topography, and other factors.

Indeed, both manpower and supplies would prove difficult to come by at Alta California's presidios. Presidio commanders struggled with a lack of support from the mother country, whether Spain or Mexico, and historical accounts of all four presidios describe them in various stages of decrepitude, understaffed and marginally defensible. In addition to lances and swords, *soldados de cuera* had at their disposal cannon and rifles, but these were, according to historians, often in sorry states of repair, and ammunition was scarce.

With the exception of the barracks on the plaza in Sonoma, Alta California's original presidio structures have been obliterated. In San Diego, grassy mounds mark excavations of the first presidio built in the Spanish colony. In Monterey,

El Castillo is also now a lawn-covered excavation site. In San Francisco, American fortifications overwhelm their Spanish progenitors. In Santa Barbara, a controversial project has relocated businesses that grew up on the historic presidio site and re-created some of the buildings that once stood there.

The Padres

There is no way to dress up the fact that, by twenty-first-century sensibilities, the Spaniards were barbaric in their treatment of Native Californians. The conquerors brought with them what can only be described in modern times as slavery, theft, rape, and murder. From leather-jacketed soldiers such behavior might be expected. That such violations occurred under the watch of priests in hooded gray robes is much more disconcerting.

Still, criticism must be tempered by recognition that the missions were established in a foreign time by foreign minds. Most of the padres who came to California were driven by evangelistic zeal. They were responsible for the eternal souls of the Indians they encountered, and they would do anything to save those souls. As a docent at the Sonoma Mission noted, Junípero Serra himself practiced self-flagellation as punishment for offenses against his God; it stands to reason that extreme punishments were used on neophytes as well. A runaway Indian might, upon his second offense, be condemned to die, but the padres would make sure he was baptized before the sentence was carried out.

The priests who established missions in California were Franciscans, members of an order established by San Francisco de Asís and characterized by religious zeal, asceticism, and strict adherence to vows of poverty and chastity. Members of the Franciscan Order were brought in to administer the mission system in New Spain after Carlos III disputed with the Jesuits, a separate Catholic order that had established seventeen missions in Baja California.

Typically, two priests were assigned to each new mission, offering each other company and support in what was generally a lonely and arduous post. Missionaries were always busy, however, carrying out both glamorous religious duties—conversions, baptisms, confirmations, marriages, and Masses—and the more mundane, including adhering to a strict schedule of daily prayer, maintaining mission records, teaching neophyte children, visiting the sick, and helping with domestic and agricultural tasks.

The missionaries kept meticulous records of the output of various mission enterprises, counting the numbers of cattle and other livestock, the bushels of grain and corn harvested, the quantities of grapes, olives, fruits, and beans brought in—even the numbers of books and household items. Examples of such tallies can be found at the various missions, as well as in historical journals and books. The records were key to assigning a value to mission property when it was later sold during secularization.

The Franciscans earned notoriety for both their goodness and their weakness. Some were devoted to the betterment of the neophytes under their care, earning the priests respect and, possibly, love. Others were disdainful and abusive, their neglect at times inciting unrest among both the Indians and their brethren. A few made contributions that reached beyond any single mission community and beyond their lifetimes.

Junípero Serra

Padre Junípero Serra is, without question, the greatest celebrity of California's missionaries. The West Coast's founding father was born in Mallorca, Spain, in 1713, entered a Franciscan convent as a teenager, and was ordained a Franciscan priest in 1738. His career in the Franciscan Order was auspicious: By the time he departed to serve as a missionary in the New World in 1749, he had earned a doctorate of philosophy and was a renowned teacher and preacher.

His penchant for walking (a Franciscan habit, so to speak) began as soon as he arrived in the New World. It was on his journey from Vera Cruz to Mexico City and the Apostolic College of San Fernando, his home base for the next seventeen years, that he was bitten on the leg or foot by a nasty bug. The bite caused a nagging disability that plagued him for the rest of his life. The story goes that Serra walked from mission to mission during his tenure in Alta California, but given his infirmity, there's a good chance that this is the stuff of legend.

In 1769 Serra was dispatched to Alta California to serve as the padre presidente of the string of missions that was to be established there. He approached this task with the zeal that characterized his life, envisioning a chain of fifty missions stretching along El Camino Real from Baja California to Alaska, according to one historian. He fell far short of this goal, establishing only nine missions, but accomplished a remarkable feat no matter the measure.

Serra and his fellow pioneer padres surely would have established more missions had they not been stymied by the political realities of the waning Spanish empire. Visitador-General Galvez was one of a succession of administrators in both the homeland and Mexico City with the ultimate power to determine if, where, and when a mission was established. Bureaucracy, coupled with military commanders hesitant to spread their forces too thinly, contained Serra's ambitions like a lantern contains a flame.

Still, that flame burned, and Serra fought for his neophytes and his missions until his death in a spartan cell at San Carlos Borromeo in 1784. His legacy remains on the ground in California, but may reach into his heaven in the future: Pope John Paul II beatified the padre in 1988, and he may one day be canonized.

Fermín Francisco de Lasuén

Like the statue that commemorates him at Mission San Fernando Rey de España, the legacy of Fermín Francisco de Lasuén is quiet, almost hidden. The wave of his predecessor's success may have crested higher, but Lasuén's was just as broad, and left as deep an impression on the California coast.

Born in Victoria, Spain, in 1736, Lasuén followed a familiar path to Alta California, first pledging himself as a young man to the Franciscan Order, then traveling to New Spain and the College of San Fernando in Mexico City to become a missionary. Lasuén worked in missions in remote parts of Mexico and Baja California until 1773, when he went north to serve at Mission San Diego de Alcalá. His successes there, and in the handful of other missions in which he served, brought his talents to the attention of both Serra and other officials in Alta California.

After Serra's death, and following the short term served by Padre Francisco Palóu, Lasuén was appointed padre presidente for the growing mission chain, and went on to found nine additional missions along El Camino Real. He died in 1803, after serving as padre presidente for eighteen years, and is buried at the Carmel Mission.

The Other Padres

Though none achieved the renown of Serra and Lasuén, a number of other padres made substantial contributions to the mission system. They are remembered for the good they accomplished; those who weren't so good have merited little or no mention in mission histories.

Francisco Palóu, one of Serra's students at the *convento* in Palma, Spain, would travel to New Spain with Serra and Padre Juan Crespí in 1749, serve at missions in the Sierra Gorda of Mexico and as padre presidente of missions in Baja California, and found Mission San Francisco de Asís on the shores of San Francisco Bay. A remarkable résumé, but Palóu is most vividly remembered for his autobiography of Serra, and other writings that recount the history of early mission times in Alta California.

The life of Juan Crespí, a contemporary of Palóu's and another student of Serra's, would be one marked by travel and chronicle: He traveled north with Gaspar de Portolá on the expedition that discovered San Francisco Bay, and his diary of that journey has become a valuable historical resource.

Pedro Font's travel diaries have also earned him fame, as has Narciso Duran's love of music—and his ability to teach it to the neophytes under his care. Antonio Peyri would lead Mission San Luis Rey for more than twenty years, transforming it into the King of the Missions. Luis Jayme would be martyred in an Indian uprising at Mission San Diego de Alcalá. And Fray Vicente

Padre Narciso Duran, who gained some fame leading neophyte choirs at Mission San José, is shown with an Indian child. This engraving was created by Duflot de Monfras.

Sarria, once padre presidente of the mission system, would drop dead of starvation in the chapel of Mission Nuestra Señora de la Soledad, having given his food to famished Mission Indians. Their stories, whether successful or tragic, parallel those of the missions they founded and fostered.

The Mission Indians

The American Indian went down fighting. That's the myth and the reality, stories told of fierce warriors and wise, well-spoken chiefs, of battles and negotiations and betrayals, of last stands and long trails stained with blood and tears.

Such stories aren't generally told of California Indians, who may have numbered as many as 300,000 at the time the Spaniards arrived, according to historian David Weber. The dramas that surrounded the destruction of indigenous cultures in the future Golden State were quiet, veneered with civility, but just as devastating.

In the years before the arrival of the Europeans, California supported a diverse Indian population—one that has been broken into at least two dozen linguistic groups by anthropologists, and then further delineated into smaller "tribelets"—but the Natives shared a lifestyle closely tied to the natural rhythms of the land. They were for the most part hunters and gatherers, securing ample sustenance by hunting game both large and small, relying on the acorn—abundant in the oak woodlands that dominate many of California's landscapes even today—as a staple food, and augmenting their diets with fruits and seeds gathered in season. They were a Stone Age people who made tools from wood and stone and bone, and developed impressive basketweaving skills. Warfare, for the most part, was on a small scale, limited to raiding neighboring villages and defending territories. The Natives also engaged in the trade of foodstuffs and raw materials such as shell and obsidian.

The different groups developed belief systems as varied and deep as the languages in which the unexplainable was explained. Shamans provided spiritual guidance. Medicines were concocted from natural sources, and sweat lodges were used as meeting places for the men in a village. Communities came together on occasion to celebrate harvests and seasons, gatherings at which they shared stories and music and the bounty of the land they inhabited.

The Spanish worldview included the right of dominion over the lands and peoples of Alta California, and charged both missionary and soldier with converting the Natives they encountered to Catholicism. These mandates were executed with gusto, forever changing the lives of California's indigenous population. Spanish law offered limited protection of Indian rights, allowing them to live in their own villages (*rancherias*), prohibiting their enslavement, and requiring them to be instructed in the lore of Catholicism. Still, the interpretation and enforcement of those laws varied widely.

Indians were lured into the missions with gifts of food, clothing, and trinkets. Some students of the mission era say they welcomed the intercession of the missionaries; others assert that the introduction of Spanish agricultural crops and domestic animals decimated indigenous flora and fauna, forcing the hungry Natives into missions where food was plentiful. Regardless, once in the system, the Indians were baptized and then compelled to stay, where their lives changed drastically.

No longer was food gathered from the woodlands; it was laboriously sown and harvested, and a diet that had once included acorn mush and wild game now consisted of a simple gruel of roasted corn and grain known as *atole*, or *pozole*, a stew of meat, beans, and corn or wheat. Where once they'd gone naked, now they wore shirts, shawls, breeches, and skirts that they'd woven and sewed themselves. They were forced to worship a single, omnipotent God, forced to work at tasks—adobe brick making, weaving, pottery making, carpentry, animal husbandry—that were foreign to them, forced to sleep in dormitories that were sometimes locked at night to prevent their flight.

The Franciscans were only minimally successful in converting the Indians in the early years of the conquest: "In the first five years of the first five missions, only 491 infants had been baptized, 462 members enrolled, and 62

This drawing by German artist Wilhelm Tilesius von Tilenau depicts California Native Americans dancing at Mission San José.

marriages performed," write the authors of Sunset's *The California Missions*. The success rate picked up in later years, however; historian W. H. Hutchinson notes that ". . . About 55,000 converts is the estimate gross harvest from Franciscan labors during the heyday of the missions."

Though never reaching the level of historical significance granted to such Indian battles as those at Little Bighorn and Wounded Knee, California's indigenous people did fight their oppressors. The destruction of Mission San Diego de Alcalá in 1775, the revolt of the Chumash Indians in the Santa Barbara region in 1824, and the Yuma Campaign of 1780, which resulted in the obliteration of two inland missions and closed the trail blazed by Juan Bautista de Anza from Sonora into Alta California, gave notice to the conquerors that the Natives wouldn't go down easy. Numerous smaller revolts and escapes kept soldiers at the presidios busy for the duration of the mission era.

The most powerful tool in the Spanish arsenal was not religion or military prowess—it was disease. Brandished inadvertently, European contagions such as measles, chicken pox, smallpox, and venereal disease swept in epidemics through both the missions and the *rancherias* outside them. Historian David Weber notes that such plagues ultimately killed up to half of the indigenous population of the coastal region of California by the end of Spanish rule there.

The mission era would eventually end, but California's Native people were never able to reassert their sovereignty. Mission lands that should have been returned to them after secularization never were, and the influx of Americans that poured into the region with the Gold Rush obliterated any opportunity they may have had to recover. It may lack the flash of the fall of the Aztecs, or the bloody majesty of battles waged by Plains Indians, but the conquest of California's Indians was just as poignant.

El Camino Real

El Camino Real, the thread that links each of Alta California's missions and presidios—both to each other and to missions in Baja California—has proved as durable as the landscape that shaped it.

The 650-mile-long highway began as Indian trails, routes used by California's indigenous people for trade and travel. In no hurry to reinvent the wheel, the Spaniards adopted these routes as they explored, then settled, both Alta and Baja California. By the time the Spaniards were overthrown by the Mexicans, El Camino Real stretched from Loreto to San Rafael; under the Mexicans, the road was extended north to Sonoma.

Today El Camino Real is still in use, lying in part under the asphalt and white stripes of U.S. Highway 101, elsewhere as city streets and rural roads, sometimes merely as a dirt trail on mission grounds. The route is marked both by historical plaques and by re-creations of mission bells placed on the landscape through the efforts of both the Native Daughters of the Golden West and the California Federation of Women's Clubs.

Ruin and Resurrection

Historic photographs of California's missions show spectacular buildings in spectacular states of ruin. Mission museums and books are resplendent with such photos: crumbling walls and caved-in roofs, churches lonely in unrecognizably empty landscapes, black-and-white documentation of the disintegration of Spain's northwest frontier. It was this fragile beauty that ultimately spurred preservation of the missions, a movement that started in the late nineteenth century and continues today.

Like their rise, the decline of the missions has international roots—in this case Spain's turn-of-the-nineteenth-century tumble from imperial powerhouse to a state hard pressed to defend its European sovereignty, much less its holdings in the New World. In 1810 Mexico launched its bid for independence, a decade-long series of revolts that ended, at least as far as California was concerned, in 1822, when the Spanish flag was lowered in California's capital, Monterey, and the Mexican flag was raised.

California under Mexican rule established one last mission, San Francisco Solano, in 1823, but during the decade that followed, Mexico proved itself unable to provide financial or political support for the mission system. The lack of supervision resulted in the seizure of mission wealth and power by *Californios*—sons of presidial soldiers and former Spanish politicians who cast a greedy eye upon ecclesiastic properties. Antonio María Osio, the son of an officer who was born in 1800, was part of a cadre of young men who wanted to see the end of the missions, decrying them in his *History of Alta California* as a part of a "detestable system . . . which was responsible for the oppression of the indigenous peoples who lived within it."

Alta California under Mexico became much more concerned with the making and hoarding of wealth than with the preservation of its borders and the conversion of its Native population. This meant, among other things, that Mexican governors allowed foreigners—including Americans—to conduct trade in its ports, pueblos, and presidios. (The Spaniards had prohibited such trade.) In turn those foreigners could see that what California lacked in gold—at that time, at least—it made up for in agricultural goods.

Greed also sabotaged the secularization process. Secularization, which required that the Franciscans return mission lands to the Indians for whom they had held it in trust, retaining only the church and padres' quarters to serve as a parish for a newly formed pueblo, had always been the goal of the mission system. But California's Mexican governors expedited the process, giving little credence to Franciscan assertions that the Indians living in the missions were not ready to manage their own lands. The padres needn't have worried; the Indians weren't given the missions they'd helped build anyway.

Instead, powerful presidial and political families were able to secure land grants that included former mission properties, their orchards, vineyards, crops, and livestock—even their household goods. Osio was among those who found himself the beneficiary of this land grab, securing a grant that included Angel Island and much of what is now Point Reyes National Seashore. Many of the padres abandoned the missions as their flocks scattered and their support systems crumbled, leaving the missions to crumble as well.

By the time Americans acquired the future state in 1848 as a spoil of the Mexican-American War, the mission system had been essentially dismantled. Still, the value of the missions, no matter how neglected, was recognized early on by the United States, which returned the buildings (and in some cases a portion of the land they'd once overseen) to the Roman Catholic Church in the mid–nineteenth century.

For many of the missions, however, the restoration of ownership did not translate into physical restoration until many years later. The early twentieth century proved most fruitful for restoration efforts, with some of the churches, *conventos*, and chapels restored by dedicated Catholic fathers or laymen, and others restored by the state. Missions that were completely destroyed by time and weather have been re-created on or near the sites where they originally stood. Others feature buildings that date back to the mission era, with church walls bearing the designs painted on them by neophytes many years earlier.

Efforts to further preserve the missions are ongoing. In 2003 a bill was passed by the U.S. House of Representatives earmarking $10 million for restoration projects, confirmation of the importance of their legacy to California's identity. At presstime, the bill was with the U.S. Senate.

The Missions

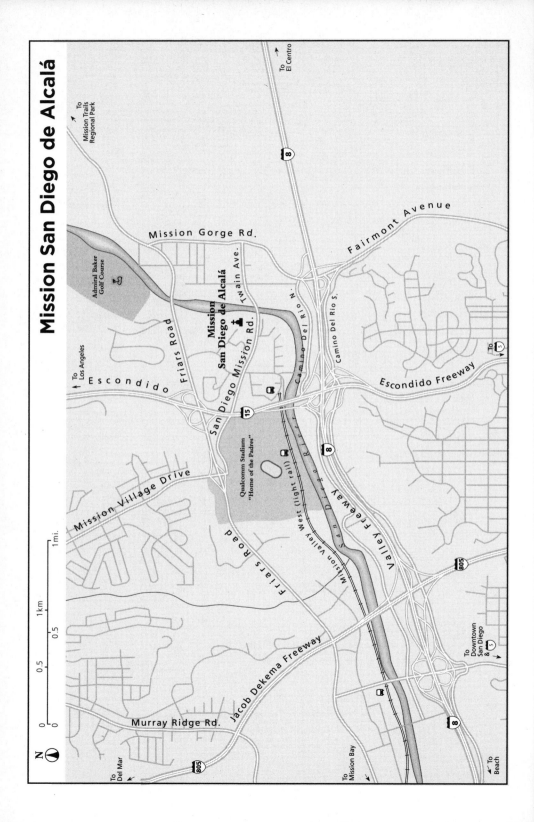

Mission San Diego de Alcalá

Mission San Diego de Alcalá

The Patron Saint: *Diego de Alcalá (also known as Saint Didacus) was a Spanish-born holy man who lived in the fifteenth century. After working as a missionary in the Canary Islands, he returned to Spain and earned renown as a miraculous healer. He died among his Franciscan brethren in 1463, and was canonized in 1588.*

FOUNDING DATE: July 16, 1769

ADDRESS: 10818 San Diego Mission Road, San Diego, 92108-2498

TELEPHONE NUMBER: Visitor center (619) 281–8449; parish office (619) 283–7319

WEB SITES: www.missionsandiego.com, www.missionbasilicasandiego dealcala.com

HOURS: The mission is open for tours from 9:00 A.M. to 4:45 P.M. daily. A small fee is levied ($3.00 for adults, $2.00 for seniors and students, $1.00 for children under twelve).

DIRECTIONS: To reach the mission from Interstate 5 in downtown San Diego, travel north to the intersection with Interstate 8. Head east on I–8 for about 6 miles to the Mission Gorge/Fairmount Avenue exit. At the stoplight at the end of the long exit ramp, go left (north) on Mission Gorge Road. Follow Mission Gorge for 0.6 mile to Twain Avenue. Turn left (west) onto Twain Avenue, which becomes San Diego Mission Road before it crosses the San Diego River. Follow Twain/San Diego Mission Road for 0.5 mile to the mission. California Historic Landmark No. 242.

PARKING: Two large parking lots front the mission, one just outside the church and *convento*, the other below that, just off San Diego Mission Road.

SERVICES AND EVENTS: Mass is celebrated daily at 7:00 A.M. and 5:30 P.M. in the mission church. Additional Masses are scheduled on Sunday at 7:00 A.M., 8:00 A.M., 10:00 A.M., 11:00 A.M., noon, and at 5:30 P.M., with a pair conducted in the St. Francis Center at 9:00 A.M. and at 11:00 A.M. (in Spanish).

The mission also hosts weddings and baptisms. An annual Fiesta, which features the ringing of the mission bells, is held on or near the mission's founding date in mid-July; call the visitor center for more information.

It doesn't boast the biggest church, the best original art, an unmatched musical legacy, or even an atmosphere that evokes mission times. But Mission San Diego de Alcalá was the mother of the mission chain, the place where Padre Junípero Serra first raised a cross within the boundaries of Alta California, the chockstone of a colonial civilization that transfigured the Golden State.

Given its historical significance, Mission San Diego is remarkably unpretentious. Not elegant like Mission Santa Bárbara, not venerable like the basilica at Carmel, not majestically decrepit like Mission San Miguel, San Diego de Alcalá is functional, plain faced, and solid. An old, comfortable soul, the mission reclines amid the palms and the ocean breezes, welcoming archaeologists, pilgrims, and parishioners with the equanimity of a contented matriarch settled in a comfortable rocking chair on her front porch. It doesn't have to claim anything or be anything, because it was the first.

The Mission Yesterday

The Kumeyaay Indians once had all of San Diego to themselves. They, like most other California Indians, were a hunting and gathering culture, skilled in the making of baskets and stone tools and weapons, infinitely knowledgeable about the natural resources that surrounded them. They belonged to a larger linguistic group known as the Yuma, a population that stretched from the San Diego coast inland to the interior boundary of California.

The world of the Kumeyaay began its transformation with the discovery of San Diego Harbor by Juan Rodriguez Cabrillo in September 1542. He named the bay for San Miguel, because he had made the discovery on that saint's feast day, but the name didn't stick. Instead, bay, mission, and presidio would be known by the moniker bestowed in 1602 by explorer Sebastian Vizcaino: San Diego.

But nearly 200 years passed before the Kumeyaay felt the impact of Spanish imperialism on their region. In 1769 a multipronged expedition commanded by Captain Gaspar de Portolá and Padre Junípero Serra traveled north to establish a Spanish colonial outpost on the bay. The soldier and the missionary selected Presidio Hill as the site for the new Spanish colony, a high point with sweeping views of the bay and estuary at the mouth of the San Diego River. With their arrival, the local indigenous people became Diegueños.

Life for the Spaniards at San Diego was not easy in the beginning. Portolá had been charged with finding Monterey Bay and choosing a site there for a mission and presidio, and he embarked on that exploration shortly after arriving in San Diego. While he was gone, Serra raised a cross at the mission site, and all members of the expedition healthy enough to help (a number of the sailors from the *San Carlos* and the *San Antonio* had sickened with scurvy during the voyage north; a third ship, the *San José*, was lost at sea) set about building structures of wood and brush for both mission and presidio.

After an arduous journey during which he serendipitously discovered San Francisco Bay, Portolá returned to San Diego to find that a number of men had perished in his absence; those who remained were starved and sick. The situation was so desperate that Portolá threatened to retreat if no help was forthcoming, setting March 19, Saint Joseph's feast day, as the deadline. As if in answer to Serra's prayers, the supply ship *San Antonio* was sighted on the horizon, and the colony was saved.

The Mother of the Missions was moved about 6 miles inland from Presidio Hill in 1774 to take advantage of better farmland and a better source of water, to be closer to the *rancherias* of potential neophytes, and to escape the presidio's soldiers, who harassed and abused the Natives. Padres Luis Jayme and Vincente Fuster built a church and compound of wood and reeds at the new site and continued their missionary work, converting more than 500 Natives in the year following the mission's relocation.

But not all the Indians were content, and in November 1775 as many as 800 rebelled. Apparently incited to the insurrection by a pair of Natives who were either unhappy with the padres' spiritual teachings, covetous of mission goods, or both (depending on the source), the Indians looted the mission before setting it afire. Padre Jayme tried to stop the rampage, entreating, "Love God, my children," but the Natives didn't listen, martyring him with blows and arrows.

In 1776 a new mission church and *convento* were erected on the site, under the supervision of Padre Serra. That mission compound was damaged in an 1803 earthquake, and another was built in 1808. Yet another temblor resulted in more rebuilding, with yet another church dedicated in 1812. Archaeological excavations and historical documents have established that at least four different churches and three different *conventos* were constructed on the site.

Though Diegueños were always troublesome for the padres, the missionaries were successful in converting a healthy number—565 in 1797—who were put to work in the mission's productive orchards, croplands, and vineyards, and who took care of abundant herds of sheep, cattle, and horses.

The mission's prosperity ended when Mexico won independence from Spain in 1821, and efforts to secularize the entire mission chain gained momentum. San Diego de Alcalá was secularized in 1833, and then granted to Santiago Arguella in 1846. The ownership of the *Californio* was short lived: In 1847 American soldiers occupied the mission, a portent of the impending transfer of Alta California from Mexico to the United States. The legacy of the U.S. Cavalry as mission keepers is one of use and abuse. Mission literature notes that in some cases soldiers shored up the disintegrating adobe structures; in others, they simply demolished them.

In 1862 the American government returned the ramshackle mission to the Catholic Church. Padre Antonio Ubach arrived in 1866, and remained at San Diego de Alcalá for more than forty years, founding an Indian school that was run by the Sisters of Saint Joseph of Carondolet, and spearheading restoration efforts until his death.

Mission restoration got another shot in the arm in 1931, as the city of San Diego prepared to host the 1935 World's Fair. Original timbers and materials uncovered at the site were incorporated into the revitalized mission, which began service as a parish church in 1941 and was named a minor basilica by Pope Paul VI in 1976. Restoration efforts are ongoing, as evidenced by recent excavations, but Mission San Diego de Alcalá is firmly rooted these days, the whitewashed bedrock of California's mission chain.

The Mission Today

Big and brilliantly white, the facade of Mission San Diego de Alcalá is impressively homely, the curves in its roofline and the columns set in relief around its heavy doors an understated ornamentation dwarfed by the plain faces that surround them.

Entrance to the mission is through the gift shop, a spacious room filled with religious and mission memorabilia, with banks of windows that open on a courtyard and fountain. The self-guided mission tour begins just outside the shop in the padres' living quarters, a sunken room in California's first rectory—the only building that survived all of the mission's hardships intact. A short flight of stairs leads down to the plain tile floor of the chamber, known as the Casa del Padre Serra, which is simply furnished with a bunk, fireplace, and rope ladder leading up into the loft.

It's a short walk from the padres' quarters to the side door of the church. A comfortable, lived-in place, the nave's height and narrowness is warmed by the Indian summer hues of green and orange used in wall decorations, by the muted yellow light that streams in through the high windows, by the earthy and uneven tile work of its floor, and by the golden sunburst—Old World symbolism for God the Father—that explodes above the main altar. The pews are padded, the communion kneelers are clothed in green brocade, and a blue ceiling stretches over all.

Beneath the sunburst at the top of the reredos, a niche holds a statue of the Madonna and Child; below that, a cross bears a tortured Christ who seems all the more gruesome given that he has no arms. The tale behind the statue is inspirational: Former pastor Monsignor I. Brent Egan, who worked to bring the mission up to date historically, purchased the armless corpus in Rome,

The facade of Mission San Diego de Alcalá is a brilliant white, with a curved roofline.

intending to have the missing pieces re-created upon his return to San Diego. But a nun with the Sisters of Nazareth reminded him of the teachings of Saint Teresa of Avila, that "the people are the arms of Christ," and the statue has remained limbless. A statue of San José stands to the left of the crucifix; the Virgin Mary is on its right.

In one of the two alcoves that flank the main altar, a vigil candle burns to the "martyred" Padre Jayme, who is interred beneath the sanctuary with four of his brethren. The pulpit on the left side of the church is shaded by a canopy, symbolic of the church's status as a minor basilica, an original painting of San Diego hanging beneath its colorful cloth. Other artwork includes a polychrome statue of San Gabriel, and a portrait of Mary painted by an artist in Cuzco, Peru. Stations of the Cross in painted frames march along the walls of the nave to the shadow of the choir loft, under which votive candles light a crucifix and the heavy confessional. A statue of Our Lady of Guadalupe is perched on a narrow shelf near the heavy wooden door. The baptismal font sits at the rear of the church in a small room blessed with a statue of Santa Ana.

The mission's *campanario* towers 46 feet above the tangled garden of bougainvillea, roses, and palms in the *camposanto* adjacent to the church. The bell on the lower right, according to mission literature, is Ave Maria Purísima, cast in 1802 and hung at the mission in 1931; the bell known as Mater Dolorosa (Our Lady of Sorrows) hangs in the lower left niche of the *campanario*.

A beautiful statue of the Pietà sits amid a cactus garden.

Tiny crosses artfully composed using tiles of the original mission rise from the ivy that carpets the garden floor, memorials to the neophytes buried here. Statues of saints and holy men also stand among the blooms: Padre Serra, San José, San Francisco de Asís at the wishing well, and San Antonio de Padua tucked in a corner. The *camposanto* is enclosed by low adobe structures that once housed the Indian School founded by Padre Ubach.

Signs for EL MUSEO—the Padre Luis Jayme Mission Museum—direct you down a corridor marked at its end by a large crucifix. The corridor swings right into a smaller patio in which a statue of the Pietà is surrounded by a cactus garden. Stations of the Cross in colorful tile mosaics decorate the wall of the corridor leading to the museum.

Inside, exhibits document and describe the various stages of mission history: the before-time of the Kumeyaay Indians, the Spanish colonial era, the Mexican era, the legacy of the American military, and the mission's reconstruction. Artifacts and documents include religious statuary and vestments; mission models, floor plans, and pictures; buttons and bottles dating back to the American occupation of the mission; and a copy of the document signed by President Abraham Lincoln reconveying the mission to the Catholic Church.

Another courtyard, this one planted with Our Lord's candle, tamarisk, and silk oak, separates the museum from the Saint Bernardine Chapel. Though built in 1977, the chapel is aged by the remarkable choir stalls that line its walls, relics from a Carmelite monastery in Spain decorated with fantastic gargoyle-like creatures. An enthroned eagle, a "symbol of resurrection," watches over the choir stalls and a display of handsome vestments in glass-fronted cases.

A large blue-tiled fountain dominates the spacious court behind the gift shop; brick walkways spin from the petals of its pool like the spokes of a wheel, stretching to the low, whitewashed buildings of the mission's rectory and the Saint Francis Pastoral and Liturgical Center, to a reconstruction of a Mission Indian shelter, to a beautiful bronze statue of the Pietà, and to the restrooms, behind which stretches a broad expanse of lawn (once the site of the mission's granaries and warehouses) from which rises a cross that honors Native Americans who lived at the mission.

Excavations are ongoing at the mission, regimented sunken squares of exposed reddish brown earth backing up to the walls of the monastery. Meticulous sifting of the earth has revealed a wealth of artifacts dating from the early 1800s to the cavalry occupation of the mid–nineteenth century. Volunteers are welcome to help with the dig, which is conducted by Dr. Jack Williams on Saturday from 9:00 A.M. to dusk.

Nearby Points of Interest

From the San Diego Presidio site in Presidio Park to scenic Mission Bay, from the San Diego Zoo to grand Balboa Park, from Old Town to the Silver Strand, all of San Diego—modern and historic—awaits exploration. The city is user-friendly and easy to navigate, but a good map and a little research will make exploration that much more fun.

Santa Ysabel Mission, an *asistencia* (auxiliary mission) of Mission San Diego de Alcalá established in 1818 in the desert east of the city, is worth a visit as well. The chapel, built in 1924, is home to an active local parish. Santa Ysabel Mission-Asistencia is at 23013 California Highway 79, Santa Ysabel, 92070. The parish office can be reached at (619) 765–0810; the Web site is www.escusd. k12.ca.us/mission_trail/SanDiego/othersantaysabel.html.

Mission San Luis Rey de Francia

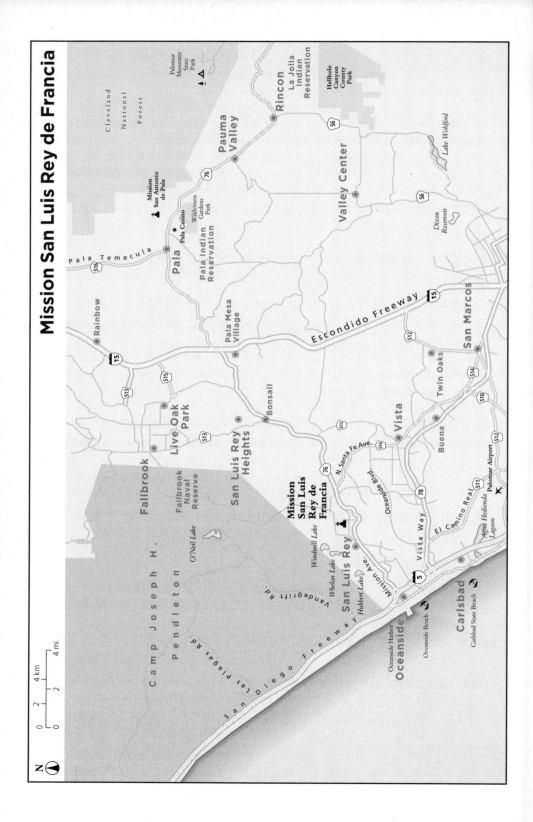

Mission San Luis Rey de Francia

The Patron Saint: Louis IX of France was born in 1215 into a deeply religious family—his uncle was King Ferdinand of Spain, patron saint of Mission San Fernando Rey de España. After leading two Christian crusades, Louis succumbed to a fever in Tunis in 1270. He was canonized in 1297.

FOUNDING DATE: June 13, 1798

ADDRESS: 4050 Mission Avenue, Oceanside, 92057-6402

TELEPHONE NUMBER: (760) 757–3651

WEB SITE: www.sanluisrey.org

HOURS: The mission gift shop is open from 9:30 A.M. to 4:30 P.M. daily. The mission museum is open for self-guided tours from 10:00 A.M. to 4:05 P.M. Monday through Sunday. A moderate admission fee is charged ($5.00 for adults, $3.00 for students, children under seven free, and $18.00 for a family).

DIRECTIONS: Mission San Luis Rey is located off California Highway 76 between Interstates 5 and 15. From I–5 in Oceanside, take the CA 76 exit and head east on CA 76 for 4 miles to Rancho Del Oro Road. The mission is on the left (north); turn left onto Rancho Del Oro, cross Mission Avenue, and enter the mission grounds. Peyri Road veers left; stay right into the parking lot. From Interstate I–15, take the CA 76 exit and head west. Travel for about 15 miles to the Rancho Del Oro Road interchange; the mission is on the right. California Historic Landmark No. 239.

PARKING: An enormous paved parking lot stretches the length of the mission and its *convento*.

SERVICES AND EVENTS: Masses are celebrated in the mission church on Saturday at 5:30 P.M. and 7:00 P.M. (the latter in Spanish). Other Masses are scheduled throughout the week and conducted in the parish chapel or the Serra Center. The parish Web site posts Mass schedules. Weddings also are conducted in the church.

The mission hosts an Annual Pepper Tree Day, celebrating both Earth Day and its venerable pepper tree, on the first Sunday of April.

It also hosts a Heritage Ball on the last Saturday in August, and a Friends of the Mission reception on the first Thursday in December. Contact the mission for more information.

Mission bells toll the hours at Mission San Luis Rey de Francia, their clear tones washing over the grounds, weaving through the arches of the *convento*, wafting through the boughs of the aged pepper tree that anchors the quadrangle. The bells are not original—in fact, they are rung electronically between 8:00 A.M. and 8:00 P.M.—but then not much of California's mission era has survived two centuries unchanged. Still, these bells, like the mission they sound over, recall past times with a poignant effectiveness. They are part of a complex that includes a unique mission church, an evocative *lavanderia*, and a powerful collection of religious statuary, all of which ensure that Mission San Luis Rey lives up to its reputation as the King of the Missions.

The Mission Yesterday

Known to Spanish missionaries and soldiers as Luiseños, the Indians who became neophytes at San Luis Rey were part of the coastal Shoshonean cultural complex. They were hunters and gatherers who lived in tule huts and wove wonderful baskets, but their lives have been further illuminated by one of their own. Pablo Tac, born at the mission in 1822, describes in a brief narrative published by the mission a people that also danced, played ball games, and battled their Indian neighbors to the south.

Life in Luiseño villages changed forever when Padre Fermín de Lasuén arrived in the San Luis Valley to establish the eighteenth mission in the chain (his ninth and last). The future success of the mission was foreshadowed on the day of its founding, with fifty-four Indians coming forth to be baptized. The priest who administered San Luis Rey from conception to secularization, Antonio Peyri, orchestrated that success.

Father Peyri, born in Catalonia, Spain, in 1769, was a remarkable overseer and shepherd, one who grew to be loved by the thousands of neophytes to whom he ministered. Part of his success may be attributed to the fact that he allowed the Indians to govern themselves, appointing Native *alcaldes* (mayors) to arbitrate disputes and levy punishments, to supervise workers in the various mission industries, and to act as liaisons and messengers between the mission and the *rancherias* that fell within its purview.

Under Father Peyri's watch, San Luis Rey became one of the biggest, most productive, and most beautiful missions in Alta California. Called a "palace" by at least one visitor, the present mission church evolved from the original tule hut to a house of worship for 1,000 Natives by 1815, incorporating unique and spectacular architectural features including a cupola with 144 panes of glass.

The quadrangle would be big enough to host bullfights, the *lavanderia* would feature spring-fed water that ran through filters, and the mission gardens would produce, in the words of Pablo Tac, ". . . pears, apples. . . peaches, quinces. . . sweet pomegranates, watermelons, melons, vegetables, cabbages, lettuces, radishes, mints, parsley," and more. The mission sold wine, butter, tallow, hides, and other goods to support itself, and maintained herds of livestock that, at their height, numbered 50,000 head.

With Mexican independence came the order to secularize the mission, a destructive process Padre Peyri couldn't bear to witness. He left the mission in 1832, departing surreptitiously to avoid the distress of farewells—a fruitless effort given that a large group of neophytes followed him to San Diego, hoping to lure him home. Mission lands that were to be handed over to the Indians were instead usurped by greedy *Californios* and added to expansive ranchos. The mission continued to function in these troubled times, though its productivity, structures, and neophyte population diminished.

Soldiers from the United States intermittently occupied the mission during the Mexican-American War and for about a decade after, looting some of the buildings and using the church as a stable. After they left, the mission was abandoned to weather and neglect—a decline that even its return to liturgical control in 1865 couldn't stop.

Restoration of the mission began in 1892, when Franciscans from Zacatecas, Mexico, moved in and Father Joseph O'Keefe was appointed mission superior. O'Keefe, who lived at San Luis Rey until 1912, became known as the Rebuilder of the Mission, overseeing a number of repair and reconstruction projects. In 1914 a boarding school opened at the mission, and in the 1920s the San Luis Rey College was built; these are now part of the parish and retreat center that occupy the north and west wings of the existing quadrangle. Restoration, excavation, and renovation have been ongoing, ensuring both the preservation of the mission and its future.

The Mission Today

The architecture of the King of the Missions blends Spanish and Moorish influences, a potent combination that gives rise to an imposing structure, a tower of white rising from a low grassy hill. Three saints occupy niches above the heavy church doors: San Luis Rey on top above a circular window, with San Francisco Solano and San Francisco de Asís below. The long arcade, with its twelve original arches, stretches toward the ocean; benches sit in the shade, offering views across the San Luis Valley.

Entrance to the mission museum and church is through a doorway off the veranda; the desk at which you pay your fee is backed by an imposing crucifix—Jesus watching all visitors with remarkable glass eyes—that dates to 1830.

Mission San Luis Rey de Francia is considered the King of the Missions.

The museum is wonderfully and professionally set up, with artifacts carefully described and presented in glass-fronted cabinets. Functional items on display include bells, pipes, gateposts, and latches; there are also Indian artifacts and mission relics, including columns from the church's original cupola, old books, historical photographs, architectural plans, and the church altar stone. Informational signs document the various stages of the mission's history. Other rooms within the museum have been dedicated to re-creations of mission living quarters, including a *sala* (living room) for *gente de razon* (people of reason, aka Spaniards), a priest's bedroom, a kitchen, and workshops outfitted with the tools of various mission trades.

But it's the statuary that sets the museum apart. Many of the pieces—from the Christo Grande in the first museum chamber to the statue of San Juan Bautista in the baptistery—are made of polychromed wood and feature glass eyes, hauntingly deep and, as a mission docent observed, known to follow you as you move around a room. Unlike the polychrome statues that decorate the mission church, distanced by their placement in altars and upon the reredos, those in the museum can be studied up close, where the artistry of their creators is powerful and intimate.

The Peyri Courtyard, with its three fountains, separates the museum from the church. A short walk through the court offers access to a mission model and a scattering of artifacts, including a brandy still, as well as a view of the "sacred" garden and yet another fountain. The Luiseño Room hosts rotating exhibits celebrating the cultural heritage of the indigenous peoples of the area.

The spacious church rings with a looping audio tour that describes various features of the building briefly, then quiets so that visitors and worshipers can contemplate what they can see, and what they can't. The walls of the nave, punched with high windows and painted with original Spanish and Indian designs, open into a high wooden dome and cupola over the sanctuary—a remarkable, airy architectural break from the design of most mission churches.

Again, the religious relics in the church are superb. The black-framed Stations of the Cross date back to the 1700s; these were removed after secularization for their protection, and returned when the Franciscans regained control of the church. Both the baptismal font, housed in a baptistery at the rear of the church, and the pulpit that climbs from the dais on the left side of the nave are original.

Though the statuary cupped in alcoves in the main reredos and side altars— the sanctuary is cruciform in design—are overwhelmed by size and space of the church, they come to the forefront within the context of the audio narration. The icons in the reredos include a statue of San Luis Rey, flanked by San Miguel on the left and San Rafael on the right. Joseph and Mary frame the crucifix, which dates back to the latter part of the nineteenth century. Two side altars present remarkable tableaux as well: On the left, a "Suffering Christ" with human hair is surrounded by San Francisco Xavier and San Antonio; on the right, San Francisco de Asís and Santa Elizabeth de Hungría bookend the "Sorrowful Mother."

The vividly painted and intimate Madonna Chapel links the church and its graveyard. Formerly a mortuary chapel, the small, octagonal room is dedicated to Our Lady of Sorrows, who stands watch as the faithful light candles that permeate the room with a waxy musk and the closeted light of winter. Though two high windows pierce the chapel's walls, which are decorated in Indian designs, they admit only a shadow of outside light, leaving the chamber moody with the flickers of tiny flames.

Encompassing old and new, the mission cemetery holds both simple crosses that date back to the mission era and new markers set flush to the grass. The older burials, overhung with trees, and the newer burials, mostly shadeless, are peppered with religious statuary and linked by a channel of water that joins two fountains. A Franciscan burial crypt and an Indian memorial can also be found here.

The grounds surrounding the church are dotted with historical signs and exposed ruins. Signs commemorate the campsites of Kit Carson and Brigadier General Stephen Kearny, combatant in the Battle of San Pasqual, as well as the mission's "capture" by Captain John C. Frémont. A chain-link fence protects

A brick archway and broad brick-and-tile stairs lead to wide pools and sunken gardens where Indian women once washed the laundry.

the ruins of the soldiers' barracks, where five to eleven *soldados* once lived and served as the "mission guard."

A gated archway serves as the entrance to the *lavanderia*, and given the setting even the most disheartened domestic servant must have found some comfort here. A broad brick-and-tile staircase drops from the arch to wide pools and sunken gardens. Water that once flowed down a narrow aqueduct spilled from the mouths of gargoyles into the pools where Indian women cleaned linens and clothing for the mission; that water was then recycled to irrigate orchards and gardens.

Informal trails explore the *lavanderia* and gardens. A short hike leads up to a lime kiln, and then switches back along an adobe wall through plantings of cactus, palm, and flowers. The trail ends at an overlook of the staircase and pools.

Another path leads uphill from the *lavanderia* toward the mission, past the Peyri Hall and Retreat Center and a bell that marks El Camino Real. An original arch frames an entrance to the mission quadrangle, part of the retreat and conference facilities and off-limits to visitors. The quad is a peaceful place, home of a lovely rose garden and a big, old, gnarly pepper tree, one of eleven grown from seeds brought to the mission by Peruvian sailors in 1830. It's a fitting conclusion to a tour of the King of the Missions.

Nearby Points of Interest

Several historic sites are associated with Mission San Luis Rey. At San Pasqual Battlefield State Historic Park (California Historic Landmark No. 533) you can explore the circumstances of the Battle of San Pasqual, in which *Californios* fought U.S. soldiers during the Mexican-American War. The park is located southeast of Mission San Luis Rey in Escondido; call the park at (760) 737–2201 for more information, or visit the Web site at www.parks.ca.gov.

The ruins of one of San Luis Rey's *asistencias*, Las Flores (California Historic Landmark No. 616), are located on the Camp Pendleton Marine Base, north of the mission. Another *asistencia*, San Antonio de Pala, located 15 miles inland from the mission, is described in detail in the next chapter.

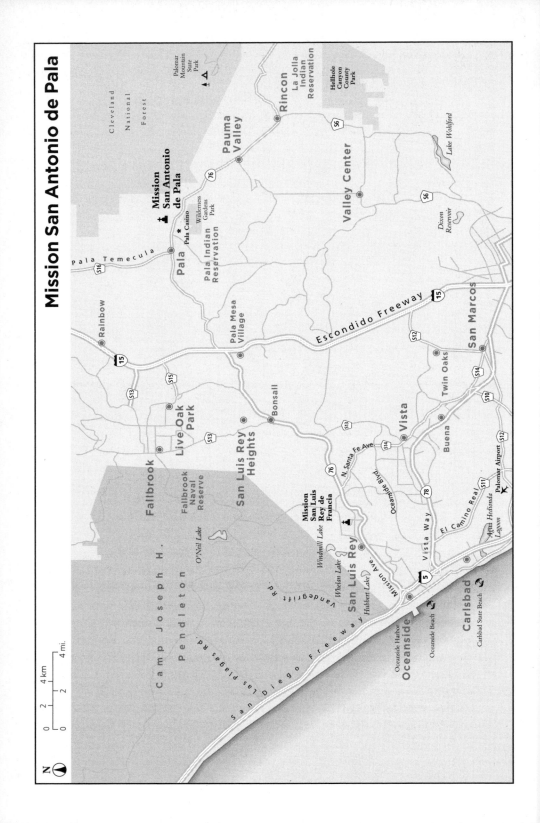

Mission San Antonio de Pala

The Patron Saint: The chapel at Pala is dedicated to Saint Anthony, renowned miracle worker, preacher, and professor of theology. The Franciscan friar is also the patron saint of Mission San Antonio de Padua in the coastal mountains of central California. He died and was canonized in the thirteenth century.

FOUNDING DATE: 1816

ADDRESS: P.O. Box 70, Pala Mission Road, Pala, 92059

TELEPHONE NUMBER: (760) 742–1600

HOURS: The museum is open Wednesday through Sunday from 10:00 A.M. to 4:00 P.M.

DIRECTIONS: To reach San Antonio de Pala from Interstate 15, drive 5.5 miles east on California Highway 76 to Pala Mission Road (San Diego County Road 516), which is opposite the Pala Casino. Turn left (northeast) onto Pala Mission Road and drive 0.6 mile to the mission. The *asistencia* is about 18.5 miles east of Mission San Luis Rey de Francia via CA 76. California Historic Landmark No. 243.

PARKING: Parking is available in the large lot at the front of the church.

SERVICES AND EVENTS: Masses are celebrated daily at 8:00 A.M., on Saturday at 5:00 P.M., and on Sunday at 8:30 A.M. and 11:30 A.M. in English, and at 10:30 A.M. in Spanish.

Mission San Antonio de Pala is an *asistencia*, or smaller "helper" mission, linked to Mission San Luis Rey de Francia. The only California mission that still serves Native Americans, Mission San Antonio de Pala overflows with informality. On a sunny Sunday morning, cars are packed in the parking lot nose to tail like fish in a tin, but no one seems to mind, because no one will be going anywhere until services are over. Worshipers stand on the veranda outside the open doors with hands upraised, unable to find either seat or standing room within the chapel, listening to a Spanish Mass. In the gardens children dressed in their Sunday best play tag among the flowers, oblivious to the damage they are doing to their starched white shirts and white patent leather shoes.

It's that informality that makes San Antonio de Pala well worth visiting. The mission is vital on a small, comfortable scale, with a current ministry and historical trappings that rival the collections of its more elite brethren—a remarkable and welcoming combination.

The Mission Yesterday

Padre Antonio Peyri, the energetic and beloved Franciscan who ran Mission San Luis Rey de Francia for more than thirty years, established San Antonio de Pala as an *asistencia* in 1816. The two missions are linked by the umbilical cord that is the San Luis Rey River Valley, open and welcoming as it nears the ocean, narrowing and scrubby inland.

The *asistencia* was prosperous almost from the first, converting large numbers of the Natives—Luiseños, Cupeños, Cahuillas—who had lived unencumbered by European influence prior to that time. In the 1820s and 1830s, the mission boasted a neophyte population of about 1,300 souls, according to mission literature.

Secularization forced the surrender of San Antonio de Pala to the *Californios*; the value of "Rancho de Pala" at the time of its sale to Pio Pico and Pablo de la Portilla was $15,363. The *asistencia* fell into disrepair in the latter part of the nineteenth century, its untended adobe eaten away by weather and time. In 1903 it underwent a partial restoration; in 1916 floods undermined the *campanario*, modeled after one in Cuidad Juarez, Mexico, which collapsed and was rebuilt. By 1959 the *asistencia* was completely restored. The chapel and museum wing are original, though the chapel received additional restoration in 1992 to repair termite damage.

The Mission Today

Today San Antonio de Pala offers visitors and parishioners everything that more elaborate missions promise in a nice, compact package, but one that departs from the plan in charmingly unpretentious ways. One example is obvious from the outset: The *campanario* stands separate from the chapel, and is home to bells that still toll for Masses, wedding, and funerals. The large bell is dedicated to San Francisco, San Luis Rey, Santa Clara, and Santa Eulalia; the smaller bell, to Jesus and Mary.

The chapel, like the rest of the mission, is intimate. The interior is typically long and narrow, but the ceiling is low and supported by exposed wooden beams. Arches are painted on the walls in warm orange hues, with the Stations of the Cross hung in the hollows between each arch. Pews sit on the original and unevenly paved tile floor. A hand-carved crucifix, its Christ modeled in an Oriental style, is the focal point of the sanctuary.

The *camposanto*—a dry patch of earth sparsely shaded—is behind the *campanario*. Hundreds of Indians and early settlers are buried at here, but stone markers are relatively few, and all the more poignant for their lack of numbers.

This outdoor shrine is just one example of the intimate and welcoming spaces at Mission San Antonio de Pala, a smaller-scale mission that serves Native Americans to this day.

There is a dearth of religious statuary in the *camposanto*, but a striking statue of a padre with an Indian child, a large arrowhead behind the two figures, stands in the parking lot outside the cemetery's rear gate.

The museum, which stretches through three rooms, is accessed through the gift shop. The small chambers hold a wealth of information and artifacts about the mission, with a distinct focus on Native cultures that includes exhibits on Indian housing, diet, crafts, and weaponry. In other rooms museum curators have re-created padres' quarters and housed religious items, paintings, and statuary, including a statue of Saint Dominic carved by Mission Indians and a wooden San Antonio that dates back to the seventeenth century. The most unique vestment among those displayed bears the skull and crossbones typically associated with pirates, not priests.

San Antonio de Pala's garden grows in the small courtyard behind the museum wing. This, too, is an intimate and friendly place, shaded by tall palms and planted with cacti, roses, and bird-of-paradises, with the soft *coo-coo* of the doves living in a small coop washing over the otherwise still enclosure. Tile paths bordered by low hedges lead to benches and shrines; these paths are watched over by religious statues, the most charming of which, arguably, is of a fat, smiling friar. A fountain forms the centerpiece of the garden, as cool as the covered corridors, cluttered with potted plants and unused furniture, that line the rectory and museum wings.

Mission San Juan Capistrano

The Patron Saint: John was born in the Italian town of Capistran in 1386. He studied law and married before leaving both occupation and wife to join the Franciscan Order. After winning acclaim as a powerful preacher, he led a crusade against the Turks in 1455 and participated in a siege of Belgrade. John perished of a fever in 1456; he was canonized in 1724.

FOUNDING DATE: November 1, 1776

ADDRESS: P.O. Box 697, San Juan Capistrano, 92693

TELEPHONE NUMBER: Visitor center (949) 234–1300; parish office (949) 234–1360

WEB SITE: www.missionsjc.com

HOURS: The old mission is open from 8:30 A.M. to 5:00 P.M. daily. It is closed on Thanksgiving, Christmas, and Good Friday afternoon. All visitors must pay a moderate admission fee ($6.00 for adults, $4.00 for children three through eleven, and $5.00 for seniors sixty years and older).

DIRECTIONS: Whether northbound or southbound on Interstate 5 in San Juan Capistrano, take the Ortega Highway (California Highway 74) exit. Head west from the interstate on the Ortega Highway for about 0.1 mile—if that. The mission, which can't be missed, occupies the right-hand block between El Camino Real and Camino Capistrano. California Historic Landmark No. 200.

PARKING: Parking is available along the streets and in public parking lots off El Camino Real and other roadways, all within walking distance of the mission. Parking may be difficult on busy weekends.

SERVICES AND EVENTS: Services are held Monday through Saturday at 7:00 A.M. in the historic Serra Chapel. Other services are scheduled throughout the week at the San Juan Capistrano Mission Basilica, which is at the rear of the old mission complex at 31522 Camino Capistrano. Basilica services are held Monday through Friday at 8:30 A.M.; on Saturday at 8:30 A.M., 5:30 P.M., and 7:00 P.M. (Spanish); and on Sunday at 7:30 A.M., 9:00 A.M., 11:00 A.M., 1:00 P.M., and 5:30 P.M.

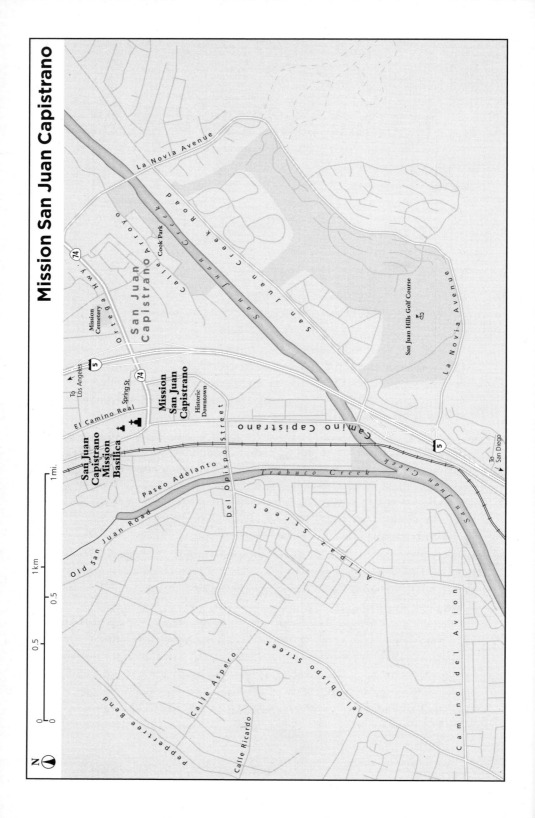

Mission San Juan Capistrano

There's the Swallows Day Festival in March, of course. (The birds return each March 19, though dates of the mission's observances may vary.) Then there is the Pirate Festival, the Russian Festival, the Lincoln Festival, the art exhibits and the World Weaving Marketplace, performances by the Capistrano Valley Symphony . . . Your best bet, if you want to enjoy a mission-sponsored event, is to acquire a copy of the Calendar and Guide for the mission, which is available by contacting the mission's special events office at (949) 234–1300 ext. 322, or by visiting its Web site.

San Juan Capistrano is the Disneyland of California's missions. It teems with visitors, especially on weekends, and that heavy population—coupled with the gated entry, the gift shops, and the colorful gardens that surround the buildings—lends it an almost circus-like atmosphere that contrasts sharply with its sometimes deserted brethren.

But this is not a bad thing—indeed, it's a well-earned compliment. This mission has it all: the swallows that return to its ruined church each spring, spectacular ruins and architecture, historical relics, a chapel with a gilded reredos, and an old cemetery. You may be hard pressed to find a place for quiet contemplation, but you are sure to enjoy what you learn and see within the mission's adobe walls.

The Mission Yesterday

When Junípero Serra founded San Juan Capistrano, the seventh mission in the chain, in November 1776, he was following through on the task he'd assigned to Fermín Lasuén a year earlier: to establish a mission between San Diego and San Gabriel. Lasuén had raised a cross on the site, but construction was halted when Indians sacked the San Diego mission, forcing Lasuén to bury Capistrano's mission bells and head south to the aid of his brethren.

The first mission church, the Serra Chapel (1777), is perhaps the oldest building still in use in California and one of the few in which Padre Serra is known to have conducted services. The church was the core of a growing and ultimately successful Christian colony, one that prospered with the help of the Juaneño Indians, members of the coastal Shoshonean language group. The Indians were persuaded to join the mission community with gifts and through the mystery of Catholic ritual, and as the neophyte population grew, so did the mission's prosperity. At its height, in 1811 and 1812, San Juan Capistrano produced an abundance of wheat, barley, corn, beans, and other crops; supported healthy herds of cattle, sheep, and horses; and included facilities for a number of trades, including the tanning of hides, candle and soap making, wine making, and metalworking.

The Great Stone Church at Mission San Juan Capistrano is spellbinding even in ruins.

The mission's Great Stone Church saw its genesis in 1797. Master stone-mason Isidro Aguilar was recruited from Mexico to direct construction, and though he died before the church was finished, he helped create an edifice that is spellbinding even in ruins. The building was cruciform in design, roofed with seven domes, with diamond-shaped tiles on its floor and walls up to 6 feet thick. Its bell tower reportedly could be seen from points 10 miles distant. It was called the Jewel of the Missions, and was the largest structure erected in California by the Spanish.

The church was dedicated in 1806, and served the mission community for six short years. In December 1812 earthquakes rattled California's central coast, wreaking havoc on missions from La Purísima Concepción to San Juan Capistrano. Services were being held in the stone church when the fateful temblor struck, causing the collapse of its bell tower and a portion of its roof and killing forty neophytes worshiping within. The mission bells, silenced by the cataclysm, were rehung in 1813 in a *campanario* next to the ruined church, but the church itself was never rebuilt.

The Indians dispersed as mission lands were sold to powerful Mexican families after San Juan Capistrano's secularization was ordered in 1834. The neophyte population dwindled so rapidly that, from 1842 to 1845, no priest served at the mission. In 1845 Mexican governor Pio Pico sold off the last of the mission to his brother-in-law, John Forster, and another man for $710. The Forster family lived in the mission for almost twenty years, but did little to preserve mission buildings other than the one they occupied. The adobe structures that framed the once bustling patio began melting into disrepair.

In June 1865, with the signature of Abraham Lincoln, Mission San Juan Capistrano was returned to the Catholic Church. Padre José Mut came to the mission in 1866 to minister to the small Catholic community living nearby, settling into a dismal room and bearing witness as the mission's adobe slowly dissolved into the earth. When he left in 1886, even the Serra Chapel was in ruins, surrounded by the brick skeletons of arches that lined the corridors of the former quadrangle.

Preservation efforts began in earnest with the work of the Landmarks Club, which put a new roof on the Serra Chapel in 1896. But it was the arrival of Father Saint John O'Sullivan, a tubercular priest who had come west with the prayer that California's sunshine might ease his illness, that proved the mission's salvation. He worked for twenty-three years rebuilding both the mission's body, using original materials and techniques where he could, and its soul, gathering a flock large enough to prompt designation of the mission as an active parish in 1918. He also oversaw the installation of the gilded altar in the Serra Chapel in 1922.

Restoration work has been ongoing since O'Sullivan's day, with each successive pastor meeting a new challenge. Given the lively cultural and spiritual support that surrounds the old mission today—its neighboring church, modeled after the Great Stone Church, was designated a basilica by Pope John Paul II in 2000—San Juan Capistrano is unlikely to be neglected in the future.

The Mission Today

It seems every mission has a nickname, and San Juan Capistrano is no exception. Known as the Jewel of the Missions—a name originally bestowed on the Great Stone Church—it has little trouble living up to the moniker, even if its namesake is little more than broken stone.

The old mission is surrounded by a high adobe wall and backed by the Mission Parish School and San Juan Capistrano Mission Basilica. The entrance is on the corner of Camino Capistrano and the Ortega Highway; visitors are funneled past a desk at which they pay fees, then through a turnstile into the sunlit plaza.

A large fountain sits in the center of the patio, surrounded by lovely plantings. Pathways lined with benches and low mission bells tarnished a coppery blue lead into the gardens, toward the ruins of the stone church, and to the low tile roofs of the mission's museum, chapel, and workrooms. You can choose any path, but if you're like most visitors you'll be drawn first to the Great Stone Church and the *campanario*, its four bells set in a brick wall in a small clearing among the roses. Each bell is named for a Catholic saint—San Vicente, San

Lovely gardens laced with walkways surround the restored structures of Mission San Juan Capistrano.

Juan, San Antonio, and San Rafael—and was cast in Mexico between 1796 and 1804. The small patio in front of the *campanario* contains a statue of Padre Serra and a neophyte. What remains of the ruined church's domed sanctuary rises behind, draped in the scaffolding and caution tape that will remain in place until emergency conservation efforts begun in 2003 are complete.

The ruin of the old church is brilliant in every detail—even the shadows are illuminating, especially those cast by the remains of the sanctuary dome upon the empty niches in what was once the reredos. The remnants of the walls that once supported other domes roll down the open nave to a fountain set among roses. The stonework is evocative; laying a hand on the rock, whether rough and broken or finished to a pearly smoothness, is like touching the hand of the Indian workman who laid it.

Paths lead from the ruins to the padres' quarters and the courtyard that fronts them, in which you'll find a copy of the mission's founding document and a replica of a Juaneño Indian home known as a *kicha*, or *kiitka*. The priests' rooms include Padre Mut's study, a humbly furnished space that only the most stalwart could find comfortable. The mission gift shop occupies the east wing, and was once the home of the Forster family.

A low doorway leads from Padre Mut's study into his bedroom, then out into the central patio. The floors of the *corredors* that enclose the patio are uneven and rustic, framed by picturesque arches of exposed brickwork. The covered arcades form the boundaries of peaceful gardens surrounding the Fountain of the Four Evangelists. The patio, which was once used by Mission Indians for domestic tasks, is now peopled with tourists and pilgrims; nary a one is disappointed by its colorful abundance.

The Serra Chapel occupies the southeast corner of the quadrangle, its vestibule forming a hallway between the patio gardens and the cemetery on the other side of the chapel. The baptismal font fronts a window that opens into the mission's gift shop; a plaque describes Padre Serra's work at the mission—including his confirmation of 213 neophytes on Columbus Day in 1783—and lists the old, original, and historical parts of the chapel.

The chapel itself, faithful to the typical architecture of a mission church, smells of burning candle wax. These wavering candles, along with two small windows that allow sea breezes to stir the scented air, shed light on the creaky wooden pews that line the nave, the choir loft that hovers over the door, and the small side chapel dedicated to Saint Peregrine. The tall walls are painted with waist-high frescoes of blue, red, and gold; the Stations of the Cross, some thought to be original eighteenth-century works, march above in frames of gold. An ornate golden pulpit and canopy rises on the left side of the chapel next to a modern statue of Padre Serra.

San Juan Capistrano is the heart of the gilded reredos, watched over by a small army of saints in niches behind him and in alcoves to either side. In the two upper niches stand Saint Peter and San Miguel Arcángel. The lower niches hold San Francisco de Asís and Santa Clara. A portrait of Our Lady of Guadalupe is at the center of the lower portion of the reredos, flanked by Saint Joseph on the left and Saint Teresa on the right. The faces of cherubs float within the gold that frames the saints. The reredos, according to mission literature, is 300 years old and was brought in pieces from Barcelona, Spain, in 1906 as a gift to the Los Angeles Diocese.

The mission cemetery is yet another pocket of blooming beauty. Among the cairns and crosses marking burials, a solitary cross memorializes those who built the mission, and a stone memorial marks the passing of Antonio Yorba I, a member of the Portolá Expedition in 1769. Father O'Sullivan, San Juan Capistrano's hero of preservation, was also laid to rest here in 1933.

Back in the central patio, a lovely mosaic of the Holy Ghost decorates the outside wall of the Serra Chapel in the eastern corridor, with adobes, roof tiles, and bricks exposed along the arcade's length. The north wing once contained warehouses and, later, a mission school; now it houses offices and dioramas depicting scenes of mission life.

Vats and furnaces used in the processing of hides and tallow are located on the west side of the quadrangle, identified as "part of Orange County's first industrial complex." Remnants and re-creations of other domestic occupations are also displayed here, including a kiln used in metalworking (the first in California), a small Indian kitchen, adobe brick and tile exhibits, wine vats, and artifacts of animal husbandry.

The mission museum, located in the west wing, is dedicated to the various incarnations of colonial life in Alta California—one room containing relics of the rancho era, another the works of the Mission Indians, a third Spanish and religious artifacts. Outside, artifacts lie ready on the "touch table" for curious little hands to fondle.

The soldiers' barracks, built in 1781 and touted as "fifty percent original," now house an art gallery and a museum in which soldiers' possessions are displayed. The *soldados* who once resided there were charged with defending the priests and neophytes living in the mission, but they were also employed in other tasks: They hunted, tended livestock, labored in the fields and orchards, worked as carpenters, tanners, and smiths, and taught these skills to the neophytes.

Outside the mission walls, you'll find San Juan Capistrano very much a mission town. One of the public parking lots (at the corner of El Camino Real and El Horno Street) is built on the site of the mission reservoir and is landscaped with stones from the great church; chain restaurants have been built where the mission orchards and vineyards once flourished; and the freeway itself runs through former mission lands. The town is also crowded with boutiques and restaurants. Explore and enjoy.

Mission San Gabriel Arcángel

The Patron Saint: Gabriel was a messenger of God, one of the three angels mentioned in the Bible. He helped the prophet Daniel interpret God's word, and foretold two momentous births: that of John the Baptist to Zacharias and that of Jesus Christ to the Virgin Mary.

FOUNDING DATE: September 8, 1771

ADDRESS: 428 South Mission Drive, San Gabriel, 91776

TELEPHONE NUMBER: Visitor center (626) 457–3048; parish office (626) 457–3035

WEB SITE: www.sangabrielmission.org

HOURS: The mission church is open daily for tours from 9:00 A.M. to 4:30 P.M. The grounds and gift shop are open from 9:00 A.M. to 5:00 P.M. A fee is charged to take the self-guided tour ($5.00 for adults, $4.00 for seniors, $3.00 for children between six and seventeen; children under six are free). The mission is closed on Easter, the Fourth of July, Thanksgiving, Christmas, and New Year's Day.

DIRECTIONS: From northbound or southbound Interstate 10 in San Gabriel, take the New Avenue exit (following the mission signs). Head north on New Avenue, which becomes Ramona Street, for 1 mile to Mission Road. Turn right (east) onto Mission Road and continue for one block to its intersection with Junípero Serra Drive. The mission is on the left (east). California Historic Landmark No. 158.

PARKING: A large parking area in front of the mission offers ample parking. Metered parking is also available along the streets surrounding the mission.

SERVICES AND EVENTS: Sunday services are held in the mission church at 7:00 A.M. and 9:30 A.M. The mission is available to parishioners and former students of San Gabriel Mission High School for weddings and baptisms; call the parish office to make arrangements.

San Gabriel's Fiesta de San Gabriel is a yearly celebration of the mission's founding held over the Labor Day weekend. Other annual celebrations include the Christmas Tree Lighting in the first week of December, and the Celebration of Our Lady of Guadalupe in the second week of December.

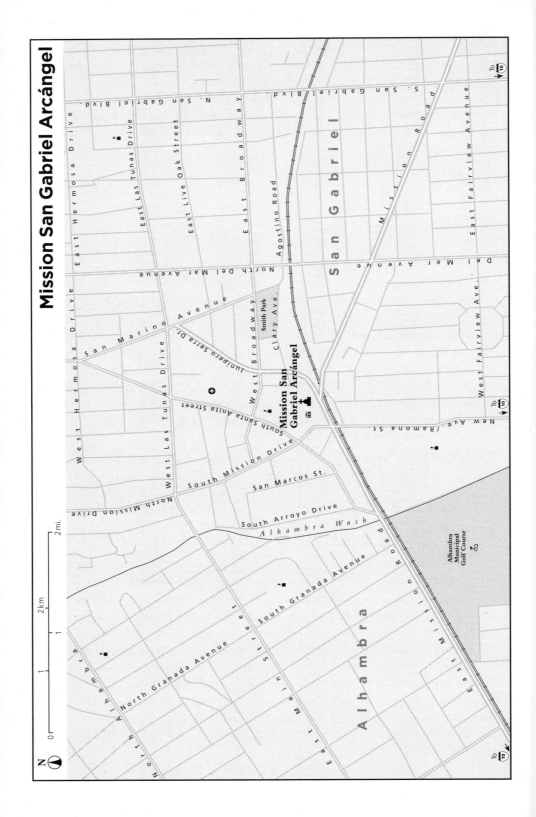

Mission San Gabriel Arcángel

Nearly everything about the exterior of Mission San Gabriel belies the historical magic within. The mission's setting is quintessentially suburban, surrounded by parking lots and busy streets, shopping centers and offices. Indeed, San Gabriel's very architecture seems un-mission-like: It is a buttressed block of a building that, were it not for the lovely six-bell *campanario* attached to its rear, could pass for a cell house.

But inside the high wall that encloses its quadrangle, Mission San Gabriel is remarkable. It's a condensed version of what you'll find at more spacious missions, with cemetery, gardens, artifacts, and atmosphere concentrated in a box as tidy as the church itself.

The Mission Yesterday

In the early days of Mission San Gabriel, meetings between the Shoshonean Indians who populated the wildlands and the missionaries who sought to convert them were tense and violent.

The culture clash colors even the founding day of the fourth mission in the chain. Two priests, Padres Somera and Cambón, had been sent by Junípero Serra to establish a community on the banks of the Santa Ana River. When they arrived at the site, they were confronted by unfriendly Indians who were, so the story goes, appeased only when one of the padres unfurled a painting of Our Lady of Sorrows (a 300-year-old piece of art that is still displayed in the mission church).

The founding fathers ended up selecting another site for the mission, one with better prospects for successful agriculture, but relations with the Natives were not destined to improve. In the early days of construction, one of the *soldados* who had accompanied the Spanish contingent raped an Indian woman, which rightfully roused the wrath of her husband and the rest of the Natives. The skirmish that ensued ended, according to one account, with the husband's head on a pole.

After yet another move, this one in 1775, and the assignment of Padres José Sanchez and Antonio Cruzado to the mission, San Gabriel began to generate the abundance for which it would one day be famous. The neophyte population began to grow; now known as Gabrielinos, the lives of Mission Indians became circumscribed by the rules and rigors of the mission tradition, which included planting and harvesting crops, tanning hides and rendering tallow, and tending to domestic chores.

The wealth of the mission was shared with visitors and travelers journeying on the three cross-country trails that passed near the mission, two that linked Alta California with Mexico, and one that reached eastward into the United States. Juan Bautista de Anza stopped at the mission on his journey northward to San Francisco in 1775, and Jedediah Smith visited as well, in 1826.

Mission San Gabriel Arcángel was designed in the Moorish style by Padre Antonio Cruzado.

The foundation of the church that stands today was laid in 1791, with the finished edifice dedicated in 1805. Its unique architecture, designed in a Moorish style by Cruzado, features walls 7 feet thick at the buttresses and 4 feet thick elsewhere. Built of stone to the height of the windows, then of burned brick above, the church was originally roofed with an impressive vault that had to be replaced after it suffered earthquake damage. Unfortunately, neither Cruzado nor Sanchez lived to serve in the grand mission they built; both died the year it was completed. The padre who replaced them, José Zalvidea, proved an equally adequate administrator; he would serve at the mission for the next twenty years.

The mission church sustained some damage in the earthquakes of 1812, but other structures were devastated. The bell tower that graced the front of the mission collapsed, as did the mission monastery. The bells were rehung in the unique *campanario* behind the church, and the mission's granaries were used as priests' quarters and a chapel until the church was restored in 1828.

Mission San Gabriel withstood yet another trial—epidemics of cholera and smallpox that decimated the neophyte population in 1825—before secularization orders were carried out in 1834. The *Californios* who were to benefit from the mission's breakup must have been ecstatic: According to mission literature, the property's agricultural holdings included more than 160,000 vines in four vineyards, more than 2,300 fruit trees in nine orchards, and more than 22,000 head of livestock, including cattle, sheep, and horses. There were four looms, four stills, three wine presses, more than 200 books, and "1,323 souls," the latter scattering as the property that was supposed to be theirs passed into private hands. By 1840 the plundering was nearly complete, with but a small herd of cattle, numbering about a hundred, left to the friars and what remained of their flock.

Mission literature asserts that "Mass has been celebrated in the mission every day since it was first founded in 1771," which means priests were on hand to witness the transfer of Alta California from Mexico to the United States, and to receive the news that the United States had returned the mission to the Catholic Church in 1862. It was employed as a parish church for the city of San Gabriel from 1862 to 1908, when it was turned over to the Claretian Missionary Fathers, who have restored, maintained, and worshiped at the mission ever since.

The Mission Today

The gift shop is a rather mundane introduction to Mission San Gabriel, but a necessary one: Here you pay the small entrance fee and pick up a brochure that describes the self-guided tour. Once out the back door of the shop, you are immediately enveloped in old mission life. There is a cluttered intimacy about the quadrangle—not a patch of ground is unmarked, whether by artifact, planting, or gravestone. Something important is revealed with every step, a density that slows the pace and quickens the mind.

Iron gates separate the cemetery, which dates back to 1778, from the fountain and benches of the small court outside the gift shop. A row of reverends rests along the adobe wall that separates the *camposanto* from the real world, a buffer for the leaf-littered brick paths that wander through wooden crosses and marble headstones marking burials in the rest of the cemetery. A stone cross commemorates the 6,000 Shoshone and Gabrielino Indians who died at Mission San Gabriel; their graves lie unmarked, while the graves of brothers and reverends lie neatly beneath the shade of grapevines more than seventy-five years old. Mosaic representations of the Stations of the Cross, made in Mexico and installed in 1939, form a loose boundary to one side of the *camposanto*.

The mission church is truly cavernous: 140 feet long, 27 feet wide, with the ceiling rising 30 feet above. A large crucifix stands under the choir loft near the rear of the church, which is darkling despite the votive candles that burn there. A smooth coating of pale adobe covers the stone-and-brick walls, and the timbers of the ceiling are painted red, green, and gold, vivid hues hovering above the heavy wooden pews and tile floor. Pillars painted on the walls separate mural-style depictions of the Stations of the Cross. Doors flanked by statues of Santa Teresa and San José open from the midpoint of the nave into the gardens.

The baptistery features a domed roof reminiscent of "the shape of half an orange," according to church literature. The baptismal font is made of hammered copper and dates back to 1771; the silver vessels used in baptisms were gifts from King Carlos III of Spain. The fresco that decorates the wall is of Saint John baptizing Christ, and portraits of the authors of the Gospels of the New Testament—Matthew, Mark, John, and Luke—look down upon the small chamber. A 300-year-old statue of the Holy Mother stands above the alcove, bathed in the green-tinted light that filters through the mission windows.

The pulpit is original and painted in red and green, harmonizing with the rest of the church's decoration. A Moorish arch hovers over the communion rail, and the stage-like chancel spreads from rail to high altar, which was created in the churrigueresque style and brought to the mission from Mexico. The reredos is only partially gilded, and overhung with tones of green. A winged San Gabriel floats above all other statuary in the niches with San Francisco de Asís on the left, San Antonio de Padua on the right, and below, from left to right, San Joaquin, La Purísima Concepción, and Santo Domingo. The painting of Our Lady of Sorrows that pacified the Indians on the mission's founding day also graces the sanctuary, casting her mournful gaze upon the eight members of the Franciscan brotherhood—and a sole neophyte—interred before the altar.

The sacristy, tucked behind the church, is touted as the "oldest and best preserved" in the mission system. The big, rounded "barrel" vault feels thick and cool, its walls hung with paintings of San Gabriel and San Francisco de Asís. It's a working space for the church, its original tile floor littered with music stands, while a vast leather-topped chest of drawers is covered with candles and other items of worship.

What were once storerooms and workrooms adjacent to the sacristy now house the mission's museum. Sunlight pouring through windows set in thick adobe walls illuminates artifacts displayed in glass-faced cases: keys, baskets, spurs, religious statuary and original art, books dating back to 1727, vestments, tiles, trunks, Bibles, and choir books. Framed pictures of important mission-era families hang on the walls, along with a baptismal record that dates back to 1778. The mission's celebrated aboriginal paintings of the Stations of the Cross are also on display here.

Outside the museum, steps lead down into a small courtyard. The rooms off the covered porches were used as padres' quarters, housing for the mission's *mayordomo*, workshops, storerooms, an infirmary, and a *monjerio* (dormitory for unmarried women). The courtyard floor is paved with original tiles and dotted with crumbling original brick pillars.

Narrow paths lead from the courtyard into other areas of the quadrangle. One section is home to the remnants of a kitchen destroyed by fire in 1812 that includes the ruins of the mission aqueduct and replicas of iron kettles in which neophytes cooked "popcorn soup." Beyond the gorgeous cactus garden you will find the mission's candle and soap factories, the enormous brick furnaces in which tannery vats once were set, and the *lavanderia* (laundry).

In the middle of the quad, an anchor from a ship built at the mission in 1930—which was then dismantled, carted to the ocean, rebuilt, and put to sea— rests near a mission cannon ("beanshooter") found in a dry riverbed in 1914. A shrine to Our Lady of Guadalupe, a replica of a mission-era kitchen, and a display of mission models share this space.

Outside the mission walls, a grassy wedge of a park separates the mission from Mission Road. Palms cast halos of shade down upon the lawn, over a mission millstone, and on a flower-shaped fountain. The palms also frame the mission's six-bell *campanario*; two of the bells were brought to Alta California from Spain, and are more than 200 years old. The San Gabriel Mission School and the rectory (offices of the Claretian Missionaries) are located behind the mission church and *campanario*.

Nearby Points of Interest

Los Angeles is thick with historical sites dating back to the mission era. A great place to start exploring is at the El Pueblo de Los Angeles Historic Monument, the site of El Pueblo de la Reina de Los Angeles, which was founded in 1781 on the shores of the Los Angeles River about 9 miles from Mission San Gabriel. Museums, adobes, and the Olvera Street Market await exploration there. Learn more by visiting www.lacity.org/elp or by calling (213) 628–3562.

A flower-shaped fountain greets visitors outside the imposing mission walls.

The San Gabriel Asistencia, built on a former rancho, is described in detail in the next chapter. To locate other mission-era sites in Los Angeles and surrounding cities—ranchos, casas, adobes, battlefields—check out the California State Historical Landmarks Web site, which is listed in this guide's appendix.

San Gabriel Mission Asistencia

The Patron Saint: The asistencia *at Mission San Gabriel's Rancho San Bernardino was also dedicated to the archangel Gabriel, messenger of God and herald of the births of both John the Baptist and Jesus Christ.*

FOUNDING DATE: 1819

ADDRESS: 26930 Barton Road, Redlands, 92373

TELEPHONE NUMBER: (909) 793–5402

WEB SITE: www.co.san-bernardino.ca.us/museum/branches/asist.htm

HOURS: The *asistencia* is open Wednesday through Saturday from 10:00 A.M. to 5:00 P.M., Sunday from 1:00 to 5:00 P.M. It's closed on New Year's Day, Thanksgiving, and Christmas.

DIRECTIONS: From Interstate 10 in Redlands, take the California Street exit. Head right (south) on California Street to Redlands Boulevard, where California jogs to the right and aligns itself with a canal. Continue 1.2 miles on California Street to Barton Road, and turn left (east). The mission is 0.6 mile down Barton Road, on the left (north).

PARKING: Parking is available in the large lot on the east side of the *asistencia*. California Historic Landmark No. 42.

SERVICES AND EVENTS: For a small fee, you can take a self-guided tour of the *asistencia*. It is also available for guided school tours. The chapel may be rented for weddings and receptions.

San Gabriel Mission Asistencia is a smaller "helper" mission linked to Mission San Gabriel Arcángel. The *asistencia* was established in the San Bernardino Mountains, which form a vast, sunbaked backdrop to Los Angeles. The peaks and valleys of the range, which have been home to California Indians, Spanish colonials, and American frontiersmen, are now traced with freeways linking nearly identical cities of shopping centers and residential developments, including Redlands, site of the *asistencia*.

The Mission Yesterday

The *asistencia* (also known as the *estancia*) was established on Rancho San Bernardino in 1819 to serve the Serrano and Cahuilla Indians, hunting and

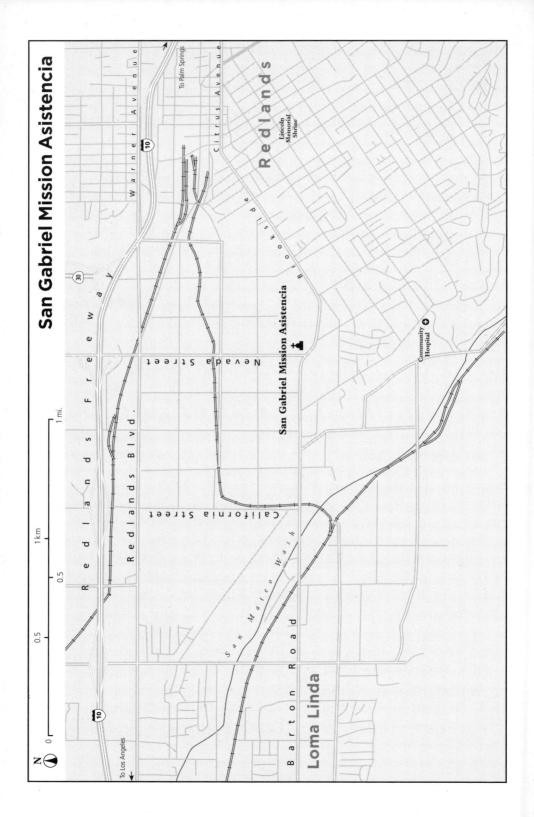

San Gabriel Mission Asistencia

Redlands

Loma Linda

Warner Avenue

Citrus Avenue

Redlands Freeway

Redlands Blvd.

Nevada Street

California Street

San Mateo Wash

Barton Road

Brookside

San Gabriel Mission Asistencia

Lincoln Memorial Shrine

Community Hospital

To Palm Springs

To Los Angeles

N

0   0.5   1 km

0.5   1 mi.

Charming artwork, such as this tiny ceramic statue and primitively painted walls, can be found at San Gabriel Mission Asistencia, a small helper mission in the San Bernardino Mountains.

gathering societies that had thrived in the desert mountains for centuries (*serrano* is Spanish for "mountaineer" or "highlander"). The rancho was integral to the agricultural wealth of the San Gabriel Mission; many of the mission's cattle were run on the rancho.

The original site of the *asistencia* lies about a mile west of the reconstructed complex, and included the Guachama *rancheria*, according to mission literature. The *asistencia* comprised a small chapel used by missionaries when they ministered to neophytes, as well as storerooms and residential quarters for both priests and the rancho overseer—a total of fourteen rooms, plus corrals and an aqueduct that siphoned water from a nearby creek.

After Mexico secularized the missions in 1834, the *asistencia* became part of the Mexican land grant given to José del Carmen Lugo, whose rancho survived through the 1840s. In the 1850s the estancia was sold to the Mormons and became the home of Bishop Nathan Tenney. Dr. Benjamin Barton purchased the former *asistencia* from the Mormons in 1859 and practiced medicine here until 1867.

The Barton family sold the ruins of the building to San Bernardino County in 1925, and restoration and reconstruction began immediately. By 1937 the helper mission had been restored by the Works Progress Administration in association with the San Bernardino County Historical Society.

The Mission Today

The revived *asistencia* sits on a low rise overlooking the Santa Ana River Valley. The site is exposed save for the few trees that shade the compound and its hallmark *campanario*, which rises just outside the quadrangle wall.

Inside the wall, a grassy patio surrounds a fountain and a statue of a Franciscan friar. The museum is in the low adobe building on the right side of the patio, a fresco of California Indians decorating its front wall. The small chapel forms the back of the quadrangle, with offices in the wing on the left.

Inside the museum you'll find a model of the *asistencia*, dioramas depicting Indian life and the Barton Ranch, displays describing the Native cultures that once thrived in the San Bernardino Valley and explaining the history of the *asistencia*, maps of Indian camps and Mexican land grants, a detailed chronology of the Spanish and Mexican occupation of Alta California, and scattered historical artifacts.

The chapel is a mission church in miniature, narrow and tall, with three lovely stained-glass windows set high in the white walls. A statue of the Holy Mother dominates the simple altar, which is set on a raised dais inlaid with plain tile.

Doors behind the chapel open into the sacristy, a large, nearly empty room in which signs of weddings past and future litter the few pieces of heavy furniture that lie within—old books and dishes, scattered roses and candlesticks.

Mission San Fernando Rey de España

The Patron Saint: *Ferdinand of Spain, born in 1198 in Salamanca, belonged to a royal family that would produce another future saint, his nephew San Luis Rey de Francia. Generally recognized as a caring monarch, this Catholic king expelled the Moors from several areas of Spain and converted at least one mosque into a cathedral. A member of the Third Order of Saint Francis, the pious Fernando was buried in a Franciscan habit after his death in 1252. He was canonized in 1671.*

FOUNDING DATE: September 8, 1797

ADDRESS: 15151 San Fernando Mission Boulevard, Mission Hills, 91345

TELEPHONE NUMBER: (818) 361–0186

WEB SITE: www.archivalcenter.org

HOURS: The mission is open daily from 9:00 A.M. to 4:30 P.M., with the exception of Christmas and Thanksgiving. A fee is charged to take the self-guided tour ($4.00 for adults, $3.00 for seniors and students; children under seven are free).

DIRECTIONS: Mission San Fernando Rey de España is located in the northeastern portion of the Los Angeles basin, within the triangle formed by Interstate 5, Interstate 405, and California Highway 118 in Mission Hills. Unfortunately, it would take an entire chapter to explain how to reach the mission from each interstate. Suffice it to say that each highway has an exit that will lead you to either Sepulveda Boulevard or San Fernando Mission Boulevard; the mission is about 0.5 mile east of the intersection of these two thoroughfares. I hope that helps . . . A good street map will help even more. California Historic Landmark No. 157.

PARKING: A large parking area fronts the mission's gift shop.

SERVICES AND EVENTS: Masses are celebrated in the mission church each Sunday at 9:00 A.M. and 10:30 A.M. Mass is also offered daily at 7:25 A.M. in the Serra Chapel. Weddings, baptisms, and *quince años* celebrations are conducted by appointment. The church and grounds are also open for school tours, which must be arranged in advance.

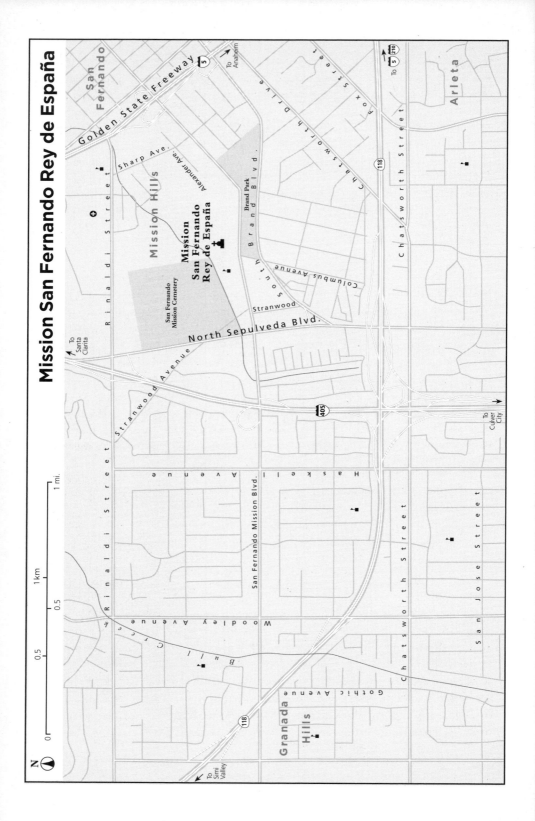

Mission San Fernando Rey de España

The Mission in the Valley, as San Fernando Rey de España is sometimes called, is just that, though the valley has changed considerably since the mission's founding in 1797. But so, too, has the mission: What was once a pastoral encampment dedicated to the cultivation of Indian souls and Indian lands is now a manicured testament to the success of the Catholic Church, both in tending its flock and in preserving and displaying its history.

You get the impression that little is left to repair or enhance at Mission San Fernando Rey. The grounds are well tended, displays in the museum and historic buildings are protected by glass or metal grilles, the paint on the walls, both interior and exterior, is fresh and bright. The battle against deterioration, which every mission in California has waged (or is still waging), has clearly been won—for now.

The Mission Yesterday

Mission San Fernando Rey's early days were peaceful and prosperous, especially in light of the difficulties encountered at its closest neighbor, Mission San Gabriel. The Native people of the San Fernando Valley, who fell under the coastal Shoshonean linguistic umbrella, had been deemed friendly by earlier European explorers, and there's nary a story in San Fernando's historical literature of neophyte uprising or unhappiness.

The mission was established by Fray Fermín Francisco de Lasuén, one of four he founded in 1797. The new mission, built on land claimed (legally or not) by the *alcalde* of El Pueblo de Nuestra Señora de Los Angeles, filled the void between Mission San Gabriel and Mission San Buenaventura. It was the seventeenth link in the chain.

The mission proved a fruitful place, outgrowing its first chapel—finished in 1799—within a year of its completion. By 1804 about 1,000 Fernandinos, as the Mission Indians were known, were counted among the mission flock, and a still-larger church was needed, this one completed in 1806.

As the neophyte population grew, so did other aspects of the mission. At its height it encompassed more than 121,000 acres, according to one source. The total count of cattle, sheep, and horses in 1819 was 21,745. Grapevines were brought to the mission from Spain via Baja California in 1797; by 1832 those few plants had reproduced in great abundance, with approximately 32,000 vines producing a good supply of claret. The mission was also known for its production of tallow, hides, soap, leather and cloth goods, olive oil, and impressive ironworks.

The *convento*, completed in 1822, took thirteen years to build, and features adobe walls that are 4 feet thick, Moorish-style arches over the windows, and twenty-one arches on the veranda, which now separate the outside corridor from the sidewalk that runs along San Fernando Mission Boulevard. In a break from the regular architectural mission plan, the *convento* was built outside the quadrangle and along the trail that led to the Los Angeles pueblo and other missions, where it served as a *hospice*, or inn, offering free respite for travelers along those routes.

The chaos of secularization came to Mission San Fernando Rey in the early 1830s. Fray Ibarra, who refused to work for the newly installed Mexican administrators of Alta California, waited as long as he could for a replacement priest who never arrived, then abandoned the mission. In 1846 Pio Pico took up residence for a time and then sold the mission, but as with other deals made by this greedy governor, the sale didn't stand up to the scrutiny of the American government that came into power shortly thereafter. Parts of the mission were returned to the Catholic Church in the early 1860s.

The mission's years of neglect are perhaps its most colorful. There was the typical looting of building tiles and materials that resulted in the exposure of friable adobe to the elements, but there were also rumors that priests had buried gold at the mission, inspiring treasure hunters to dig up the floor of the church in what was ultimately a fruitless excavation. Other mission facilities were used as warehouses and stables, and the quadrangle was, at one point, a hog farm.

Restoration efforts began at the turn of the twentieth century, with renewed interest in preservation of California's mission heritage by such organizations as the Landmarks Club. The mission was placed under the supervision of the Oblate Fathers in 1923; the Archdiocese of Los Angeles has operated the mission since the mid-1950s.

In 1971 an earthquake rocked Mission San Fernando Rey, this one accomplishing what the earthquake of 1812 and more than a century of neglect hadn't; it toppled the church built in 1806. The present church is a replica of its long-lived predecessor.

The Mission Today

That San Fernando Rey is more formal about mission history than its brethren is apparent as soon as you enter the extensive gift shop (once a dormitory for neophyte girls). After paying the fee, you are given a brochure that describes the self-guided tour of the mission grounds, and buzzed into the beautifully manicured interior of the quadrangle. Devotional music wafts over the moist lawns and rises to the sighing fronds of palm trees that surround a huge flower-shaped fountain—not original, but still an impressive work of Cordovan design. The exterior of every building is painted an earthy yellow with black accents, neat and trim. It's orderly, impeccable, and ready for business.

The tour brochure directs you first to the mission's museum, where pictures illuminate the disintegration San Fernando Rey underwent following secular-

Mission San Fernando Rey de España is well kept and well preserved.

ization, reduced by neglect and weather to a crumbling structure amid the empty rolling hills that then constituted the landscape of southern California. Religious icons, Spanish, Mexican, and English dinnerware, and examples of the basketry and beadwork created by local Indians are displayed behind glass in clean and quiet rooms, along with a collection of miniature mission bells, priestly vestments, a Franciscan habit, and remembrances of the visit Pope John Paul II made to the mission in 1987.

The back door of the museum empties onto a walkway fronting the Archival Center of the Archdiocese of Los Angeles and other administrative offices. Head left through an archway to the *mayordomo*'s house, a re-creation of what the residence may have looked like in the early days of the mission, with a dining table, humble beds, and housewares sparely and cleanly presented.

The two-story *convento*, also called the "long building" and described in mission literature as the largest original building still standing in California, adjoins the *mayordomo*'s quarters. The rooms on the ground floor have been filled with mission-era artifacts, including pictures, statuary, furniture, and musical instruments (including an old organ with hammered pipes). You can peer through the wire door into the wine cellar, watch a historical film in the Teatro de Fray Junípero Serra, and visit a simple friar's bedroom (larger than many of those in other missions); a living area (*la sala*) called "one of the largest and most elegant . . . of any among the missions"; the grandly appointed bishop's chamber, outfitted for Francisco Garcia Diego y Moreno, the first bishop of California; and an impressive library that serves as repository for volumes dating back to the mission era. Known as the Bibliotheca Montereyensis-Angelorum Dioceseos, the library holds more than 600 books: Bibles, histories, dictionaries, epistles, and instructional manuals in many different languages. Even a skeptic would be impressed by this collection of theological tomes.

Exit the *convento* at the meat-curing chamber, then reenter farther along into a room featuring a very old crucifix and one of two original confessionals from the original church. Out again, then back, into a chamber that houses a replica of a Wells Fargo coach, various historical displays, and a room dedicated to the Madonna, where music dances over a huge collection of busts, statuettes, paintings, and stamps bearing the image of the Holy Mother. Walking deeper into the building, you'll find displays of period furniture, oil paintings and other pieces of religious art, and the Governor's Room with its canopy bed.

Outside the *convento*, paths drift through well-cared-for grounds dotted with grinding wheels, old beams, and barrels. A statue of Fray Lasuén is tucked in an ivy-hung niche; follow the walkway around the West Garden to an arched doorway that leads into the mission church.

Walls painted in muted shades of red and blue on a white backdrop, a high dark roof, high deep windows, an immaculate tile floor, worn wooden pews, a choir loft, dark renderings of the Stations of the Cross—even the glow of burning votive candles and the faint scent of incense—these are familiar variations on the trappings of a mission church. The enormous gilded altar at the front of the church, which dates back to 1687 and once graced a chapel in Ezcaray, Spain, is another matter entirely.

San Fernando, king of Spain, is in the central niche of the glowing reredos, with a golden sunburst illuminating him from behind. He is surrounded by representations of the Holy Trinity, the dove at the apex symbolizing the Holy Spirit. The larger statues outside the Trinity are Saint Dominic and Saint Philip Neri, while Mary Magdalene and Junípero Serra occupy the niches below. The brightly painted pulpit, capped with an equally ornate "sound chamber," climbs the left side of the church in front of the sanctuary; on the right side, a statue of Nuestra Señora del Pilar stands on a pedestal, and a picture of Our Lady of Guadalupe hangs on the tall white wall.

Two doors open opposite each other in the middle of the church. One door leads to the tidy cemetery, where a sign and cross commemorate the 2,425 Mission Indians buried at San Fernando Rey. The other door leads down a flight of steps into the central quadrangle. The bell tower rises a story above the roof of the church, partially hidden from view behind the canopy of a tree. A statue of Junípero Serra, protected within an alcove of greenery much like his confrere Fermín de Lasuén, is just outside the mission doors.

One of the mission's original fountains can be found in Brand Park, across the street from San Fernando Rey's convento.

The mission workrooms are the final stops on the mission tour. The smithy, the saddlery, the carpenter's shop, the weaving room, and the pottery room all illustrate the industries at which the neophytes worked within the mission. The Estenaga Room houses uniforms of various religious military orders that date back to the Christian Crusades. Here, too, you'll find mission models and relics of the Wells Fargo legacy.

Nearby Points of Interest

There is no lack of opportunity for entertainment and exploration in Los Angeles. But in the immediate vicinity of Mission San Fernando Rey, the most obvious destinations are Brand Park and the San Fernando Mission Memory Garden (California Historical Landmark No. 150), which occupy the strip of land between San Fernando Mission and Brand Boulevards. The park holds one of the mission's original fountains and its soap works, as well as arbors draped in flowers, lovely rose gardens, picnic facilities, and meandering paths laid out on what was once part of the mission's original land grant.

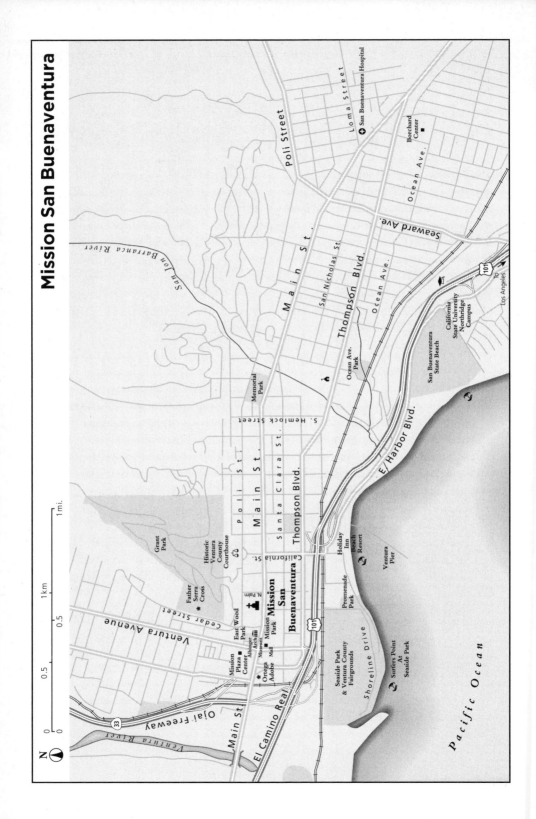

Mission San Buenaventura

Mission San Buenaventura

The Patron Saint: *According to legend, Giovanni di Fidanza, born in Italy in 1221, acquired his saintly name as a child when he cried "O buona ventura!" (O good fortune) after being healed by San Francisco de Asís. The fortunate man went on to join the Franciscan Order and become a respected philosopher, teacher, and peacemaker. He was appointed cardinal-bishop of Albano, and was considered by some the second founder of the Franciscan Order. He died in 1274, was canonized in 1482, and was declared a doctor of the church in 1588.*

FOUNDING DATE: March 31, 1782

ADDRESS: 211 East Main Street, Ventura, 93001

TELEPHONE NUMBER: (805) 643–4318

WEB SITE: www.sanbuenaventuramission.org

HOURS: The mission and its museum are open for self-guided tours from 10:00 A.M. to 5:00 P.M. Monday through Saturday, and from 10:00 A.M. to 4:00 P.M. on Sunday. A nominal fee ($1.00 for adults, 50 cents for children) is charged for the tour.

DIRECTIONS: To reach Mission San Buenaventura from southbound U.S. Highway 101 in Ventura, take the Main Street exit (on the north end of town). Pass under the freeway and continue straight on Main Street for 1 mile, crossing Ventura Avenue. The mission is at the intersection of Main Street and the Figueroa Plaza walking mall.

From northbound CA 101, take the California Street exit. Head north on California Street for 2 blocks to Main Street. Turn left (west) onto Main Street; the mission is 2 blocks ahead, on the right. California Historic Landmark No. 310.

PARKING: Parking is available at Holy Cross School, on the west side of the mission; along Main Street; or in the east parking lot, on Palm Street at Junípero Serra Way.

SERVICES AND EVENTS: Mass is celebrated Monday through Friday at 7:30 A.M.; on Saturday at 7:30 A.M, 5:30 P.M., and 7:30 P.M (Spanish); and on Sunday at 7:30 A.M., 9:00 A.M., 10:30 A.M. (Spanish), and noon, with a Tridentine Latin Mass at 1:30 P.M.

The mission also hosts two Fiestas, one on the Fourth of July and one on the first Sunday of December, in conjunction with street fairs sponsored by the city of Ventura.

When compared to its more renowned neighbor to the north—which it inevitably will be—Mission San Buenaventura comes across as refreshingly unpretentious, imparting a beachside hominess that Mission Santa Bárbara, with its expansive grounds and impressive architecture, can't begin to compete with. This is an urban mission, parked on Ventura's main thoroughfare and hemmed in by businesses and a school, but it also anchors a cultural corner, in agreeable partnership with a neighboring art museum and archaeological museum. It's a working mission, frequented by both worshipers and visitors. It's a simple mission, just church and garden and views that stretch from star pines to the beach.

The Mission Yesterday

The modern understatement that is Mission San Buenaventura belies its importance at the time of its founding. The church was the first established on the Santa Barbara Channel at the midpoint between missions on San Diego and Monterey Bays, a site originally intended by Junípero Serra and Spanish officials for the third mission in the chain. But politics and other difficulties prohibited Serra from establishing this link until the end of his career; San Buenaventura's was the last cross he raised, the ninth and final mission he founded.

The locale of the Mission by the Sea was desirable not only because of its geography, but also because its fertile hills and valleys were home to a number of Chumash Indians, a wealth of souls to save and laborers to employ. The Chumash were a prosperous and numerous people—padres who had previously traveled this stretch of coastline counted a population in the thousands, and almost universally characterized them as smart and welcoming. Their anthropological classification as a hunting and gathering society doesn't do justice to the depth of Chumash culture and the expertise displayed in the craftsmanship for which they became known, as weavers of beautiful baskets so tight they held water and as navigators of finely fashioned plank canoes.

Though they helped the Spaniards build Mission San Buenaventura and never waged a major revolt against it, the Chumash weren't eager converts. Still, some eventually became neophytes: At the mission's height, in 1816, some 1,300 Indians were counted among the faithful.

The first mission building was a brush structure on the beach; this was replaced by a second church that was lost to fire. The foundations of a third church have been uncovered in excavations near the present mission, but this one was never finished because the site was prone to flooding. Construction on the fourth and final church began in 1792 and was completed in 1809; its 6.5-foot-thick walls have withstood nearly 200 years of use and abuse.

The final mission included a quadrangle that stretched east down present-day Main Street, complete with attendant warehouses, workshops, dormitories, kitchens, and storerooms. The *camposanto* was on the west side of the church. A 7-mile-long aqueduct siphoned water from the Ventura River to the mission and its fruitful gardens, which earned the praise of British explorer George Vancouver when he visited in 1793, as well as kudos from other travelers.

In 1812 the earthquakes and tsunamis that struck the central coast proved so unnerving and caused so much damage that the priests fled the mission for a short time. The church and buildings were repaired, only to be briefly abandoned again when Argentine privateer Hippolyte Bouchard, who had just sacked the presidio at Monterey, was sighted offshore in 1818.

The secularization of San Buenaventura was ordered in 1835. The mission was rented for a time to two *Californios*, then sold by the ubiquitous Mexican governor Pio Pico to one of those renters. As with other dubious transactions authored by Pico, this one was voided by the Americans after they acquired California in the late 1840s, and the mission was returned to the church with the signature of President Abraham Lincoln in 1862.

Another earthquake in 1857 forced the replacement of the church's tile roof, but it suffered its most profound physical degradation at the well-meaning if misguided hands of one of its pastors, who decided in the late 1800s to modernize the mission by covering its tile floor and beamed ceiling, removing its small high windows and replacing them with bigger ones of stained glass, and demolishing the sacristy to make way for a school. Restoration work, much of which was carried out under the supervision of Father Aubrey O'Reilly starting in 1956, uncovered both original floor and ceiling, and returned the windows to their original size and height. The mission now looks much as it did in its heyday.

The Mission Today

The plain front of Mission San Buenaventura nestles against the sidewalk, flanked on one side by a campanile outfitted with five bells in two tiers, two of which date back to 1781. A pair of enormous star pine trees, which were planted with the intent of one day using them as masts for sailing ships, provide shade for both the mission and its small garden. A flight of stairs between mission and trees seems the obvious place to start, but to take a formal tour you must enter through a decidedly unremarkable storefront next door.

After perusing the gift shop's selection of religious items and books, head upstairs into the historical exhibit room. This tiny museum has the feel of a crowded antiques shop, with relics and artifacts jammed together in display

Mission San Buenaventura was the last mission established by mission system founder Junípero Serra.

cases, against the walls, and on shelves. Chasubles and chalices, missal stands and monstrances, crucifixes and statues, Chumash Indian baskets and a library of old Spanish books, relics from Junípero Serra's day, wooden mission bells, and the original mission doors, carved with the river of life, clutter the small room. It's a fascinating and educational treasure hunt.

The mission garden is outside the museum's back door. Four paths of tile spin from the fountain (not original) at the center of the small plaza: one to the museum, one to the street, one to the church, and one to the parish rectory, at the rear of the patio. The star pine trees are the most unusual flora in the garden, which also encompasses an old mission olive press and a shrine dedicated to Our Lady of the Apocalypse.

Opening the small door at the back of the church softly illuminates the vestibule, with the low roof of the choir loft sinking onto the tops of the bulky confessionals. The Junípero Serra Chapel is opposite the doorway, a small space protected by a grille painted green and gold, its hammered copper baptismal font most likely the work of a Chumash Indian metalworker.

The nave and sanctuary of Mission San Buenaventura are open and welcoming. Red carpets protect the original floor tiles, upon which are set light-colored pews. The high walls are painted in hues of pink and red, with a fresco of flowers in pink and green separating the shades and painted columns stretching upward between high windows and 250-year-old renderings of the Stations of the Cross. The beams of the high ceiling are painted a mottled green, and from them hang wooden chandeliers fashioned by Sir Harry Downie, famed restorer of the Carmel Mission.

The main altar and two side altars of the sanctuary host a holy assemblage. Votive candles illuminate the Shrine of the Crucifixion, its central figure a 400-year-old corpus from the Philippines that is flanked by San Antonio de Padua and Our Lady of Sorrows on the left and Saint John the Apostle and Saint Thomas Aquinas on the right. A 250-year-old painting of Nuestra Señora de Guadalupe is the focus of the right-hand altar, with Saint Dominic and Saint Gertrude on her left and Saint Isidore and San Francisco de Asís on her right. The Chumash symbols incorporated into the designs painted around the side altars form interesting frames for their subjects. Similar Native designs enliven the reredos behind the main altar, its four golden columns set against a marbleized background. The columns separate three niches painted a vivid blue. The figures housed in these alcoves depict, from left to right, Mary the Immaculate Conception, San Buenaventura, and San José holding his son, the Christ child. The mission's patron saint overlooks a simple crucifix.

The exterior decorations over the center side doors of the church are a Chumash representation of the mission and its surroundings, with the upper line denoting the hills behind the mission, the sloping lines on either side of the central niche representing the Ventura River on the west and the Santa Clara River on the east, and the statue of the Blessed Mother in the niche representative of the mission itself. The doors are re-creations of the originals crafted by Downie, who was faithful to the river of life design.

As for the rest of the mission, that's mostly been buried under the city of Ventura. The quadrangle, with its residences and workshops, stretched down what is now Main Street; Holy Cross School is built on the *camposanto*. Behind the church, you can check out the exposed brickwork of a settling tank that dates back to 1829, and if you climb the stairs that lead into the modern plaza separating the Serra Center from the mission, you can visit the graves of a triumvirate of padres, Vicente de Santa María, José Señan, and Francisco Suñer.

Nearby Points of Interest

A walk down Figueroa Plaza offers visitors a chance for respite with a view, and an opportunity for the little ones to cool their jets. Located directly across Main Street from the mission, the plaza stretches to Santa Clara Street, with blue-tiled fountains at each end linked by a shallow blue tile aqueduct—an irresistible invitation to water play for anyone under the age of ten. The plaza is lined with businesses and restaurants, and borders the lawns and small groves of trees that surround Ventura County Museum of History and Art (www.vcmha.org; 805–653–0323).

The Albinger Archaeological Museum (805–648–5823), located opposite the art and history museum and next to Holy Cross School, encompasses ongoing excavations of Ventura's history from the time of the Chumash. Digs have uncovered a Chumash *tomol* (canoe) and exposed mission-era adobes, roof tiles, and foundations, including those of the abandoned church.

Other mission-era sites, described in detail in a Mission San Buenaventura pamphlet sold at the mission gift shop, include Serra's Cross (La Loma de la Cruz) on the hill behind the mission, and the Olivas Adobe Historical Park.

If you want to eat and shop, Main Street offers a plentitude of options, including inexpensive taco shops and thrift stores. And there's always the beach.

Mission Santa Bárbara

The Patron Saint: Barbara is as much fairy-tale princess as she is saint, her very existence a matter of faith more than verifiable fact. Born in the early days of Christendom, the beautiful Barbara was sequestered in a tower by her father to protect her from suitors, but a hermit was able to convert her to the new Christian religion. Her devotion to this new and controversial faith enraged her father; he turned her over to judges, who condemned her to death. She was martyred in the fourth century.

FOUNDING DATE: December 4, 1786

ADDRESS: 2201 Laguna Street, Santa Barbara, 93105

TELEPHONE NUMBER: Parish office (805) 682–4713 ext. 121; gift shop (805) 682–4149

WEB SITE: www.sbmission.org

HOURS: The mission is open from 9:00 A.M. to 5:00 P.M. daily. A moderate fee ($4.00) is levied for the mission tour, and includes an informational brochure. The mission archive library is open from 9:00 A.M. to noon and from 1:00 to 4:00 P.M. Monday through Saturday and can be entered by appointment only; the telephone number is (805) 682–4713 ext. 152.

DIRECTIONS: To reach the mission from northbound or southbound U.S. Highway 101 in Santa Barbara, take the Mission Street exit. Head northeast on Mission Street, toward the mountains, for about 1 mile to Laguna Street. Turn left (north) onto Laguna Street; the mission is directly ahead. California Historic Landmark No. 309.

PARKING: Parking is available in a large lot that spans the front of the mission, and in a second lot immediately to the mission's left (west). Overflow parking is available along residential streets.

SERVICES AND EVENTS: Masses are celebrated weekdays at 7:30 A.M., Saturday at 4:00 P.M., and on Sunday at 7:30 A.M., 9:00 A.M., 10:30 A.M., and noon.

Living up to being the "Queen of the Missions" is not easy. Other missions have bigger churches, fabulous collections of mission-era art and statuary, extensive grounds upon which lie intriguing archaeological remains, impressive cemeteries,

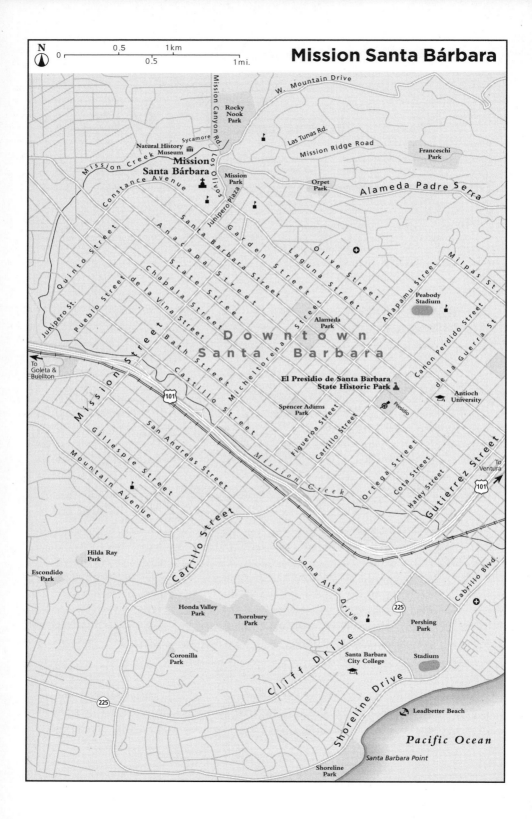

Mission Santa Bárbara

N

0   0.5   1km
0   0.5   1mi.

W. Mountain Drive

Rocky Nook Park

Las Tunas Rd.

Mission Ridge Road

Franceschi Park

Natural History Museum

Sycamore

Mission Creek

Mission Canyon Rd.

Los Olivos

Mission Santa Bárbara

Mission Park

Constance Avenue

Mission Park

Orpet Park

Alameda Padre Serra

Junipero Plaza

Quinto Street

Anacapa Street

Santa Barbara Street

Garden Street

Laguna Street

Olive Street

Junipero St.

Pueblo Street

Chapala Street

State Street

de la Vina Street

Bath Street

Micheltorena Street

Alameda Park

Anapamu Street

Milpas St.

Peabody Stadium

Mission Street

Castillo Street

D o w n t o w n
S a n t a   B a r b a r a

Cañon Perdido Street

de la Guerra St.

To Goleta & Buellton

El Presidio de Santa Barbara State Historic Park

Antioch University

Gillespie Street

San Andreas Street

Spencer Adams Park

Figueroa Street

Carrillo Street

Presidio

Mountain Avenue

Mission Creek

Ortega Street

Cota Street

Haley Street

Gutierrez Street

To Ventura

101

Carrillo Street

Loma Alta Drive

225

Hilda Ray Park

Escondido Park

Honda Valley Park

Thornbury Park

Cliff Drive

Pershing Park

Cabrillo Blvd.

Coronilla Park

Santa Barbara City College

Stadium

Shoreline Drive

225

Leadbetter Beach

Pacific Ocean

Santa Barbara Point

Shoreline Park

and beautiful gardens. These other missions, arguably, have just as much claim to a royal title as does Mission Santa Bárbara.

But no other mission combines these attributes with such elegance and authority. Mission Santa Bárbara, haughty on its hilltop overlooking the Santa Barbara Channel, its two towers rising in majestic complement to the green peaks of the Santa Ynez Mountains, does all of this. It is a gilded crown, polished, poised, and as nearly perfect as a mission can be.

The Mission Yesterday

The Spaniards who cruised the California coast in the 1500s and 1600s with an eye toward expanding their empire recognized Santa Barbara's potential from the first. But it wasn't until 1782 that Spain manifested its claim to the region, establishing a presidio near the shoreline on April 21 of that year. Padre Junípero Serra envisioned a mission to accompany the presidio, but politics and military matters delayed its construction for four long years. Serra died in the interim, leaving his successor, Fermín Francisco de Lasuén, to break ground in 1786 on Mission Santa Bárbara.

The missionaries found a generous population of Chumash Indians near their newest mission. Headed by Chief Yanonali, the village of Siujtu alone was home to 500 people, just a small portion of the more than 5,000 Chumash who may have lived along the channel at the outset of the mission era. The Chumash were a remarkable people, called "friendly," "intelligent," and "resourceful" by various historians. Occupying large villages between San Luis Obispo and Ventura, they developed a thriving hunter-gatherer culture, fishing the waters of the channel in plank canoes called *tomols* and augmenting that staple of the California Indian diet, the acorn, with seafood and small game. They made watertight baskets into which they wove wonderful designs. And they maintained dynamic social and spiritual lives that incorporated dances, the creation of mystical rock art, and ball games.

The padres wooed the Indians with gifts and food, converting more than 4,700 of them over the years, according to historian Maynard Geiger. Recognizing that these were a powerful and numerous people who could overrun both mission and presidio if provoked, the padres were lenient in their imposition of religious order on the Chumash, which no doubt made mission life all the more palatable to the Natives. In 1807, according to mission literature, more than 1,700 neophytes lived in a mission *rancheria* of about 250 adobe homes, working at typical mission trades such as animal husbandry and harvesting olives. Mission historians detail the bounty they generated: In 1814 the mission supported more than 15,000 head of livestock (cattle, sheep, horses, and pigs); in 1821 more than 12,800 bushels of wheat, barley, corn, beans, and peas were harvested. The Indians also helped construct the mission quadrangle

Henry Chapman Ford created a number of evocative images of California's missions, including this rear view of Mission Santa Bárbara, perched on its hill overlooking the sea.

and all the workrooms, dormitories, and other buildings that it comprised, as well as the *convento*, and the dam and aqueduct that supplied the mission with water.

Four churches were raised in succession on the site, the first of wood (1787) and the next two, built in 1789 and 1794, of adobe. The last adobe mission was destroyed in the earthquakes that rattled California's central coast in 1812; Padre Antonio Ripoll undertook construction of the stone church that would replace it. Built under the supervision of a master stonemason, the facade of the new church was sculpted of local sandstone and anchored by two bell towers, and was sturdy enough to stand for more than a century. It was finished in 1820.

For many of Alta California's missions, the secularization order issued by the Mexican government in 1834 was a raging disaster, with mission lands sold into private hands or incorporated into ranchos granted to powerful *Californios*. Much of the property that once fell within the bounds of Mission Santa Bárbara wasn't exempt from this redistribution; it was first rented, and then sold into private hands in 1845.

But the church remained with the Franciscans who had founded it. In 1842 Francisco Garcia Diego, the first Catholic bishop of both Alta and Baja California, took up residence at the mission, as did Narciso Duran, then padre presidente of the system. The presence of these two preeminent religious figures instilled caution in greedy *Californios* itching to pillage the queen. But when both men died in 1846, Pio Pico hovered over the mission like a buzzard over a wounded doe; his attempt to sell the church was foiled just in time by the American occupation of Alta California.

Still, secularization and the transition from Spanish to Mexican to American governance had scattered the mission's neophytes and stripped it of its original mandate, which meant the Franciscans had to find other ways to keep Santa Bárbara viable. In 1856 an apostolic college was brought to the mission; in 1903 a Franciscan seminary was established on the grounds.

The earth rumbled beneath Santa Barbara's mission and town again in 1925, causing massive damage to the old mission church. It was restored—the exterior true to the 1820 design and the interior completely refurbished—and rededicated in 1927. The external repairs cracked and frayed over the next thirty years, and the mission underwent another face-lift in the 1950s. Today it shines, as a queen should.

The Mission Today

Mission Santa Bárbara is a busy place, especially on weekends, with visitors gathered in clumps around the arches of the two-story *convento* and crowding the museum exhibits. But there's plenty of space and plenty to see; patience will result in an appreciation of why crowds have gathered here.

A tour of the mission begins in the *convento*, which houses the museum and the parish offices, as well as the archives, repository for many mission-era records and documents. Doors etched with the river of life offer entry into the mission's gift shop, where a wall-sized display succinctly recounts the mission's history from the discovery of the Santa Barbara Channel by Juan Rodriguez Cabrillo in 1542 to the reconstruction of the church in 1925.

The museum fills a line of *convento* rooms. The culture of the Chumash, showcasing the tribe's fine basketwork and novel plank canoes, dominates one chamber. In a second, the history of the mission is captured in photographs and artifacts. In other rooms, you'll find portraits of San Antonio de Padua, San Buenaventura, and San Francisco de Asís; more historical photographs; Indian-carved statues of Hope, Charity, and Santa Bárbara, which were once part of the mission's facade; and polychrome statues of the Virgin Mary and Saint Ildephonse, a Spanish monk who lived in the seventh century.

The museum also contains re-creations of a missionary's room—with an original bed and a frayed friar's hat—and of a *cocina* (kitchen), the original adobe bricks and other artifacts protected by a wall of glass. Mission industry is on display as well: blacksmithing, pottery making, weaving, and the creation of paints using natural and imported pigments. Upscale artifacts associated with California's first bishop, Francisco Garcia Diego, include an inkstand and a "bishop's doll."

The last few chambers of the museum hold pieces of devotional and modern Chumash art. In the small theater, vestments and musical artifacts are displayed, along with a corpus from the Philippines in which every wound suffered by Christ in his last torment is grotesquely depicted.

A narrow doorway leads from the museum to the mission's central patio, planted with palms and roses. A fountain centers the quiet, lovely garden. The rustic walls of the *convento* and the church, as well as church offices and classrooms, enclose the space. Access to the Blessed Sacrament Chapel and the mission church is provided by a ramp and a short flight of stairs.

Inside the church, the choir loft shelters the confessionals and baptismal font in the back of the nave. In an alcove on the left, a fabulous statue of Jesus and Mary at his tomb rests under a painted dome; on the right, under a painted dome of their own, stand Santa Clara and San Francisco de Asís. A short hallway leads to a small, colorful room at the base of the church's bell tower, the repository for the mission's first altar and tabernacle. The cross on the altar dates back to 1786, was created by the local Indians, and is set with glowing abalone shells.

The nave is ornately painted in blues, greens, oranges, and golds, with deep reds accenting columns that reach to the high finished ceiling. The original Stations of the Cross (1797) and impressive paintings decorate the walls: Archangels Michael, Gabriel, and Raphael are on the left, and Saints Agnes, Clare, and Margaret of Cortona are on the right. Two mural-sized portraits hang at the transition from nave to sanctuary, one of the crucifixion, the other portraying the Assumption and Coronation of Mary. An alabaster statue of the Pietà is on the left above the communion rail.

A grand reredos rises behind the main altar, painted in a swirling marble of yellow and gold. A crucifix backed by a golden sunburst is the centerpiece; beneath, in a large niche, is a statue of Santa Bárbara. Mary the Immaculate Conception, Saint Joseph, Saint Francis, and Saint Dominic occupy niches on either side of the crucifix.

The Blessed Sacrament Chapel is intimate and warm, with windows that allow the afternoon sun to set aglow both the room and the lovely tabernacle within it. A window opens onto the sanctuary of the church, so that overflow crowds can witness the celebration of Masses on Sundays and holy days.

The central patio is linked to an even smaller courtyard behind the chapel; from there a flight of stone steps leads to the retreat center behind the church and to the back of the mission cemetery. The stone walls of the church, broken in places by circular windows, form an impressive backdrop for the *camposanto*, as does the old Moreton Bay fig tree whose gnarly roots spread among the graves like those of a mangrove in a swamp.

The cemetery was established in 1789, and is the final resting place for more than 4,000 Chumash Indians and a number of Spaniards as well. Those interred here include Padre Narciso Duran and Chumash Indian chief Pedro Yanonali, as well as Juana Maria, the "lone woman of San Nicolas Island." Burials also were made in a crypt below the church floor, where Padre Antonio Paterna, one of the mission's first fathers, and Governor José Figueroa, the first Mexican-

Mission Santa Bárbara, known as the Queen of the Missions, boasts an impressive facade anchored by two bell towers.

born governor of California, are interred. Mausoleums line the back of the *camposanto*; museum literature notes that one of those vaults was a charnel house, in which the bones of neophytes dug from the burial grounds to make room for more dead were stored. The artistic imagery of the cemetery is suitably dark: a skull and crossbones carved over the entrance to the church, a crucifix with rust like blood staining Christ's hands and feet, a sundial marking time that means nothing to the dead.

The gate that issues from the cemetery is nestled against one of the campaniles, which holds two tiers of bells that toll the call to services. Outside the gate you'll find yourself in the shadow of the church's formidable facade, eyes drawn upward to the two domed towers. A wide bank of stairs drops from the heavy doors to the parking lot and the lawn beyond, and also down to the veranda of the *convento*, its weathered adobe walls lined with benches that face the sea.

The grounds surrounding the mission are dotted with the remains of the more functional aspects of its operation. A 200-year-old fountain, its waters paved in lily pads, sits beside the long pool of the *lavanderia*, which was built in 1818 and features spouts sculpted into the heads of mountain lions. Tanning vats, the jailhouse, and other ruins lie in neighboring Mission Park. And at the base of the sloping lawn that spreads oceanward from the mission's doors, a fabulous rose garden blooms, heady with fragrance and vivid with color.

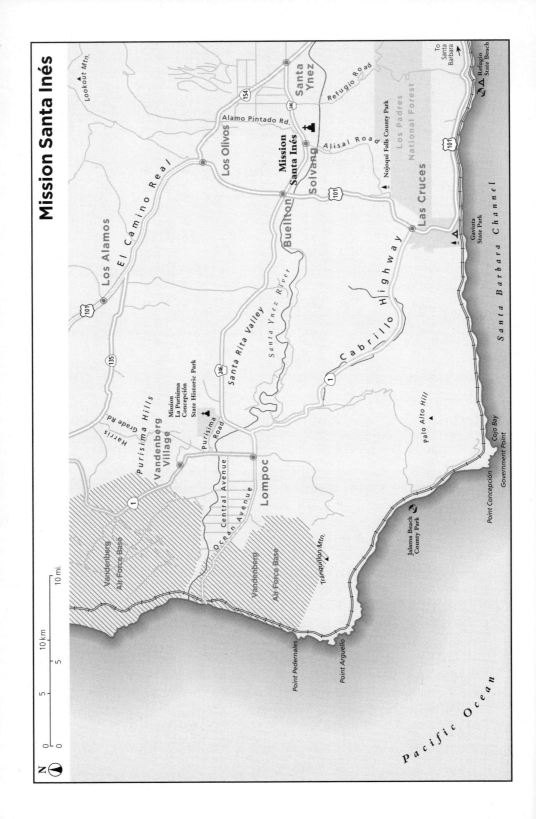

Mission Santa Inés

Mission Santa Inés

The Patron Saint: *Saint Agnes was a fourth-century Roman girl (thought to be only thirteen when she was martyred) who refused marriage because of her faith in the fledgling Christian religion. Her declaration of betrothal to Christ prompted authorities to send her to a brothel, but she was spared the humiliations of this sentence when her hair grew thick and fast enough to obscure her nudity, and when a man who attempted to see her was struck blind. Condemned to death for her devotion, the flames of the pyre on which she was to be burned alive were miraculously extinguished, so she was beheaded instead.*

FOUNDING DATE: September 17, 1804

ADDRESS: 1760 Mission Drive/P.O. Box 408, Solvang, 93464

TELEPHONE NUMBER: (805) 688–4815

WEB SITE: www.missionsantaines.org

HOURS: The mission is open from 9:00 A.M. to 5:30 P.M. daily; the gift shop is open during the same hours, and until 7:00 P.M. in summer. A small fee ($3.00 for adults, $2.50 for seniors) is levied for the self-guided tour. The door between the museum and church is locked during Masses.

DIRECTIONS: To reach Mission Santa Inés from U.S. Highway 101 either northbound or southbound, take the California Highway 246 exit for Solvang and Lompoc. Head east on CA 246 for 3.6 miles, through downtown Solvang, to the mission, which is on the right (south). California Historic Landmark No. 305.

PARKING: A large paved lot spans the front of the mission.

SERVICES AND EVENTS: Masses are celebrated daily at 8:00 A.M., on Saturday at 5:00 P.M. and 7:00 P.M. (Spanish), and on Sunday at 8:00 A.M., 9:30 A.M., 11:00 A.M., 12:30 P.M. (Spanish), and at 5:00 P.M. Marriages and baptisms are performed by appointment.

The mission hosts several annual celebrations, including Art Under the Arches, held over the Memorial Day weekend, a Fiesta held during the second week of August, and the Rancheros Vistadores horseback-riding event held during the first week of May.

Mission Santa Inés and its setting are a study in melding—blending the old with the new, the Spanish with the Danish (yes, Danish), the secular with the holy. Such juxtapositions could be jarring, but the mission strikes an interesting balance, one in which you are aware of disparities, but not disturbed by them.

That Santa Inés, the "Hidden Gem" of the California mission system, is the heart of a working Catholic parish is obvious from the moment you turn into the parking lot. It is as clean and polished as Mission San Fernando Rey de España, its buildings well maintained, its cultural heritage meticulously documented, its old face and its new presented with pride and care.

The Mission Yesterday

The nineteenth founded in Alta California, Mission Santa Inés was established by Padre Presidente Estevan Tapis to bridge a gap between the Santa Bárbara and La Purísima Concepción missions, to provide a buffer for those missions against the unfriendly Tulare Indians, and to bring the benefits of Christianity to the Chumash Indians living on the west side of the Santa Ynez Mountains.

Fray Fermín Francisco de Lasuén had selected the site years earlier, after Tapis and Captain Felipe de Goicoechea of the Santa Barbara Presidio scouted the inland valley and determined that the Indian population was rich enough to support another mission. But death and politics intervened: Both Lasuén and the governor who had approved the mission passed away, leaving Tapis to convince a new governor that the new endeavor should move forward, and to dispel concerns that the standard contingent of six *soldados* might not prove sufficient against a potential Indian attack.

This the padre accomplished in 1804, and construction began on the site even before the mission was formally dedicated. Santa Inés was considered an immediate success—112 converts were recorded by the end of its founding year, construction of a second wing of quadrangle was completed in 1805, a third wing was built in 1806, and new quarters for the padres were finished in 1807. Historians note that Santa Inés benefited from more than twenty years' experience in the mission-founding business, the willingness of the Chumash Indians to support the missionaries, and the proximity of the well-established Santa Bárbara and Purísima missions. In 1817, one of its most productive years, the mission boasted a population of livestock—horses, cattle, pigs, sheep, and mules—numbering more than 12,000, and harvested more than 4,000 bushels of wheat, 4,300 bushels of corn, and 300 bushels of beans.

The mission's history isn't entirely one of success, however. It was hit hard by the earthquakes that rattled the area in December 1812, which damaged the original church, knocked down a number of adobe dwellings, and toppled the second floor of the *convento*. Repairs were made during the next four years under the guidance of Padre Francisco Xavier Uria, who oversaw construction of the adobe-and-brick church that stands to this very day.

In February 1824 the Indian attack that had been a concern at the time of the mission's founding finally materialized. Santa Inés was the locus of a violent and destructive neophyte rebellion that also affected the missions at Santa Bárbara and La Purísima. Disgruntled by a lack of monetary support from officials in the newly independent Mexico (according to some sources), soldiers living at the missions had been taking out their frustrations on the neophytes. The soldiers forced them to work harder, longer, and without compensation, which in turn fueled dissension among the resident Chumash. The flogging of an Indian by a soldier at Santa Inés pushed unrest into revolt, and the Chumash attacked the mission, holding both priests and soldiers hostage and burning barracks and workshops. (They stopped short of burning down the church, reportedly because their quarrel was with the soldiers, not the missionaries.) When the rebellion at all three missions was finally quashed, more than a dozen Indians were dead and many others had fled, fearing military reprisals.

The mission was secularized in 1834, but the Franciscan fathers who ran it were able to keep both the church and their quarters, enabling them to carry on with their ministry. A land grant was issued to Bishop Francisco Diego Garcia to establish a college east of the mission in 1844; this is often confused with a seminary dedicated to Our Lady of Refuge that was established at the mission itself in 1835, and later moved to Santa Barbara. When Pio Pico became the Mexican governor of Alta California, the mission was sold for $7,000, but the onset of American rule in 1846 rendered his nefarious deal moot.

President Abraham Lincoln restored Mission Santa Inés to the Catholic Church in 1862, but by then the Franciscans had left the mission in the hands of other religious orders, and the buildings had begun to suffer the disrepair and disintegration common to its brethren. In 1882 an Irish family, the Donahues, moved into a part of the rectory and did some restoration work, but still the adobe crumbled. It wasn't until 1904, the centennial of its founding, that the mission began to see the benefits of restoration efforts. Undertaken by Father Alexander Buckler, those repairs included adequately roofing the buildings to protect fragile adobe from erosive winter rains.

Restoration efforts have continued under the watch of Capuchin Franciscan priests, who arrived at the mission in 1924. The Capuchins revived the mission garden, installed electricity and plumbing, and oversaw extensive restoration work—work that is ongoing, and might one day result in the regeneration of the original quadrangle in its entirety.

The Mission Today

Mission Santa Inés's exterior is polished and functional, its simple facade and the arches of its *convento* painted a creamy yellow and trimmed in a dark brown that gives depth to the pilasters on either side of the church and matches the brown of the heavy wooden doors. The *campanario*, a re-creation of the original, holds

The reredos at Mission Santa Inés, with its mix of Spanish and Chumash Indian influences, is a visual feast.

three bells, including one that was cast in Lima, Peru, in 1817. The original bells are on display in the mission museum.

The mission's gift shop doubles as the entrance to the museum, which shares the *convento* with parish offices. The audio tour, accessed by pressing buttons in each of the museum rooms, is informative; artwork and artifacts within the museum are also labeled thoroughly, in the event you choose not to listen to the recordings.

The museum's first room is a festival for the eyes. Paintings of various saints, including a depiction of the martyrdom of Santa Inés and a portrait of Saint Raphael composed by a neophyte, complement a lovely display of vestments dating back to the seventeenth and eighteenth centuries, including one worn by Junípero Serra.

More religious art is displayed in the museum's second room, along with a map of Spain's holdings during its days of empire, an old confessional, a mission model, and a library of historical photographs of California's missions. In the third room you'll find missals and Bibles, polychromed wood statuary, and domestic items that shed light on the lives of Indians before and during the mission era, including pottery and basketry, adobe bricks and candlesticks, metates and metalwork.

The last room is dedicated to the Madonna. A polychrome statue of Our Lady of Sorrows gazes upward at a crucifix; other images of the Holy Mother and her son occupy the small chamber. A tile in the floor holds the footprint of a Mission Indian, a tangible relic left by one of those who worked so hard to build the mission.

A narrow hallway carved through a 12-foot-thick adobe wall leads into the church. The artistic imagery of the Chumash Indians enlightens the high walls of the nave—wispy, shadowy images in green similar to those that decorate the walls at neighboring La Purisíma mission. The walls are also hung with renderings of biblical events—Christ at the well of Jacob, Christ and the fisherman—and Stations of the Cross brought to the mission from Mexico in 1818.

An entire room is dedicated to the Madonna.

Inside the baptistery, near the rear of the nave, a font of zinc and copper made by the mission's neophytes rests beneath a polychrome statue of Saint John the Baptist. Statues of Saint Anthony holding an infant Jesus and scenes from Christ's nativity are set in alcoves along the church walls.

The tiles on the mission floor are original, as are all but two of the ceiling beams; a red carpet leads up the center aisle to the sanctuary. The fertile, swampy images of the Chumash, rendered with pigments generated from native sources, decorate the reredos. A statue of Santa Inés dominates the sanctuary, which she shares with the Madonna of the Rosary and a 200-year-old wooden cross from Mexico.

The mission's gardens are superbly manicured and maintained. Stone paths form the shape of a cross with the fountain at its heart. Prickly pear and salvia thrive under the scant shade of palm and olive trees, and roses bloom toward the rear of the garden, where part of the floor of the Seminary of Our Lady of Refuge of Sinners—California's first college—has been unearthed. A shrine dedicated to the Capuchin Franciscans rests amid cacti and roses near the back wall of the mission enclosure; a plaque and map show where you stand within the original quadrangle, and also describe portions of the present mission that are original: the church, a section of the *convento*, and the nineteenth arch of the arcade. The tale of Pasquala, a Mission Indian girl who ran from her home among the Tulare Indians to warn Padre Uria of impending rebellion in 1824, is described in this corner of the garden as well.

As many as 1,700 souls were laid to rest in the *camposanto*, which stretches along the north side of the church. There aren't nearly enough wooden crosses and marble headstones to account for all the dead, but those that remain are poignant and creative: the broken cross of Noble Lizzie, headstones set with seashells, a tiny marble memorial marked simply BABY. The headstones of the priests and brothers interred in the cemetery are tucked close against the yellow church wall, surrounding a statue of the Madonna and Child.

The rest of the quadrangle is off-limits, a closed gate barring access to the parish offices housed in the rest of the *convento*. The back door of the gift shop leads through to the grounds in front of the mission, which hold other remnants of Santa Inés's past. The original reservoir, dating back to 1808, splits the parking lot in two. The gristmill built by Joseph Chapman in 1820 can be sighted from an overlook on the far side of the lot; at the end of the colonnade fronting the mission, the original arch, its heart of brick exposed, rises heavenward.

Nearby Points of Interest

The quaint little Danish village of Solvang, complete with windmills, backs up to the mission. The town offers a variety of activities for visitors, including the opportunity to shop for European gifts and antiques, and to enjoy European cuisine. More information is available at www.solvangusa.com, or by calling the Solvang Conference and Visitors Center at (800) 468–6765.

Mission La Purísima Concepción

The Patron Saint: *La Purísima Concepción de Maria Santisima (the Immaculate Conception of Mary Most Holy) is not a saint in the traditional sense, but Mary is an important intercessory figure in the Catholic Church.* Immaculate conception *refers to the belief that Mary was conceived without original sin.*

FOUNDING DATE: December 8, 1787

ADDRESS: La Purísima Mission State Historic Park, 2295 Purisima Road, Lompoc, 93436

TELEPHONE NUMBER: (805) 733–3713

WEB SITE: www.lapurisimamission.org

HOURS: La Purísima Mission State Historic Park is open daily from 9:00 A.M. to 5:00 P.M. Mission buildings close at 4:30 P.M. A moderate admission fee is charged ($4.00 for vehicles, $1.00 for a park map). The mission is closed on Thanksgiving, Christmas, and New Year's Day.

DIRECTIONS: To reach La Purísima mission from northbound or southbound U.S. Highway 101 in Buellton, take the California Highway 246 exit for Lompoc and Solvang. Go west toward Lompoc on CA 246 for 13.8 miles to Purisima Road, which is marked with signs for both the mission and Vandenberg Air Force Base. Turn right (northwest) onto Purisima Road and continue for 1 mile to the park entrance, which is on the right. California Historic Landmark No. 340.

PARKING: Ample parking is available in the large lot behind the entry kiosk.

SERVICES AND EVENTS: No Masses are celebrated at this Mission. However, school tours and docent-led tours are offered. Tours are slated Monday through Friday at 2:00 P.M., and on Saturday, Sunday, and holidays at 11:00 A.M. and 2:00 P.M. Tours take one to two hours to complete, and encompass an easy walk of about 1 mile.

A number of special events are held at La Purísima. Those held once a month from March to September or October include Mission Life Days (generally held on the third Saturday of the month) and Purísima's People Day (generally held on the first Saturday of the month). Village Days and Mountain Men Days are held twice annually;

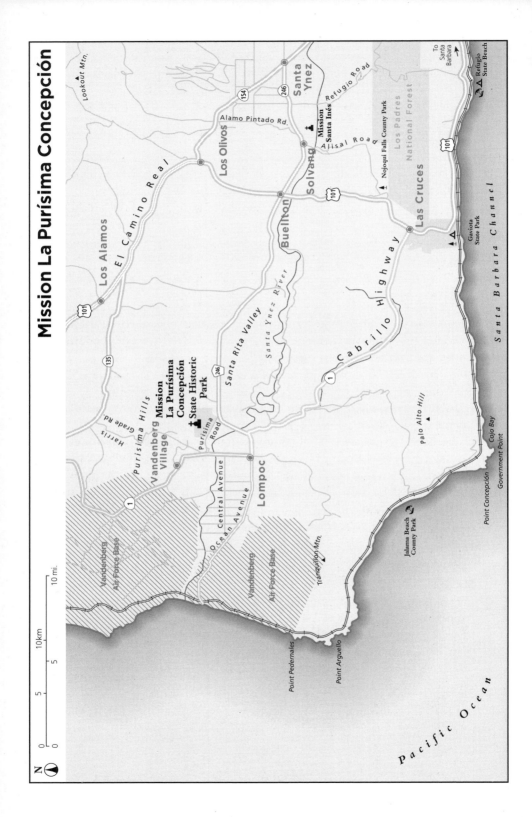

Mission La Purísima Concepción

the dates are subject to change but are posted on the mission Web site. Candlelight Tours are held during the second weekend in October, and the Founding Day celebration is held on December 8 of each year. Contact the park or visit the mission Web site for complete details.

It would be tough to find a prettier setting for a mission. Visual aesthetics probably were not a consideration—nor hard to come by—when La Purísima Concepción was established, but the centuries that have passed since its founding have eliminated the wilderness familiar to missionaries and the indigenous people they sought to convert, making the undeveloped loveliness of the site all the more remarkable.

It would also be tough to find a place that better exemplifies what mission life was like. La Purísima is a living history museum, the most completely and truly reconstructed mission in the world. Its adobe chambers are redolent with the smell of extinguished candles and wood fires, yarn remains strung on its loom, tools in the carpenter's shop and the smithy are ready for use. The hands that work the loom and hold the tools these days are those of well-trained docents, but the activities they re-create and the images they evoke faithfully recall the lives of those who came before.

The Mission Yesterday

La Purísima's mission days were turbulent and troubled, but the story of its renaissance is inspirational.

Padre Fermín Francisco de Lasuén founded the mission, the eleventh in the mission chain, to bring Christianity to the Chumash Indians. Amply sustained in the years prior to European contact by an abundance of foodstuffs gathered from their environment, the Chumash had perfected the crafts of basket making and canoe building; had developed a spiritual and social complex that included ball games, ceremonial dances, and the creation of rock art; and presented a healthy population of souls to be saved.

The first La Purísima mission was constructed 4 miles distant from the present site, in what is now downtown Lompoc. It was productive from the first, with 95 baptisms recorded the first year; by 1798 the mission had outgrown its first church, with 920 neophytes on the books. Construction of a second church was finished in 1802, the focal point of a mission that included workshops, granaries, barracks, dormitories, storehouses, and more than one hundred tule houses for neophytes, as well as orchards, gardens, and pens for a wealth of livestock. It wasn't all good—about 500 neophytes perished from contagion between 1804 and 1807—but overall the mission flourished.

By 1812 the mission, under the leadership of Padre Mariano Payéras, who is universally remembered as a just administrator, boasted a neophyte population of about 1,000 souls, and supported more than 20,000 head of cattle, sheep, horses, and other livestock. Then came the December earthquakes, which ravaged the coast and leveled much of the mission. What the temblors didn't take out, the mudslides and rainstorms that followed did.

The Franciscans selected a different site, in the "canyon of the watercress," upon which to rebuild their mission, and again generated success. Adjacent to El Camino Real, the reinvigorated La Purísima enjoyed a vigorous trade in hides and tallow. It was built in a linear fashion rather than upon a quadrangle—a design diversion that some writers attribute to a desire to make the buildings easier to escape in an earthquake—and its holdings sprawled across the bottomlands of the Santa Ynes River Valley. The main compound included the church; residences for the padres, the *mayordomo*, the *soldados*, and the neophytes; and warehouses, workshops, and infirmaries. Farther flung were orchards, cultivated fields, and the springhouse, which supplied the mission with fresh water via a complex system of aqueducts, cisterns, and fountains.

In 1824 the mission suffered yet another blow. According to several sources, the new Mexican government found itself unable to financially support its distant holdings in Alta California, which engendered dissatisfaction among the *soldados*. The soldiers vented their frustrations on the neophytes, who in turn grew disgruntled. The beating of an Indian at Santa Inés sparked an insurrection, and sympathetic Chumash at La Purísima took up arms, occupying the mission for a month before soldiers from the presidios at Monterey and Santa Barbara reclaimed it. The incident resulted in a number of Indian dead, as well as in the deaths of Native leaders executed in the aftermath of the revolt.

A declining neophyte population drove the padres from the mission in the early 1830s, and secularization in 1834 brought about its sale by Mexican governor Pio Pico to rancher John Temple for a little over $1,000. Though La Purísima was returned to the Catholic Church in 1874, its deterioration, like that of its sister missions, was well under way. By the time restoration efforts began at La Purísima in 1934, not much of the original structures was left.

The Civilian Conservation Corps, whose Depression-era public works projects resulted in the preservation and restoration of a number of cultural and natural treasures, worked with the National Park Service, the state of California, and Santa Barbara County to re-create at La Purísima what the neophytes and padres had wrought more than a century before, from the construction of buildings using mission-era methods to the replication of mission-era tools and artifacts. Their work was halted in 1942 with the onset of World War II.

La Purísima State Historic Park, which now includes nearly 2,000 acres and 25 miles of trail surrounding the historic mission, works in conjunction with Prelado de los Tesoros de la Purísima (Keepers of the Treasures of La Purísima), a volunteer organization, to support the reconstructive and living history programs that are ongoing at the mission.

The Mission Today

It's one thing when it is crowded with visitors and docents, quite another when it is empty. To describe La Purísima during one of its living history events would be like trying to describe a summer carnival—it could be done, yes, but to truly get the picture you'd have to be there. Consider this a snapshot taken after the carnival has closed.

The services that will be housed in a new visitor center, slated to open in December 2004, resided at press time in two humble adobes once used as infirmaries. The first adobe, distinctly evocative of the Spanish frontier with heavy wooden floors and roof beams held in place with rawhide straps, served as a small museum. Exhibits included Chumash Indian artifacts (among them a floor tile inscribed with a Native symbol), artifacts from the mission era (ax head, spinning wheel, scissors), succinct historical information about the mission from founding to restoration, and a wonderful diorama that depicted in miniature La Purísima as it appeared in 1825. The neighboring adobe housed the mission gift shop and bookstore, as well as restrooms.

Cross the bridge outside the adobes, and step back in time to 1825. Paddocks for sheep, cattle, and horses border the broad gravel path that leads to the mission *camposanto* and *campanario*. A sign marks the passage of El Camino Real, and a cluster of racks slung with dried hides is on the left. A narrow aqueduct severs the ground fronting the mission, and a gigantic prickly pear blossoms from the pink adobe wall next to the cemetery entrance. The red-and-yellow flag of Spain flutters from a pole in the open court fronting the church.

The *camposanto* is studded with a single cross commemorating all the dead buried at the mission. The bell wall, which holds reproductions of two original mission bells, links the mission church to the cemetery. A wooden ladder leads up from the dusty hallowed ground to a platform from which the bells can be struck.

Functional aspects of mission life back up to the spiritual, with soap vats and tallow vats just outside the back door of the cemetery. A covered veranda runs the length of the back side of the church, birds nesting in its eaves and dirt caught in waves on the adobe walls.

The doorways to the church are flanked by prickly pear, and give entry to a high, cool nave. Benches are pushed up against the walls, as is a lonely confessional hung with a faded purple cloth. The choir loft hovers over the back of the nave, its underside painted and the wall at its base warped by a spring. Oil paintings of the Stations of the Cross hang above pale frescoes in blue and gold that decorate the walls to waist height, bordered by scrollwork of faded orange; more abstract and copious wall decorations cover the walls below the choir loft.

Though this is clearly a secular building, its historical function is not neglected. Abalone shells perch in wall niches flanking the doorways, receptacles for what, in a mission church, would be holy water. A baptismal font rests on its pedestal by the rearmost doorway. Opposite the forward door, a statue of San Miguel stands with hand upraised behind glass. Large oil paintings, including one of the Arcángel Miguel, hang on the walls near the sanctuary.

The pulpit climbs the right side of the church, painted with the same abstract design that decorates the walls under the choir loft, reminiscent of light passing through lake water. The sanctuary, furnished with a bell wheel among other pieces of furniture, is backed by a reredos indented with three niches. A crucifix sits atop the bright blue altar, heavy candlesticks set to either side. The Immaculate Conception occupies the central niche, her hands pressed together in prayer. The pattern of heavy wooden planks that makes up the floor of the sanctuary is broken by the grave marker for Padre Payéras, born in Mallorca, Spain, in 1769, and buried in this distant Spanish outpost in April 1823.

The *cuartel*, or soldiers' quarters, are adjacent to the church, outfitted with cots, shields, weapons, and other military paraphernalia. Doors open along the shops and quarters building to the corporal's apartments and the interior courtyard, with its chicken coop, *hornos* (ovens), olive trees, grapevines, picnic tables, and barbecue pits. Other rooms include apartments for married soldiers, a candle-making room, and the master weaver's quarters.

Behind the *mayordomo*'s apartment, with its carved canopy bed and armoire, there is another patio, this one enclosing an olive mill and press. The carpenter's shop is next to the *mayordomo*'s rooms, and beyond that is the weaving room featuring a reproduction of an original loom upon which docents transform yarn spun from the wool of the mission's churro sheep into shawls and blankets.

The private padres' chapel dominates the residence building, with its great buttress and long portico of both original and reproduced arches. Again, a statue of the Immaculate Conception occupies the middle of the reredos behind the altar. The walls are hung with religious paintings; a small choir loft is suspended over an ornate confessional at the rear of the chapel. Two tiers of windows wash the chapel with sunlight, which reflects off heavy wooden floors and white walls painted with a simple wainscot of orange and blue.

A smaller chamber off the chapel holds a baptismal font; here you'll also find vestments on display. In the schoolroom artifacts include spurs used by vaqueros, hand tools, adobes, choir books, a mission bell, and a painting of Saint Michael rescued from the mission chapel in the 1860s. Several tables are spread with

This hut is part of a re-created Indian village on the grounds of Mission La Purísima Concepción.

items to be touched: metates and manos, yokes and hides, roof tiles and clay pipes. (These items will be moved to the new visitor center when it is opened.)

Other rooms in the monastery include a leatherworking shop, an unfinished room that demonstrates how original and new adobe walls were married during restoration, the padres' quarters, *la sala* (the living room), a dining room, and a guest room that was once used, according to mission literature, by trappers and sea captains. The mission office occupies the final room, outfitted with a fine couch, a desk, and a collection of books.

Outside the office, trails lead to the vegetable garden, the pigpen, and the blacksmith's shop (*la herreria*). The path opposite the shop leads between a plowed field and fragrant scrub to the mission aqueduct and springhouse. In front of the mission complex, paths wander through a re-created Indian village and a garden of native and exotic plants—ceanothus, Apache-plume, artichoke, Rose of Castile, toyon—each identified with signs describing its medicinal or traditional uses. The gardens surround the *lavanderia*, a pool in which Natives both bathed and washed clothing, a pair of fountains, a sundial, and an enormous wooden cross.

A path leads from the gardens to the horse paddock, then curves to a bridge, continues through a picnic area, and deposits you back at the parking lot.

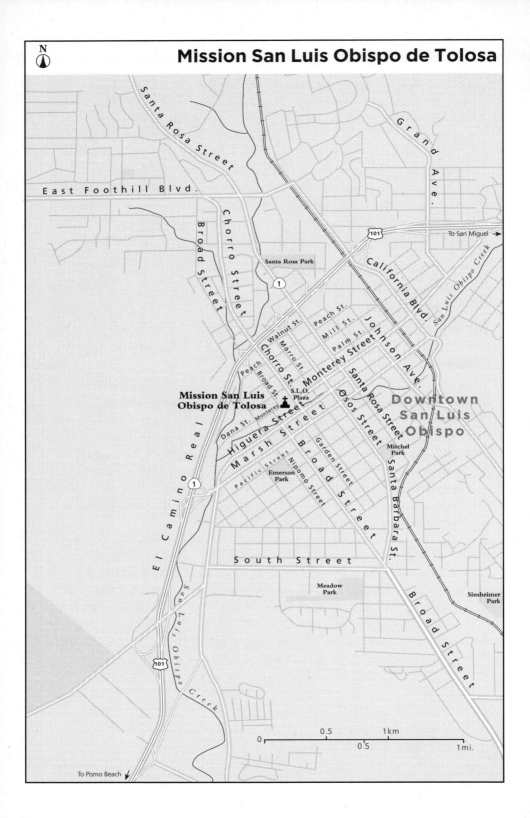

Mission San Luis Obispo de Tolosa

The Patron Saint: A son of kings, Louis was born a prince of Naples in 1274. After his father lost a war in Spain, he and his brothers were sent as hostages to that country, where they studied with Franciscans. After being set free, Louis remained with the order, was ordained a priest in 1297, and then was quickly promoted to the bishopric of Toulouse. He held the post only a short time, dying at the youthful age of twenty-three. He was canonized in 1317.

FOUNDING DATE: September 1, 1772

ADDRESS: 751 Palm Street, San Luis Obispo, 93401

TELEPHONE NUMBER: Parish office (805) 781–8220; gift shop (805) 543–6850

WEB SITE: www.missionsanluisobispo.org

HOURS: The mission and gift shop are open from 9:00 A.M. to 5:00 P.M. daily during the summer months, and from 9:00 A.M. to 4:00 P.M. in winter. Donations are accepted.

DIRECTIONS: To reach the mission from northbound or southbound U.S. Highway 101, take the Broad Street exit in the town of San Luis Obispo. Follow Broad Street south for about 0.2 mile (four blocks) to Monterey Street; mission buildings border Broad Street for the last block, and the city plaza forces motorists right onto Monterey Street. California Historic Landmark No. 325.

PARKING: A very small parking lot is located behind the mission off Palm Street. Metered parking is available along city streets and in public parking lots scattered around downtown San Luis Obispo. The town is a busy place, especially on weekends, so be patient, and be prepared to walk.

SERVICES AND EVENTS: Mass or communion service is celebrated daily at 7:00 A.M. and 12:10 P.M., with a Spanish Mass on Thursday at 7:00 P.M. Saturday's Vigil Mass is held at 5:30 P.M. On Sunday, Mass is celebrated at 7:00 A.M., 9:00 A.M., 10:30 A.M., 12:10 P.M. (bilingual), and 6:00 P.M.

The mission holds a couple of annual events: the Fiesta of Our Heritage in late August, and the Our Lady of Guadalupe celebration on December 12.

Worshipers overflow the church, spilling onto the staircase that descends into the city plaza. At the doorway, the priest stands with a young mother and father, holding their infant child. The baby, soon to be baptized, is blessed and introduced to his religious family with an inviting mix of the formal and the informal, with a friendly intimacy and a distance born of mystery.

This blend of mystery and familiarity permeates Mission San Luis Obispo. The center of a working parish in the heart of a busy downtown district, it wears its place in California's history like a rich mantle. But there is a strictly modern facet to this mission, an appeal that stretches forward in generations, as if it were a painting by a master artist that has been updated in colors true to the original, but vivid and somehow trendy.

The Mission Yesterday

In California autumns, the fog that cools the coastline in summer is blown offshore, leaving beach and valley exposed to a hot and brilliant sun. Shade probably wasn't a consideration when Fray Junípero Serra established Mission San Luis Obispo in 1772, marking the site of the fifth mission by hanging a bell in a sycamore alongside San Luis Obispo Creek, but that riparian canopy would prove a relief to many a future mission resident—and visitor—on hot fall days.

Actually, Serra had selected the site in part because of the abundance of meat that could be found nearby—meat of the California grizzly bear, which abided in great numbers in a region that became known to the Spaniards as the level (or plain) of the bears. Gaspar de Portolá and members of his expedition had noted the populous and dangerous omnivores when they marched through in 1769; later, when missionaries, soldiers, and neophytes at the Carmel and San Antonio de Padua missions found themselves starving, a group of hunters was dispatched to the valley. They carted twenty-five mule loads of jerked bear meat and seeds back to the famished colonists.

The valley was home to Chumash Natives, an amiable and intelligent people with whom the Spaniards shared the spoils of their bear hunt and who later would be recruited as neophytes of the mission. San Luis Obispo was established by a handful of Spaniards—Fray José Cavaller was initially the sole padre (there were usually two), supported by a skeletal crew of five soldiers and two neophytes—but this handicap was overcome with relative swiftness. Native laborers helped them erect the first crude mission structures, composed of brush and branches, and the conversions began. By 1804 mission records would reflect a population of more than 800 neophytes at San Luis Obispo.

Not all of the Indians were friendly to the Spaniards or neophytes, however. Hostile tribes to the east plagued the mission in its early years, once using flaming arrows to set fire to the wooden structures. When a new mission church was constructed in 1793 and 1794, the padres incorporated a building material introduced to Alta California at Mission San Antonio—baked red clay tiles—rendering the church roof both fire- and waterproof. The tiles were shaped over wooden molds and became a standard feature for missions built thereafter.

By 1820 San Luis Obispo was a successful working mission. Its quadrangle, completed in 1819, included a *convento* with a portico (today supported by round columns), warehouses, storerooms, workrooms, and residences. Tanning vats, a gristmill, corrals, vineyards, gardens, and orchards surrounded the quad, as did a Mission Indian village. Indeed, San Luis Obispo was successful enough to merit an *asistencia*—Santa Margarita. The combination porch/bell loft of the mission, a unique structure incorporated into the front of the building, was outfitted with bells cast in Peru in 1818.

Many of San Luis Obispo's most prosperous years were overseen by Padre Luis Antonio Martinez, remembered in mission literature as a popular and able priest who would serve for more than thirty years. Martinez was an outspoken critic of Mexican rule, which came to the missions in the early 1820s after independence was won from Spain; his stewardship ended in 1830, when he was arrested and falsely accused of treason by the Mexican governor of California, then sent into exile.

Mexico's order to secularize the missions in 1834 sparked the beginning of a period of decline at San Luis Obispo. Its properties were turned over to secular authorities, though the priests were allowed to continue their ministries. Padre Ramon Abella, the last Franciscan to serve at San Luis Obispo, died in 1842; three years later the mission was sold by Mexican governor Pio Pico to a trio of men for $510.

Pico was ousted in 1846 when the United States gained control of California. The mission was returned to the Catholic Church in 1859, and fell under the supervision of Joseph Alemany, bishop of Monterey, who had petitioned for and won claims to some of California's mission lands in the 1850s and 1860s. But this victory didn't translate into religious revitalization, and in the last half of the nineteenth century San Luis Obispo found itself used not only as a parish church, but also as the town's first school, a jailhouse, and the county courthouse.

In the 1870s the mission was extensively remodeled: Its porch/bell tower was removed, its interior and exterior were clad in clapboard, and a steeple was erected over its church. It also saw enough growth that in 1893, Father Valentin Aguilera built part of the current annex to accommodate new parishioners. After a fire damaged the sacristy in 1920, efforts to restore the mission to its original form were instigated; by 1934 all the wood had been removed, and the porch/bell loft with its trio of bells rebuilt. In the late 1940s Harry Downie, the restorer of Carmel Mission, helped with restoration of the church, as well as an addition to the annex. Wall decor on the church's interior has been completed in recent years.

The Mission Today

High and humble on its tree-shrouded hill, Mission San Luis Obispo overlooks a shady plaza bounded by San Luis Obispo Creek, which flows through a narrow channel enclosed by bulkheads and the concrete foundations of businesses and restaurants. Clean and straightforward, a splash of red tile, white walls, and black trim, it greets shoppers in the busy downtown district, couples strolling along the creek or sitting in the shade of sycamore and bay laurel, and children playing in a fountain decorated with statues of a Chumash child and grizzly bears.

Stairs converge on the church and its *convento* from both the plaza and Chorro Street. The climb lends the mission a lofty presence, made all the loftier by the fact that the bell tower is flush to the canopies of the trees that crowd it. To watch the bells ring, a carillon that beckons the faithful to Mass, you must descend into the plaza and then crane your neck—and still they are screened by leaves and boughs.

The inside of the church is long and narrow, lit by small windows, painted white with a fresco of flowers low on the walls. The dark cement floor is a break from the more common tile floors found in other missions. In an alcove a few pews inside the door hangs a painting of the Madonna and Child; opposite is a memorial to Adeline Eliza Dana, a small child buried within the church wall. Stations of the Cross proceed up the nave to the altar, whose wood reredos is composed of columns and simulated marble fronted by Christ on the cross. Saint Joseph and Mary the Immaculate Conception flank the crucifix, with a newly restored statue of San Luis Obispo facing the annex that stretches to the right.

The annex is narrow and high ceilinged like its older counterpart. The tabernacle sits in an alcove to the immediate right of the sanctuary. Niches and shelves along the annex walls hold statues and candles, and a small prayer room glows with the flickering light of votive candles. The doors of the annex open onto a sunny garden that stretches alongside the church, well-tended shrubs and flowers surrounding a circular fountain.

The mission garden proper lies on the other side of the church, bounded by the museum and gift shop on the south, the church on the east, and the parking lot and youth center on the north. Brick paths lined with little mission bells lead to a wishing well and into the shade offered by an arbor hung with grapes. Roses dominate the plantings, abundant and colorful.

The entrance to the mission museum is through the gift shop, a three-room complex in the *convento* packed with religious items and mission memorabilia. The museum is housed in a series of well-lit, whitewashed rooms, the first and third of which contain an extensive collection of Chumash Indian artifacts, including shell and stone beads and necklaces, flintknapped points, stone tools, basketry, and information about how the Natives lived both before and during missionary times. Other rooms contain missionary furniture; religious relics

Brick paths lead to a wishing well in the gardens of Mission San Luis Obispo de Tolosa.

such as vestments, crosses, statuary, and fonts; a spectacular altar behind glass; and a marvelous collection of historical pictures, including some of the mission taken at the turn of the twentieth century, some of the priests who served here, and some of surrounding adobes. An exhibit that traces California's transition from an outpost of the Spanish empire to a state of the Union includes such artifacts as old dolls, women's dresses, old cameras, sewing machines, guns, tea, historic pictures of the town of San Luis Obispo, an Edison Amberola dating back to 1898, and the original mission doors.

Nearby Points of Interest

San Luis Obispo is a bustling tourist town, as well as home to one of the most prestigious universities in California. Bookstores and clothing stores, upscale restaurants and coffeehouses, candy shops and boutiques line the grid of streets that surrounds the mission. For the shopper and the gourmand, it's a delight.

If you don't feel like eating or shopping, the little path that runs along San Luis Obispo Creek provides a pleasant interlude. Pathways of stone, brick, and wood lined with benches drop from the plaza to a small amphitheater, then down to the creek itself, where stepping-stones allow kids (and adults) to skip from one side of the waterway to the other. Staircases lead up from the creek to the restaurants and shops that hover above.

Ten minutes on the freeway leads visitors from San Luis Obispo to the Pacific Ocean and its beaches. Avila Beach is the first off US 101; Pismo Beach lies farther south.

Mission San Miguel Arcángel

The Patron Saint: Saint Michael, one of the three angels mentioned in both the Old and New Testaments, is a warrior angel, captain of the armies of God, and protector of both Jews and Christians.

FOUNDING DATE: July 25, 1797

ADDRESS: 775 Mission Street/P.O. Box 69, San Miguel, 93451

TELEPHONE NUMBER: Parish office (805) 467–2131; gift shop (805) 467–3256

WEB SITE: missionsanmiguel.org

HOURS: The mission is open daily from 9:30 A.M. to 4:30 P.M. Museum tours are halted at 4:15 P.M. Donations are accepted.

DIRECTIONS: From southbound U.S. Highway 101, take the Tenth Street exit in San Miguel, which is marked by a CALIFORNIA HISTORIC LANDMARK sign for the mission. Follow Tenth Street east for two blocks to Mission Street. Turn left (south) onto Mission Street to the mission, which is on the right.

From northbound US 101, take the Mission Street exit. The mission is located no more than 0.1 mile from the end of the exit ramp. California Historic Landmark No. 326.

PARKING: A parking area sprawls the length of the mission's *convento*.

SERVICES AND EVENTS: Because earthquake damage has forced closure of the mission church, Masses are conducted at Casa San Miguel, located at Fourteenth and Mission Streets in San Miguel. Masses are held Monday through Friday at 7:00 A.M., Saturday at 9:00 A.M., and Sunday at 7:00 A.M., 11:00 A.M., and 6:00 P.M. (Spanish).

Note: Mission San Miguel was badly damaged in an earthquake that struck in December 2003. While the gift shop and museum have since reopened to the public, the historic church must undergo significant repairs that, according to mission spokespeople, will cost millions and take years to complete. To assist in the efforts to revitalize the mission, donations to the Mission San Miguel Preservation Fund are encouraged; visit the mission's Web site for more information.

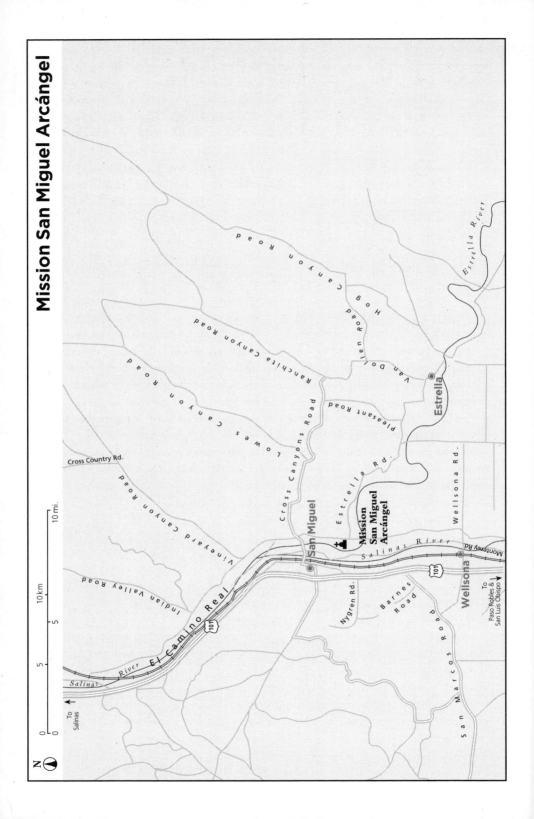

Mission San Miguel Arcángel

It shows its age. Inside and out, Mission San Miguel is venerable, chipped and frayed by neglect and hard use, bleached by the omnipresent southern California sun. Outside, the adobe veneer has peeled away from the brickwork of the arches supporting the veranda, and the paint that remains on the front of the church and *convento* has weathered to the same mosaic of blonds and browns as summer-dried grasses on the surrounding hills. Inside the long, hollow church, cracks split the painted walls, and the edges of the niches that hold the holy water have been nibbled away, as though time were a hungry mouse.

But it's a vibrant old age, with beauty still clear beneath the laugh lines, the frown lines, and the sunspots. It's a phoenix not readying for rebirth, but settled comfortably into its ragged, colorful, serviceable feather coat.

The Mission Yesterday

One of four missions founded in 1797 by Padre Fermín Francisco de Lasuén, and the sixteenth mission in the California chain, San Miguel Arcángel filled a long gap along El Camino Real between Missions San Antonio de Padua and San Luis Obispo. It also occupied land inhabited by the Salinan Indians, who were hailed by the padres as friendly and eager to join the mission community. Historians surmise that the Indians welcomed the mission because of the stability it promised—they would no longer have to range the coast and inland valleys hunting and gathering with the seasons, as the mission provided reliable meals and permanent shelter.

But stability was not the experience of one of the missionaries stationed at San Miguel in its first year. Padre Antonio Horra went insane shortly after being assigned to the new outpost—driven mad by ants and loneliness, according to one historical account—and was shipped back to Mexico. He was replaced by a hardier soul, Padre Juan Martin, who would remain with the mission for twenty-seven years and see it through its major trials and triumphs.

The neophyte population of Mission San Miguel grew steadily through the early years of the nineteenth century. The first church was replaced within a year of the mission's founding to accommodate the growing neophyte population, which topped 1,000 in 1805 and by 1814, the mission's apex, included 1,076 souls. Indians weren't the only living beings who abided at the mission in abundance—there were also herds of cattle, horses, and sheep totaling more than 20,000 head, according to mission literature.

The healthy neophyte population, with the assistance of neighboring missions, helped San Miguel recover swiftly from a devastating fire in 1806. Flames damaged the church and several other buildings, and destroyed all of the mission's cloth and leather goods, plus about 6,000 bushels of wheat. The destruction, though profound, proved but a hiccup: Within a year the mission was operating smoothly again, the center of a vast network of ranchos and outposts

Mission San Miguel's long deterioration was well under way by the late 1800s, when Henry Chapman Ford created this image. Restoration efforts continue today as the mission struggles to recover from a December 2003 earthquake.

that at its height would stretch 18 miles north and south from its core, westward to San Simeon by the sea, and inland for 66 miles.

San Miguel's final church—the one that stands today—was built between 1816 and 1818. The huge edifice—144 feet long, 27 feet wide, and 40 feet high, supported by walls 6 feet thick—was raised in that astonishingly short amount of time because of the industry of the neophytes in the years after the fire, during which they made tens of thousands of adobe bricks and clay tiles. Estevan Munras, a native of Barcelona, Spain, was recruited to decorate the interior of the new church in 1821, but San Miguel's neophytes were employed there as well. Munras and the Indians used stencils and local pigments moistened with cactus juice to render the colors of their passion on the walls of the nave, creating the frescoes that are celebrated to this day.

In 1836, in accordance with Mexico's secularization order, the Franciscans were dispatched from mission control and a secular administrator was installed. The last mission to be secularized, San Miguel declined swiftly: By 1841 a scant thirty neophytes remained, along with a lone padre, Ramon Abella, who died in that year. In 1842 the mission fell under the direction of Padre Miguel Gomez at Mission San Luis Obispo. And finally, in 1846, the mission and its properties were put up for sale by Mexican governor Pio Pico, and purchased by Petronilo Rios and William Reed. The price was $600.

The mission's history grew both tragic and bawdy after its sale. William Reed and his family, who'd taken up residence at the mission, were murdered by a gang of miscreants who'd come to California in search of gold; the murderers were then hunted down by a posse and executed in Santa Barbara. In subsequent years the site was used as a saloon, a dance hall, and a warehouse. Though it passed back into the ownership of the Catholic Church in 1859, the mission wasn't assigned a priest until 1878.

After a long hiatus, Mission San Miguel was placed back in the hands of the Franciscans in 1928. Under the restrained and respectful watch of the order that founded it, the mission has seen preservation and restoration efforts that haven't altered its historical beauty or power.

The Mission Today

A long yard enclosed by a low fence stretches from the plain-fronted church to the end of the picturesque *convento*. Within this yard a desert garden of hardy cacti and sunburned roses flourishes. Beehive ovens, metates, a gristmill, an olive press, a sundial, and a statue of Padre Junípero Serra have been placed under the occasional shade of an olive tree in the succulent garden, and a lily-filled fountain sits at its center.

Twelve arches of different shapes and sizes, their adobe worn away in spots to reveal their brickwork bones, support the portico; the floor is brick as well, the roof constructed of tiles laid on wooden slats. The side-door entrance to the church opens off the arcade near the mission bell, which hangs in the curve of an arch.

The church (visited prior to the December 2003 earthquake) was cool and dark, rough edged and ponderous. The rough brick floor supported dark, heavy pews; broad planks that appeared unfinished formed the distant ceiling. It was a somber place, one in which martyrs were venerated and sorrows lay thick.

The Stations of the Cross, carved in relief on wood panels, stretched from the darkness under the choir loft forward to the altar; muted oil paintings hung among them. A Madonna stood above a small altar near the side door, surrounded by flowers and flames that fluttered behind the thick glass of the holders in which they burned.

The remarkable frescoes that decorated the nave were illuminated by a sparse light that flowed bluish through the high windows piercing the adobe walls on the *convento* side of the church. Still, from sanctuary to choir loft, the artwork was simply spectacular. The sun rose between the first row of pews and the chancel, splashes of red and green shot from a great blue orb. A dove decorated the crown of the pulpit, the sanctuary was framed in ornate painted columns, and the all-seeing Eye of God gazed out over the statue of San Miguel at the center of the reredos. The frescoes, which had remained untouched through the more than 150 years since their rendering, were clearly a source of great pride at Mission San Miguel. And rightfully so.

Chips and cracks in the adobe at time-worn Mission San Miguel Arcángel enhance the structure's venerable charm.

In the reredos San Francisco de Asís sat in the niche to the left of the mission's patron saint, while San Antonio de Padua occupied the niche on the right. An aged statue of Saint Joseph was the focus of the side altar on the right; on the left stood a more modern statue of the Holy Mother. Two priests are buried in the church: Padre Juan Martin, who guided the mission for more than a quarter century, and Padre Marcelino Cipres.

The mission's gift shop and museum occupy several rooms in the *convento*. Religious artifacts dominate the museum collection (and gift shop selections), with a large, wonderful statue of San Miguel that dates back to the sixteenth century commanding the first chamber. In the second room, once used for wine making, the mission's history is described in a time line and illustrated with historical photographs, and two mission models constructed by inmates at San Quentin Penitentiary capture Missions San Miguel and San Antonio de Padua in miniature. Vestments, basketry, choir books, and other relics round out the museum collection.

The mission garden lies beyond the museum doors. The public is not permitted to wander the garden paths, but from the shade of the interior veranda, you can look out across the lovely, well-tended landscape, its blossoms and greenery surrounding a fountain. The other boundaries of the garden are marked by the mission's living quarters.

The corridor behind the museum is brightly painted, and the mission's original doors, as well as other artifacts, lie along the walls. Doorways beckon from the corridor, opening into rooms and alcoves in which different aspects of mission-era life are modestly showcased. In a dark hallway that once was a sheep gate, deteriorating harnesses and other tools of animal husbandry hang from the rough, original adobe walls, illuminated by shafts of light that eke through the roof tiles above. From the *cocina*—with its original beehive oven, kettle, griddle, and soot-darkened pots—duck through a low doorway into a high-ceilinged living chambers. Old pottery, an old trunk, an old bed, an old piano, an old hide chair, old timbers bearing signs of termite damage, old painted roof tiles, and an old loom and spinning wheel rest evocatively in the dim yellowish light that filters through windows made of thin sheets of sheepskin.

The cemetery huddles between the patched, streaked wall of the church and a high adobe wall. The *camposanto* dates back to March 1798, when the first neophyte was buried here; more than 2,000 Mission Indians would follow, but no headstones survive to mark their graves. The bronze statue of Christ on the cross that towers above the cemetery paths once adorned the inside of the church. A three-bell *campanario* rises from the rear of the church near the back of the graveyard, a narrow stone staircase climbing to a platform from which the bells could be rung. One of the bells, cast in San Francisco in 1888, weighs 2,000 pounds, according to mission literature. The stone-and-brick foundations of the bell tower are adobe-free and of a startling textural beauty.

Nearby Points of Interest

The Rios-Caledonia Adobe and Museum (California Historic Landmark No. 936) is next door to the mission, and houses collections—dresses and dolls, furniture and kitchenware—that illustrate the lives of the residents who settled in the area. The two-story adobe was built in 1846 by Petronilo Rios and named Caledonia in the 1860s; it served as the Rios family home and headquarters for its cattle operations, then as a hotel, and as a stage stop between Los Angeles and San Francisco. For more information, call the adobe's gift shop and museum at (805) 467–3357.

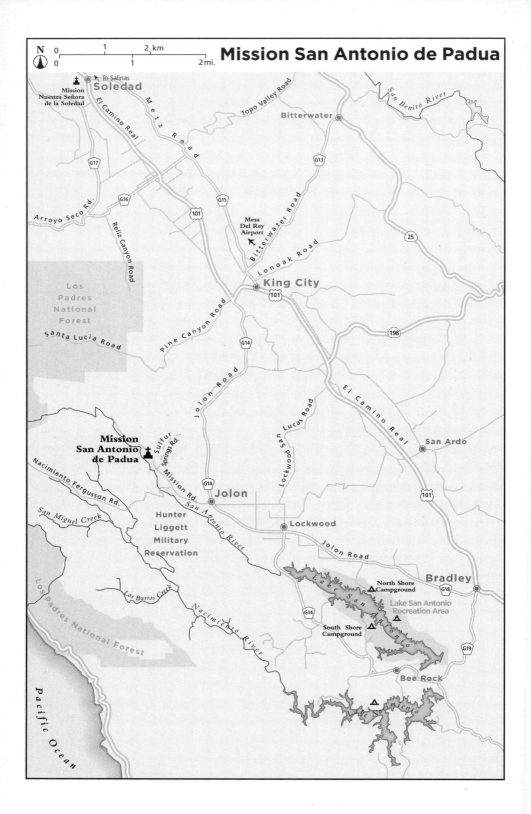

Mission San Antonio de Padua

The Patron Saint: *Christened Ferdinand when he was born in Portugal in 1195, the future saint joined the order of Saint Augustine as a young man. He later joined the Franciscan Order, took the name Anthony, and became a professor of theology and a celebrated preacher. Anthony also was reported to have performed a number of miracles in his lifetime. He died in Padua in 1231, and was canonized in 1232.*

FOUNDING DATE: July 14, 1771

ADDRESS: P.O. Box 803/End of Mission Creek Road, Jolon, 93928

TELEPHONE NUMBER: (831) 385–4478

WEB SITE: Mission San Antonio de Padua has no dedicated Web site.

HOURS: The mission museum is open for self-guided tours from 8:00 A.M. to 5:00 P.M. daily during the winter months, and from 8:00 A.M. to 6:00 P.M. daily in summer. The gift shop is open from 10:00 A.M. to 4:00 P.M. Monday through Saturday, and from 11:15 A.M. to 4:00 P.M. on Sunday. A $1.00 donation is suggested.

DIRECTIONS: From U.S. Highway 101 southbound in King City, take the Jolon Road (Monterey County Road G14) exit. Follow scenic Jolon Road southwest for 18 miles to Mission Road and the entrance to Fort Hunter-Liggett. Turn right (west) onto Mission Road, and pass the entrance gate to the military post. Stay straight on Mission Road, through the post, to the driveway for the mission, which is on the left and marked with a large sign.

From northbound US 101 in Bradley, take the Jolon Road (Monterey County Road G18) exit. Follow Jolon Road northwest for 21 miles to Mission Road at the Fort Hunter-Liggett entrance. Turn left (west) onto Mission Road, and follow the directions above to the mission. California Historic Landmark No. 232

PARKING: Plenty of parking is available in the large lot fronting the mission.

SERVICES AND EVENTS: Mass is celebrated Sunday at 10:00 A.M. in the mission church, and daily in the chapel at 7:30 A.M. Weddings and baptisms are performed at the church. The mission hosts its annual Fiesta on the second Sunday in June.

Mission San Antonio de Padua's setting, in a high mountain valley where tall grasses and wildflowers swim around the burly trunks of oak trees, harks back to the time of the missions with great effectiveness. Instead of manicured gardens and sloping green lawns, this mission is pillowed by a woodland in which you can feel, if not see, the snakes, lizards, and crickets at home in the grass, the hawks, buzzards, and jays watching from the treetops, the deer and the hare hiding in the brush.

The mission itself is as raw and picturesque as its surroundings, a weathered and natural place. The church and its arcade, their exteriors weathered to muted shades of brown, cream, and red, are a complement to the mountain backdrop, and the exposed foundations and rustic adobe walls of structures that re-create its quadrangle lend the site an enhancing poignancy.

The Mission Yesterday

Mission San Antonio de Padua was built in a secluded hollow in the Santa Lucia Mountains near the confluence of the San Antonio River and Mission Creek. Known as the Valley of the Oaks, the area was inhabited by Salinan hunters and gatherers who had created a rich and sustainable culture finely tuned to the environment they found themselves a part of. The valley would prove equally hospitable to Franciscans and their Spanish attendants.

Junípero Serra established the mission a scant two years after he arrived in Alta California, hanging a bell in an oak tree at a spot 1.5 miles from the present mission site. The story goes that even though no Indians were around to

The setting of Mission San Antonio de Padua remains much as it appeared in the late 1800s, when Henry Chapman Ford set its image onto paper. The Valley of the Oaks is still relatively remote and pastoral.

witness the founding ceremonies, Padre Serra summoned them exuberantly, ringing the bell and shouting out a welcome.

Eventually the Indians did come, lured by gifts and the persuasive arts of the missionaries who offered them. The third mission in the chain was moved to its present site, near a better water source, in 1773, and by the end of that year 163 neophytes called San Antonio de Padua home. The marriage of Juan Maria Ruiz to Margarita de Cortona, "a Salinan neophyte," was performed in 1773 as well, their nuptials representing the first Catholic marriage conducted in Alta California, according to mission literature.

Padres Miguel Píeras and Buenaventura Sitjar were assigned the task of building the mission into a self-sufficient entity, a goal they accomplished with relative alacrity. When San Antonio de Padua reached its height, in the early nineteenth century, it was home to about 1,300 neophytes and encompassed housing for the Indians and the padres, a gristmill (said to be the first in California), a threshing floor, a cemetery, storerooms, workshops, and barracks for the three to six *soldados* assigned the task of providing protection for the settlement. In addition, an aqueduct sluiced water from the San Antonio River, 3 miles distant, into reservoirs used to irrigate extensive vineyards, orchards, and gardens.

A "great church" was erected on the mission's quadrangle between 1810 and 1813, a building 200 feet long and 40 feet wide, with timbers supporting its roof and adobe walls up to 6 feet thick. The neighboring *convento*, with its long arcade, was completed in 1816. And the distinctive burned-brick facade, which incorporates a *campanario* hung with three bells, was added in 1821, just as the fruitful Spanish era was ending and the turbulent years of Mexican rule commenced.

Mexico, unable to provide sufficient financial support for California's missions, ordered their secularization in 1834. For most missions, that meant the sale of land and resources to wealthy *Californios*. This was not the fate of San Antonio de Padua, however, for although the mission was placed under the purview of a civilian administrator, its padres limited to providing religious services for those few neophytes who lingered, a buyer was never forthcoming.

And the mission's spectacular decline began. By 1841 only 150 neophytes remained. A single stalwart padre sustained a ministry at the mission until his death in 1882, but without a vigorous resident population, he couldn't fend off the inevitable deterioration. Uncle Sam returned the mission to the church in 1862, but that, too, did little to alter the pitch of its downhill slide.

The mission's abandonment in 1882 was a boon to looters, who robbed the buildings of everything valuable, including the roof tiles. Rain and wind now ate at the structures, melting them down until nothing was left but the brickwork cores of the church walls, its distinctive facade, and the arches that once fronted the *convento*.

Beginning in 1903, interest in the preservation of California's missions reached the secluded Valley of the Oaks, and work on San Antonio's restoration got under way. Sir Harry Downie, renowned for his work at the Carmel Mission, played an important role in the restoration of the mission, as did funding from the William Randolph Hearst Foundation. The mission's revival also included the return of the Franciscans in 1928; under the guidance of the order that established it, San Antonio found itself once again a parish church, and later a brothers' school.

By 1952 the mission's reconstruction was complete, reborn from its own adobe dust. San Antonio de Padua today is an active parish and retreat center, and a revitalized link to days long gone.

The Mission Today

Under a blistering summer sun, the gardens fronting Mission San Antonio de Padua are more noteworthy for the artifacts scattered among the plantings than for the prickly plants themselves. Metates and figureheads from sailing vessels brought inland by sailors recline on the parched ground under the serene gaze of a statue of Junípero Serra. A mission olive tree and a mission grape scrabble water and life from the dry soil, plants that, according to signs, may have been brought to San Antonio de Padua by the padres who arrived in Alta California in 1769.

Burned bricks were used in the construction of the church's distinctive *campanario*, or bell wall, its red-checkered appearance antiqued by exposure. The same burned bricks were used to build the pillars that support the roof of the arcade. Three bells are slung in openings in the *campanario*; the bronze bell that hangs in the center is touted as the first mission bell made in California. Three markers lie in the ground below the bells, identifying the graves of Edward and Mary McDonagh and Mary Grayson.

The church's interior is dark and cool, lit by shafts of sunlight from the high windows and a rainbow of red, orange, and blue prayer candles. Small statues of Christ, San Antonio de Padua, and Our Lady of Sorrows decorate the spaces in and around the baptistery; a heavy confessional sits to the left. Dark oil paintings (copies of original French works) and Stations of the Cross have been hung on the walls of the nave, above a fresco of Native imagery that includes a flowing river of life. Older-looking pews are set up toward the rear of the church; newer pews have been placed nearer the altar.

A great painted arch is slung high over the communion rail and pulpit; the altar in the sanctuary is spread with an Indian blanket, upon which is set a crucifix. Above rises the reredos, with a winged San Miguel in the highest niche. San Antonio de Padua stands below, with San Buenaventura on his left, and San Francisco de Asís on his right. The Immaculate Conception is the focus of a small altar on the right side of the chancel, and San José resides on the left. All of the statues, with the exception of San José, once blessed San Antonio's orig-

A sun-parched courtyard and a statue of Padre Junípero Serra welcome visitors to Mission San Antonio de Padua.

inal church; they were kept safely at Mission San Miguel during the mission's decline. San José is also a mission-era statue, but came from Mission Santa Bárbara to the south.

A small army of Spanish priests is buried at San Antonio de Padua, including Padre Buenaventura Sitjar, who spent thirty-six years at the mission; Padre Francisco Pujol; Padre Juan Bautista Sancho, who worked for twenty-six years at the mission; and Padre Vicente de Sarria, who "died of want and hunger" at Mission Nuestra Señora de la Soledad, more than 40 miles to the north, in 1835. The sole Mexican priest, Doroteo Ambris, served at the mission from 1851 until his death in 1882.

Heavy turquoise doors lead from the arcade into the mission museum. The thick walls insulate the artifacts within from heat and cold, which is a good thing given the abundance of the collection housed at San Antonio de Padua.

Though perhaps not as slick as other mission museums, this one is extraordinary in its completeness.

A long series of rooms linked by thick doorways lined up shotgun fashion hold display cases filled with trade beads and children's toys, tools used in "home industries" during mission days, arrowheads and basketry employed by Salinan Indians in Native industries, collections of native foodstuffs and medicinal herbs, and other artifacts that recall mission priests and the leather-jacketed soldiers that protected them, including vestments and religious art, firearms and shields.

And there's more: an exhibit of mission tiles and adobes, both original and from reconstruction; examples of textiles and the looms and dyes used in their manufacture; the bellows and anvils of the blacksmith's shop; candle-making apparatus; the skull of a tule elk, once abundant in the area and now flourishing only in small protected herds; musical instruments; photos of the mission in various stages of deterioration; pictures of Indian cave art; mission maps and models; a chronology of significant events in the mission's history; re-creations of a typical padre's room and a Spanish colonial kitchen . . . you can even descend a dimly lit staircase into a cool wine cellar that still smells like fermenting grapes, and climb into the chamber where the grapes were crushed, also redolent with aromas of wine making.

An archway between church and *convento* leads to the mission garden, where a sundial and a fountain stand amid rosebushes, fruit trees, and a circle of slender, towering evergreens. The garden also holds original grapevines, as well as statuary and a display of cauldrons and metates.

The adobe foundations of other buildings are scattered in the grasses surrounding the mission church and museum. The barracks, adjacent to the *convento*, once housed up to six soldiers, including a corporal. Narrow trails lead to other ruins: You can visit the tile shop, the bathing pool, the mission reservoir, the donkey-powered mill, the stone threshing floor, the tannery (which dates back to 1808), the ruins of the *mayordomo*'s house, and the Indian cemetery, a vast overgrown plot of land within low crumbling adobe walls. El Refectorio, the low structure attached to the church, houses private offices; the chapel is located here as well. The brand of the mission is scored into the base of the Camino Real bell in the front courtyard. And in the distance—with a sign on the mission's access road serving as the only clue to its identity—stands the *matanza* (slaughter) tree where cattle were killed. This solitary oak, solid and impassive, has withstood the vagaries of time with an ease that the human-made constructions of San Antonio de Padua couldn't hope to equal.

Mission Nuestra Señora de la Soledad

The Patron Saint: The mission was dedicated to Our Sorrowful Mother of Solitude, the Holy Mother heartbroken and lonely after the crucifixion of her son, Jesus Christ.

FOUNDING DATE: October 9, 1791

ADDRESS: 36641 Fort Romie Road, Soledad, 93960

TELEPHONE NUMBER: (831) 678–2586

WEB SITE: Soledad Mission has no dedicated Web site.

HOURS: The mission is open from 10:00 A.M. to 4:00 P.M. daily. It is closed on Easter, Thanksgiving, Christmas Day, and New Year's Day. Donations are accepted.

DIRECTIONS: To reach the Soledad Mission from U.S. Highway 101 northbound or southbound, take the Arroyo Seco exit in the town of Soledad. Follow Arroyo Seco west for 0.9 mile to its intersection with Fort Romie Road (Monterey County Road G17). Follow Fort Romie Road for 1.5 miles to the Soledad Mission entrance, which is on the left (west). The route is well signed. California Historic Landmark No. 233.

PARKING: Ample parking is available in the large lot to the north of the mission compound, as well as in a smaller lot on the west side, near the mission garden.

SERVICES AND EVENTS: Regular masses are held at the mission on the first Sunday of every month at 10:00 A.M. It is also used for the celebration of religious holidays, including Easter and Christmas, as well as for weddings and baptisms. The mission hosts two annual Fiestas—one on the last Sunday in June and one on the first Sunday in October—with proceeds earmarked for ongoing restoration efforts. A Mass is celebrated before each Fiesta.

Could Padre Fermín Francisco de Lasuén, who dedicated this mission to "Mary, Our Sorrowful Mother of Solitude," have known that the name would prove so apt? Could the venerable Franciscan have known that Mission Nuestra Señora Dolorosísima de la Soledad, the thirteenth mission in the chain, would stand so alone more than two centuries after it was founded?

Not likely. But the fact remains that the Soledad Mission, surrounded by the

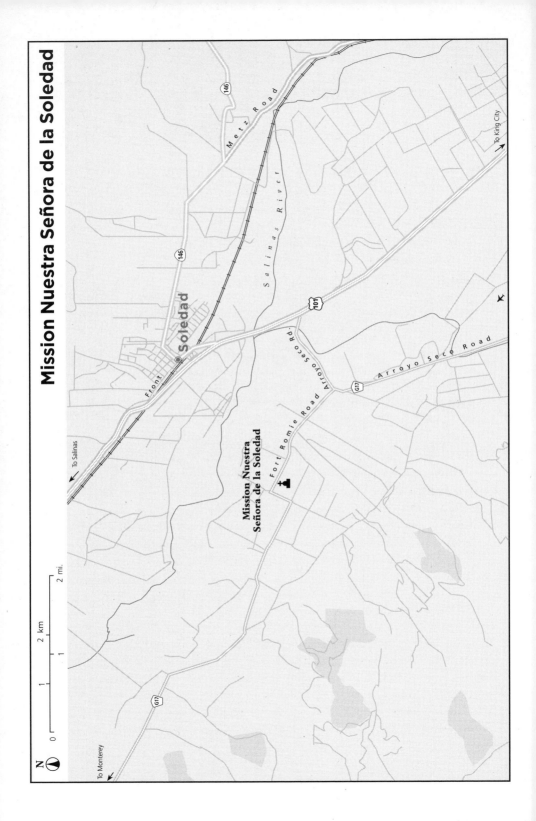

Mission Nuestra Señora de la Soledad

fertile fields of the Salinas Valley and buffered on the west by the rounded but rugged Santa Lucia Mountains, endures a modern seclusion. Part of a panorama of well-tended croplands and scattered farmhouses, the mission's setting is pastoral and singular, especially when compared to the bustle that has grown up around most of its sister missions.

But Nuestra Señora de la Soledad is well served by this solitude, for whether you're standing in the remains of its hot, dusty quadrangle or beneath the shady eaves of its reconstructed portico, you get a tangible sense of what it was like to live here in mission days. The landscape is lovely, either peacefully quiet or deafeningly so, drenched in scorching summer sunshine or chilled by a wet winter cold that frosts the bottomlands. So it was then, and so it is today.

The Mission Yesterday

Mission Nuestra Señora de la Soledad was established as a way station for travelers on El Camino Real, linking Mission San Antonio de Padua to the south with busy Mission San Carlos Borromeo on the banks of the Carmel River. The site was scouted by the Portolá Expedition in the early days of Spanish colonial exploration, and later by Junípero Serra; both parties heard Esselen Indians refer to the valley with a word that resembled *soledad*, according to several mission histories. There is little doubt that Padre Lasuén had that nugget in his mind when he named the new mission.

Soledad's history is more a tale of woe than of success, its growth hampered by transient padres, drought, floods, and epidemic disease. There were Natives to be ministered to in the area, but they were scattered and few in number. Esselen Indians lived in villages in the Santa Lucia Mountains, isolated from each other, other tribes, and the mission by terrain, and probably by temperament as well. The peak neophyte population at Soledad, recorded in the early 1800s, numbered no more than 700 souls.

Padres seldom remained at the mission long enough to truly lead it. Historians note that thirty priests attempted to endure the seclusion of Soledad over the years, with little success. One pair of young Franciscans stationed at the mission early on were particularly dissatisfied with the assignment, and are said to have complained almost constantly, particularly about a lack of "altar wine." The mission's most prosperous years—and there were some, in which thousands of head of cattle and sheep were pastured on mission ranchos and its gardens and orchards, irrigated by water from the Salinas River, produced abundant crops—were overseen by Padre Florencio Ibañez, who arrived at the mission in 1803 and remained until his death in 1818. His was the longest tenure of any mission priest.

The first structures at the mission were of brush; it wasn't until 1797 that an adobe church was erected at the site. That building was destroyed by a flood in

1824—both the Salinas and Arroyo Seco Rivers were wont to overflow their banks in the wet season—and never rebuilt. A chapel erected to serve in place of the church was taken out by another flood in 1828; when the waters rampaged again in 1832, its replacement was also demolished and not rebuilt.

Soledad was in decline by 1825, suffering the deprivations of a new Mexican government that couldn't afford mission upkeep and was destined to enforce secularization orders that would end the mission era. The Franciscan friar who oversaw the last years of the mission under Mexican rule, onetime padre-presidente Vicente Francisco Sarria, was essentially martyred by Mexican neglect: According to mission literature, Sarria "died of starvation while saying mass, because he was giving all his food to the handful of natives that remained."

After Sarria's death in 1835, the mission was essentially abandoned. Its neophyte population, which had been in decline since an epidemic swept the mission in 1802, dropped to just seventy-eight by 1839. In 1845 Mexican governor Pio Pico sold what remained of the mission for $800. Soledad's roof tiles were removed at about that time as well, to pay off its debts, a move that resulted in the nearly complete deterioration of its adobe structures in later years.

After the United States gained control of California, the missions were returned to the Catholic Church, and Soledad fell under the purview of the bishop of Monterey in 1859. Still, it continued to suffer from neglect and weather, and was in ruins by 1874.

Though humbler than other missions at which he undertook restoration projects, the Soledad Mission nonetheless received the ministrations of Sir Henry Downie, who was the driving force behind the reconstruction of the neighboring Carmel Mission. The Native Daughters of the Golden West were also significant contributors to the mission's revival in the mid–twentieth century, when the chapel that stands today was resurrected from the dust of the adobes that once made up its predecessor. The mission's *convento* was rebuilt in 1963. And restoration efforts are ongoing, a process that, as it exposes the ruins of the old mission, may also alleviate its solitude.

The Mission Today

Soledad Mission's agrarian soul is evident from the moment you drive into the parking lot. Ancient grapevines bound the garden behind the chapel, and poppies bloom in arid soil in spring; on the opposite side of the lot grows the revitalized olive orchard. Chickens roam the churchyard, braving even the most withering summer sun. And it is completely surrounded by the fertile croplands of the Salinas Valley.

The plain front of the chapel, and the 200-year-old Mexican-made mission bell that dates back to 1799, face the Santa Lucia Mountains to the west. The west wing of the quadrangle also faces the mountains; the greenery of the mission garden and a verdant lawn buffer the buildings from the parking area. Covered picnic tables and a large barbecue pit are on the far side of the parking lot, along with a chicken coop and a beautiful rose garden. A statue of Junípero Serra presides over a corner of the gardens, with orderly fields stretching into the distance behind him.

The adobe *convento* is lined with inviting benches and lemon and orange trees. A sign invites visitors to pick a fruit from one or the other, and to purchase chicken feed for the resident fowl, along with an admonition not to allow the young ones to chase or harass the birds.

The entrance to the chapel is at the north end of the arcade. Everything about Soledad is compact and spare, evocative of the honorable humility of mission life here, from the

A statue of Junípero Serra presides over the gardens at Mission Nuestra Señora de la Soledad. The fertile fields of the Salinas Valley are the backdrop.

small vestibule with its lovely painting of the Virgin Mary to the intimate chapel, in which a high blue-painted ceiling floats above narrow rows of pews. Three windows illuminate the nave's high places with streams of sunlight, and votive candles burn in shallow alcoves. Dark paintings depicting the Stations of the Cross—original works that are 200 years old and were saved from the looting that accompanied secularization by being returned to Mexico for safekeeping until their security at Soledad could be guaranteed—hang on the chapel walls. Our Lady of Sorrows, sad faced and shrouded in black lace, looks out into the shadowy chapel from her simple niche in the painted reredos, a small crucifix at her feet.

The entrance to the gift shop and small museum is near the chapel entrance. The first room of the reconstructed *convento* is dedicated to the gift shop; the museum begins in the second chamber. Here you can read about how the Soledad Mission became known as the Olive Mission. One account describes how cuttings from Soledad olive trees were used to build California's olive "nursery industry" in the mid-1900s, and others document the work that has gone into regenerating the mission's original olive grove.

Other artifacts in the museum, many excavated in the 1980s, include nails, spades, saddlery, plates, and bottles that were used by mission residents. Also of interest are the vestments, incense burners, and an example of the simple robes worn by Franciscan friars assigned to work at Soledad Mission.

The mission church formed the southwest corner of the original quadrangle, both of which exist only in history. Three graves that were once inside the church now lie exposed, flush to the ground and linked by a slender pathway of broken red tile—the former floor of the church. One is unmarked and belongs to a Native woman; mission literature notes that at the time, only the most important people—almost exclusively "male and European"—were buried in mission churches, "so to have a native woman honored by burying her in the Church was unusual then and intriguing now." The two other graves belong to Spanish men and bear inscriptions, one for Padre Florencio Ibañez, who died in 1818 after serving the mission for fifteen years, and one for José Joaquin de Arrillaga, governor of Alta California and a friend of Padre Ibañez, who died at the mission in 1814.

The grave sites and the church ruins form the southern boundary of an arid patio in which olive trees, poppies, and other hardy plants surround a central fountain. On the east and north sides of the garden lie the broken adobe walls and foundations of other buildings that once made up the mission quadrangle—Indian workshops, the smithy—formless and unidentifiable save for the signs, but evocative and strangely beautiful nonetheless. The ruins, according to mission literature, are coated with mud each year to preserve the fragile remnants of original adobe. More original adobe is preserved within the walls of the museum wing and the chapel.

A large cross rises to the northeast of the chapel, facing the parking area and the olive grove; this marks the site of one of three Native cemeteries that served the mission. The olive trees that crowd the northern edge of the parking area, which visitors can read about in depth in the museum, were propagated "using cuttings taken from 200-year-old Padre-planted trees" at Mission La Purísima Concepción to the south. Olive oil from the mission's trees is used by the Diocese of Monterey as holy oil.

Mission San Carlos Borromeo del Rio Carmelo (Carmel Mission)

The Patron Saint: *Yet another saint from a royal family, Charles of Borromeo, archbishop of Milan, was related to the Medicis and the nephew of Pope Pius IV. Born in 1538, Charles began his climb to greatness at a young age, earning a doctorate at twenty-two and playing an influential role in both the generation and reformation of the Catholic doctrine of the time. He also adhered to the Franciscan vow of poverty by giving of his own wealth to the poor. He died in 1584, and was elevated to sainthood in 1610.*

FOUNDING DATE: June 3, 1770

ADDRESS: 3080 Rio Road, Carmel, 93923

TELEPHONE NUMBER: Parish office (831) 624–1271; museum gift shop (831) 624–3600

WEB SITE: www.carmelmission.org

HOURS: The Carmel Mission and its museum store are open weekdays from 9:30 A.M. to 4:30 P.M., and on weekends from 10:30 A.M. to 4:30 P.M. A moderate fee is charged ($4.00 for adults and seniors; $1.00 for children from five through seventeen; those under five are admitted free).

DIRECTIONS: To reach Mission San Carlos Borromeo from either northbound or southbound California Highway 1 in Carmel-by-the-Sea, take the Rio Road turnoff and head west. Follow Rio Road for 0.7 mile to Lasuen Drive; the mission is on the left (west) side of the road.

PARKING: Large parking lots wrap around the mission on Rio Road and Lasuen Drive. California Historic Landmark No. 135.

SERVICES AND EVENTS: Masses are scheduled weekdays at 7:00 A.M., noon, and 5:30 P.M. in the Blessed Sacrament Chapel. A Saturday vigil is held in the basilica at 5:30 P.M. Masses are celebrated in the basilica on Sunday at 7:00 A.M., 8:00 A.M., 9:30 A.M., 11:00 A.M., 12:30 P.M., and 5:30 P.M.

The mission also hosts educational and historical lectures and concerts. Contact the parish office or visit the Web site for more information.

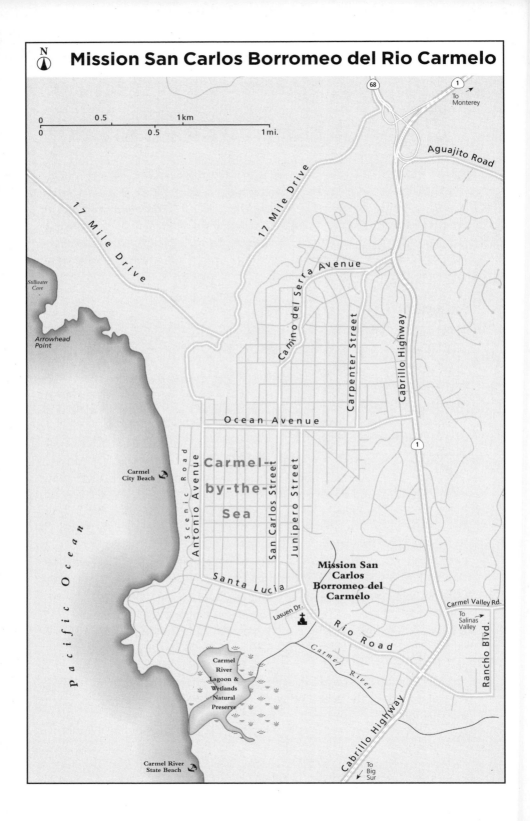

Mission San Carlos Borromeo del Rio Carmelo

N

0   0.5   1km
0   0.5   1mi.

68

1
To
Monterey

Aguajito Road

17 Mile Drive

17 Mile Drive

Stillwater
Cove

Arrowhead
Point

Camino del Serra Avenue

Carpenter Street

Cabrillo Highway

Ocean Avenue

Carmel
City Beach

Scenic Road

Antonio Avenue

San Carlos Street

Junipero Street

1

Carmel-
by-the-
Sea

Pacific Ocean

Santa Lucia

Mission San
Carlos
Borromeo del
Carmelo

Lasuen Dr.

Rio Road

Carmel Valley Rd.

To
Salinas
Valley

Rancho Blvd.

Carmel River

Carmel River
Lagoon &
Wetlands
Natural
Preserve

Carmel River
State Beach

Cabrillo Highway

To
Big
Sur

Mission San Carlos Borromeo is the final resting place of Junípero Serra, the charismatic Franciscan who dedicated the latter part of his life to establishing missions in the wildlands of Alta California. He made this his home base, and it's clear why—the mission commands a superior site near where the mouth of the Carmel River kisses the sea. The weather is mild, the landscapes are inspiring, and it's close to Monterey, which was to serve as the capital of frontier California for much of the mission era.

Save that Monterey is no longer California's political center, much of what appealed to the missionary then remains true today. The hospitality of Carmel and the legacy of Serra and his compadres draw a small multitude of visitors to Mission San Carlos (also known at the Carmel Mission) each year. These pilgrims cannot help but be satisfied by what they find here, for the spirit of the legendary padre informs every brick in the church, every article in the museum, and every blossom in the garden.

The Mission Yesterday

Mission San Carlos Borromeo was originally founded on the shores of Monterey Bay, hailed by Spanish explorers as a desirable harbor on the new frontier and the ultimate prize sought by the overland expedition led by Gaspar de Portolá in 1769. Junípero Serra raised the cross establishing the second of the mission chain at the site where Carmelite priests had performed the first Mass in Alta California during the expedition led by Sebastian Vizcaino in 1602. His Mass, like theirs, was sparsely attended, but that would soon change.

A presidio was established at the same time as the mission, a marriage of colonizing parties that didn't suit the missionary as well as he'd hoped. Proximity to the less-than-holy influences of the Spanish military, coupled with a less-than-suitable water source and less-than-fertile soils, prompted Serra to relocate the mission to the outlet of the Carmel River, a site that enjoyed arable land, abundant fresh water, and a larger population of Native souls for the saving—not to mention a buffer of 5 miles from the irreverent *soldados* at Monterey.

The padre raised a cross on the new site on August 24, 1771, and set about his business. The indigenous people of the area, hunters and gatherers of the Ohlone and Esselen tribes, were converted as swiftly as they could be recruited. Over the next sixty years, more than 4,000 would be baptized at Mission San Carlos, and they would be taught the rudiments of European civilization—to be laborers, agriculturalists, artisans—as well as indoctrinated in the Catholic religion that motivated the padres for whom they worked.

The first mission structures were meager and rough—a chapel, granary, kitchen, residences, and palisade constructed of wood, brush, and turf. This poverty extended to the mission's subsistence in its first years, when it repeatedly faced the specter of famine. Supply ships from New Spain had a hard time reaching the far-flung California outposts, leaving the colonists chronically short of food. They were saved from starvation in 1772 by the bounty of the valley of the bears (future site of Mission San Luis Obispo), from which hunters would return with cartloads of bear meat. By 1774 San Carlos began to prosper, with nearly 500 bushels of wheat, corn, and beans available to feed mission residents; by 1775 the yield had gone up to 980 bushels, according to historians.

A series of log structures were erected over the next few years, with an adobe church finally taking shape in 1782. It wasn't until 1793, after Padre Serra had died and been buried within that adobe church, that work began on the stone church that stands today. It was built during the tenure of Fermín Francisco de Lasuén, Serra's successor as padre presidente, and raised under the supervision of a master stonemason from Mexico using sandstone quarried in the Santa Lucia Mountains. The church took four years to build, and featured an arching roof, two bell towers of different sizes, and walls covered in a plaster made from burned seashells.

The population of San Carlos peaked in 1794, with almost a thousand Indians living in the mission's *rancheria*, according to mission histories. Those numbers would fall off sharply by the time Mexico won its independence from Spain; disease brought by the Spaniards to the New World essentially demolished the Natives' health, and by 1823 only 381 were left.

Padre José Maria del Real had been installed at San Carlos in 1833, and would oversee the execution of Mexico's "Order of Secularization," which was handed down in 1834. Del Real moved many of the mission's religious items to Monterey and others were sold, as was all of the mission property save that on which the church stood.

Now under the care of civilian authorities, it didn't take long for the mission to fall into disrepair. By the early 1850s the chapel's stone roof had collapsed, forcing services to be held in the sacristy. The U.S. government returned the mission to the possession of the Catholic Church in 1859, and Father Angelo Casanova was able to put a wooden roof on the church in 1884 to help preserve what was left, but it wasn't until the 1930s, and the arrival of Harry Downie, that the mission would be truly resurrected.

Downie, a talented and dedicated layman, worked for fifty years on the mission's restoration, conducting extensive research and excavations to make sure he got it right. For his efforts Downie was eventually knighted, and his talents were employed at various other missions, including San Antonio de Padua and San Juan Bautista.

As if the work of Downie and the parish priests who supported him weren't validation enough of the mission's revival—and of its historical significance—it was named a minor basilica in 1961 by Pope John XXIII. Padre Serra would be proud.

The Carmel Mission is noted for its Moorish design, including the onion-shaped dome on its bell tower and its unique star window.

The Mission Today

While a tour of the mission formally starts in the gift shop, the experience begins once you enter the courtyard in front of the basilica. An ivy-covered archway leads into this garden patio from the parking lots outside the mission walls. Inside, sentinel saints stand on either side of the archway, keeping watch over visitors who wander narrow pathways through lovely plantings and pause to contemplate the simple, circular fountain at its center. But the basilica, with its striking architecture, and the little museum tucked in the greenery on the north side of the courtyard, beckon visitors indoors.

In the museum, which focuses on the work of restoration wizard Harry Downie, you can view fragments of the original cross erected by Fray Serra, an altar missal that was used by the officiating fathers from the mission's founding to the 1920s, and other artifacts from the mission era—including tools used by Mission Indians before they came under the oversight of the Franciscans, and vestments worn by the priests who ministered to them. The mission's history is recounted on plaques and via an audio tour broadcast within the museum.

The basilica represents the seventh incarnation of the mission chapel. Its design is described as "Moorish," with a vaguely onion-shaped dome atop the largest bell tower and a striking star-shaped window above the arched doors of the entrance. This window is said to be unique among the missions, though it was copied in the re-creation of Mission San Rafael.

Heavy doors open onto a warm, cavernous nave. The baptistery is at the rear of the church and contains the original baptismal font. Beneath the narrow, arched ceiling of the basilica hang paintings of the Stations of the Cross. The pews are plain, as is the hard red floor; the windows, small, high, and deeply recessed, admit a shadowy light that, augmented by lovely candelabra, lends a creaminess to the white walls of the nave. The altar is ornate and vivid, with San Carlos Borromeo at the top, above a central alcove in which Our Lady of Sorrows and Saint John the Evangelist gaze upward at Christ on the cross. Other holy figures depicted in the reredos include the Immaculate Conception, Saint Michael Archangel, Saint Peter and Saint Paul (both in ovals), Saint Anthony of Padua, and Saint Bonaventure. The reredos and the pulpit were created by the ubiquitous Downie, who strove, as in all his work, to re-create what would have originally adorned the church.

The grave of Padre Serra, along with that of Juan Crespí, his fellow missionary and friend from Mallorca, Spain, and that of another Franciscan padre, Julian Lopez, lies before the altar. Padre Lasuén was laid to rest beside them after his death in 1803.

Our Lady of Bethlehem Chapel, once the mortuary chapel, is on the left side of the basilica's nave, furnished with a simple prayer bench watched over by a lavishly dressed statue of the Holy Mother. The chapel door opens into the mission's quadrangle, which is fragrant with flowering plants, shaded by trees, cooled by a large fountain, and decorated with statues of holy men including Padre Serra. A large replica of the cross that Serra erected in 1774 now rises from the foundations of the original.

The corridors that line the west and south walls of the quadrangle are modern, their verandas sheltering the classrooms of the Junípero Serra School. The corridors on the east and north sides of the quadrangle are older, overhung with wisteria that scents the cool air in spring. The east wing houses the mission's rectory and the Blessed Sacrament Chapel; the north is dedicated to the mission's wonderful museum.

The Serra Cenotaph, a bronze statue of the body of Father Serra surrounded by three of the padres who accompanied him from Spain to America, is the centerpiece of the first museum room. Juan Crespí stands by Serra's head; Fermín de Lasuén, Serra's worthy successor, and Padre Julian Lopez stand at his feet. This poignant sculpture, created by local artist Jo Mora and unveiled in 1924, lies beneath the blue-painted ceiling of the chamber, below a great carved cross set against one wall.

Artifacts of mission life at San Carlos Borromeo are displayed and explained with great care and deliberation in other museum rooms, including priestly vestments and Catholic statuary. Re-creations of the mission's library, kitchen, and dining room, and a spartan padre's bedchamber with adjacent sitting room,

Ivy covers the graves of those buried at Mission San Carlos.

are also presented. Mission plans and a model are on display, as is an oil painting of Padre Serra conducting his first Mass in Monterey.

But most poignant is the re-creation of the chamber in which Serra died, reconstructed by Downie using materials found on the site. The cell is small and spare and dark, a humble setting for the repose of a holy soul.

In the cemetery, gravestones float in a sea of ivy. A cross has been erected in memory of the Indians who lived and died at the mission, but no markers bear their names. Parish priests and others are remembered in granite and marble, their names darkened on their stones by time.

Behind the basilica is the Casa Munras, which recalls the home of Estevan Munras, a trader who arrived in Alta California is 1812 and later became the *alcalde* (mayor) of Monterey. Munras was the artist who created the remarkable frescoes at Mission San Miguel and the recipient of two land grants following secularization. Artifacts of life on a rancho are displayed here, including saddles and branding irons, clothes and books, cooking utensils and photographs.

Nearby Points of Interest

Mission San Carlos Borromeo is a scant mile from the shopping bonanza found in downtown Carmel. To reach this hub of high-end boutiques, art galleries, bakeries, coffee shops, and restaurants from the mission, head north on Junipero Street to Ocean Avenue. Parking is available along the streets or in public lots.

The mission is also a short distance from world-class golf courses, the spectacular beaches and wild areas that stretch along the coast from Monterey to Big Sur, and Monterey itself, with its wharf, museums, and renowned aquarium. To reach Monterey and Pacific Grove, drive north from Carmel on CA Highway 1, or take the scenic 17-Mile Drive (follow the signs). Big Sur lies south of Carmel on Highway 1.

Mission San Juan Bautista

The Patron Saint: *John the Baptist is best known as the man who baptized Jesus Christ in the River Jordan, and the one who called him the Lamb of God. His birth foretold in the Old Testament by the prophet Isaiah, he was well known in his time as a preacher. He was killed when Salome, the daughter of King Herod, demanded that his head be brought to her on a platter.*

FOUNDING DATE: June 24, 1797

ADDRESS: P.O. Box 400/Second and Mariposa Streets, San Juan Bautista, 95045

TELEPHONE NUMBER: (831) 623–2127

WEB SITE: www.oldmissionsjb.org

HOURS: The mission is open from 9:30 A.M. to 4:45 P.M. daily. It is closed on major holidays.

DIRECTIONS: To reach the mission from either northbound or southbound U.S. Highway 101, take the San Juan Bautista/California Highway 156 East exit. Follow CA 156 east for 2 miles to the San Juan Bautista town limits. Go left (north) at the sign onto Monterey Street. At the stop sign, turn right (east) onto Muchelemi Street, and follow it for about 0.4 mile to the center of town and the mission. California Historic Landmark No. 195.

PARKING: Parking is available along the streets surrounding the mission and the state park.

SERVICES AND EVENTS: Services are held on Saturday at 5:00 P.M. and on Sunday at 8:30 A.M., 10:00 A.M., and noon (Spanish). On weekdays Mass is celebrated in the Guadalupe Chapel at 8:00 A.M.

Everything about San Juan Bautista—both mission and town—reflects California's colonial heritage. The abundance that both Native peoples and Europeans found in the San Juan Valley is still obvious, with neatly cultivated fields spreading north below the plaza to the gentle hills in the distance. The stately old mission retains the flavor of its heyday, with meticulously groomed gardens and a spectacularly restored church stationed on what is hailed as the last original Spanish plaza in the state. The historic buildings of San Juan Bautista State

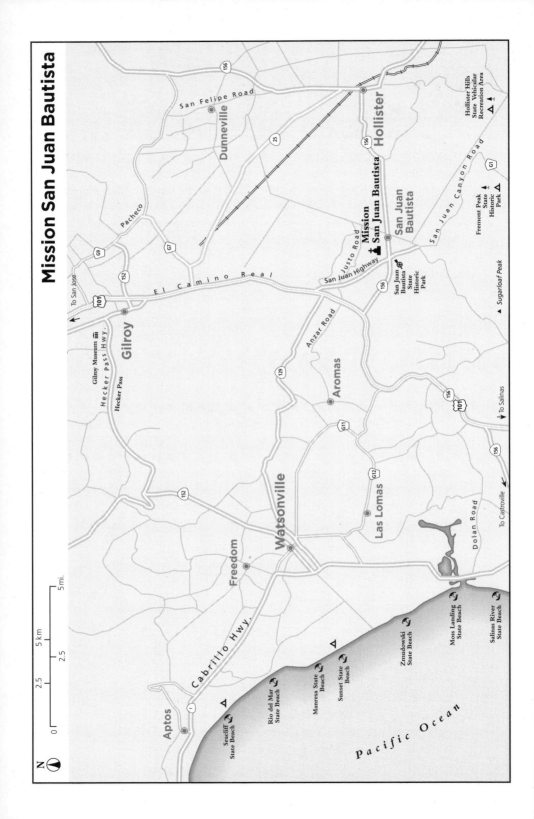

Mission San Juan Bautista

Historic Park, every one preserved as well as the mission, flank the plaza to its east and south, augmenting the frontier atmosphere of the small but vital town that flourishes around it.

The Mission Yesterday

Fray Fermín Francisco de Lasuén established Mission San Juan Bautista during his busiest season; it was one of four he established in 1797, and it helped close the gap between Carmel Mission and Mission Santa Clara de Asís.

There was no way the missionaries who raised the cross on the site could have known that they were building on top of the future Golden State's most notorious fault line. They were concerned only with the security of good water and arable land, as well as a healthy population of friendly Ohlone Indians who could be converted to Catholicism. The ground would shake beneath their feet a number of times, but the padres stood fast, making San Juan Bautista one of the few missions in the chain that has seen an unbroken ministry since the time of its founding.

The fifteenth mission was an immediate success. Indians in the area—one source notes there were twenty-three tribelets in the region—received the Franciscans with relative eagerness. Newly converted neophytes helped the mission's first priests, Padres Jose Manuel de Martiarena and Pedro Martinez, erect an adobe church, a granary, barracks, a monastery, and residences by winter of 1797.

By 1800 the neophyte population had grown to 500; in 1805 the numbers had more than doubled. They worked at tasks common to Mission Indians throughout Alta California—they cooked, cleaned, farmed, made candles, tanned hides, and built adobe structures. They would eventually succumb in large numbers to disease—there would be only about 500 living at the mission in 1812—and some fled the mission, returning to villages inhabited by Indians who didn't buy into the system. Still, the congregation was populous enough to prompt the building of what would become the biggest church in the mission chain.

A cluster of earthquakes rumbled along the San Andreas Fault in 1800, rending both ground and adobe wall at San Juan Bautista, but temblors didn't inhibit construction plans. The cornerstone for the new church was laid in 1803. When it was completed in 1812, the edifice boasted three naves separated by great archways and 3-foot-thick adobe walls. Nineteen arches made up the portico of its cloister, and three bells were erected on posts adjacent to the church. Thomas Doak of Boston, who had jumped ship in Monterey and is identified in mission literature as the first American resident of Alta California, would paint its reredos.

Today Mission San Juan Bautista looks remarkably like it did when this image was created, before the turn of the twentieth century. The mission has proven resilient, despite the fact that it lies virtually atop the infamous San Andreas Fault.

San Juan Bautista thrived under the ministrations of two capable and caring padres. The first, Felipe del Arroyo de la Cuesta, would arrive in 1808 and supervise much of the construction of the grand church. He is remembered as being fluent in many native dialects, and as being well loved by the neophytes.

Estevan Tapis, former padre presidente of the mission system and founder of Mission Santa Inés, was also well loved. He came to San Juan Bautista in 1812, and, freed from the responsibilities of higher office, indulged his passion for music. The Indian choirs under his tutelage were so well respected that San Juan Bautista became known as the Mission of Music. The mission's celebrated barrel organ also contributed to its reputation as a musical mecca: The story goes that when a band of Tulare Indians threatened the mission, a quick-thinking padre grabbed this novel instrument and began to play, with the Mission Indians singing along. The aggressors were not only appeased by the music, but wanted to stay at the mission to hear more.

After the Mexicans won independence from Spain, San Juan Bautista, along with the other missions in Alta California, was transferred from religious control to secular. The neophytes scattered, and mission structures were used as residences for José Tiburcio Castro, a *Californio* who would come to lead Mexican military forces in Alta California, and members of the Breen family, late of the infamous Donner Party. The church, however, would continue to serve the parish, its ministry uninterrupted.

The pueblo that had grown up around the mission prospered in the mid-1800s, first under the Mexicans and then under the Americans, who brought with them the wealth of the Gold Rush and other enterprises. But later in the nineteenth century, various catastrophes, both natural (fire, disease, and the 1906 earthquake, which badly damaged the mission) and human-made (the railroad that might have served the town was routed instead through neighboring Hollister), led to a decline. Still, there was enough prosperity to warrant the maintenance of the mission, which never suffered the monstrous disintegrations that plagued its brethren.

Which is not to say that the mission didn't warrant restoration. Some efforts were misguided, like the installation of a steeple in the 1860s, but most were necessary, and the biggest was precipitated by the disastrous 1906 earthquake. Sir Harry Downie, renowned restorer of the Carmel Mission, had a hand in San Juan Bautista's upgrades. Restoration efforts are ongoing, revealing the visage of the mission in its youth while it enjoys an honorable old age.

The Mission Today

Tours of the mission begin in the southwest corner of the plaza, where the last arch of the *convento* meets Second Street. A mission bell and commemorative plaques mark the spot. The gift shop serves as portal to the mission complex: Beyond the memorabilia, at the back of the boutique, a door opens into a long open corridor bordering the spectacular mission garden.

Cacti and zinnias, roses and flowering herbs, drowsy olive trees and vine-covered arbors, small benches and graceful statuary conspire to create a dell of contemplation bordered by church, *convento*, and adobe walls. The loveliness of these gardens, and the peace they inspire, is best summed up by a poem found on a small sign among the greenery:

> *The kiss of the sun for pardon*
> *The song of the birds for mirth*
> *One is nearer God's heart in a garden*
> *Than anywhere else on earth.*

The corridor that borders the garden is studded with low doors and windows topped with heavy wooden lintels, and artifacts of mission life run along its length. The history lesson begins just outside the door of the gift shop, where a *calderon* that dates to the 1830s and was used to render tallow rests on stubby legs in the shade.

The *pozoleria*, a re-created 1812 kitchen complete with baskets and pots, mortars and pestles, and information about the foodstuffs processed and consumed at the mission, is in one room. In the first gallery of what might be called the museum proper, walls are hung with priestly vestments. In other rooms display cases are crowded with religious statuary, carpentry tools, Indian baskets and arrowheads, women's clothing, old photos, books and maps, mementos of the Breen family—a bountiful sampling. A music room, a sitting room, and a living room are preserved in their representative entirety. Cast a coin into a wishing well, inspect the mission model made at Atascadero State Hospital, and then exit the museum to visit the church.

San Juan Bautista's trio of naves are flooded with light—sunshine issuing through the gold and white panes of the high windows and a duller glow emanating from flickering votive candles. Painted arches separate the narrower side aisles from the main, where

The spectacular gardens at Mission San Juan Bautista create a peaceful place for contemplation.

plain wooden pews stretch from the vestibule at the rear of the church to the sanctuary at its head. The lower portions of the arches are painted in celebratory shades of orange and green; the colors infuse the nave with warmth that rises from the red tile floor to the rough ceiling.

The ornate high altar is set with six niches. In the upper three, from left to right, are polychromed wood statues of San Antonio de Padua, Saint Dominic, and San Francisco de Asís. In the lower niches, from left to right, are San Isidro, a life-sized statue of San Juan Bautista y el Cordero de Dios (John the Baptist and the Lamb of God) that dates back to 1809, and San Pascual de Baylón.

The church houses other exceptional examples of religious art and memory, including the Stations of the Cross, grand portraits of the Holy Apostles, the grave of Padre Stephani (Estevan) Tapis, a cross dedicated to Maria Antonia Castro, and two baptismal fonts—large sandstone basins used to receive local Indians into the Catholic Church.

The original mission, today called the Chapel of Guadalupe, was built between 1799 and 1803, and is located behind the main church. The chapel is as ornate and festive as its larger counterpart. Here worshipers sit on chairs, not in pews, and in place of a formal reredos, large paintings focus contemplation, including a 200-year-old portrait of Nuestra Señora de Guadalupe, to whom the chapel is dedicated, in a gilded frame.

The church cemetery is on the north side of the church, shaded by olive trees and protected by high adobe walls. More than 4,000 neophytes are buried here, including Ascension Solorzano, believed to be the last full-blooded San Juan Mission Indian.

A portion of El Camino Real runs just north of the cemetery and parallel to the San Andreas Fault. A set of steep steps leads down from the plaza fronting the mission church to the dirt track, from which you have unobscured views of the verdant fields in the valley below. The sun-splashed plaza, with its scattering of benches, serves as the perfect venue from which to check out the *campanario*, the bronze statue of San Juan Bautista, arms raised to the heavens, and the complete panorama of the mission.

Modern structures attached to the mission stretch down Second Street to San Jose Street, including low, whitewashed brick offices and weathered adobe walls enclosing an open field. The Catholic rectory and the residence of the Franciscan Sisters of the Atonement are at Second and Polk Streets.

San Juan Bautista State Historic Park

A cornucopia of artifacts illustrating San Juan Bautista's history, including those that belonged to Mexican military leaders, survivors of the Donner Party, and prosperous local businessmen, are preserved within San Juan Bautista State Historic Park. Exhibits are located in a cluster of impressive buildings in and around the Mission San Juan Bautista's historic plaza, including the Plaza Hotel, the Plaza Hall, and the Plaza Stable. The park is open from 10:00 A.M. to 4:30 P.M. daily, and admission is $2.00. For more information about the park, write to San Juan Bautista State Historic Park, P.O. Box 787, San Juan Bautista, CA 95045, call (831) 623–4882, or see www.parks.ca.gov.

Begin a tour of the park at the Plaza Hotel, located at the corner of Mariposa and Second Streets on the plaza. The dining room, barroom, parlor, office, and bedrooms have been outfitted as they were in the 1860s, when the hotel was run by builder and successful local businessman Angelo Zanetta. The hotel also hosts a slide presentation that captures San Juan Bautista's history in pictures and stories.

The Plaza Stable is packed with the historic wagons, buggies, phaetons, and rockaways that used to travel the stage routes that passed through town; a stuffed cougar keeps watch over the door that links the two rooms of the structure. Inside Plaza Hall, a narrow hallway illuminated with red light leads to bedrooms and sitting rooms set up as they would have been in the late nineteenth century, with heavy wood bedsteads and other impressive pieces of period furniture, as well as dolls and cribs—even an old wheelchair. The adobe portion of the hall was once a dormitory for the female neophytes of the

The church houses exceptional examples of religious art, such as this evocative painted cross.

mission. Behind the hall and stable is a blacksmith's shop stocked with an extensive display of tools and the San Juan Eagle fire engine.

The Castro-Breen Adobe is on the corner of Second and Washington Streets. Fronted by a rustic plank walkway, the adobe was used first by Don José Castro under the auspices of the Mexican government, and later was part of the Patrick Breen estate. Breen was one of the survivors of the ill-fated Donner Party; many of his fellow pioneers perished in their attempt to cross the Sierra Nevada in the harsh winter of 1846–47, and some of those who survived did so by consuming the flesh of those who weren't so lucky.

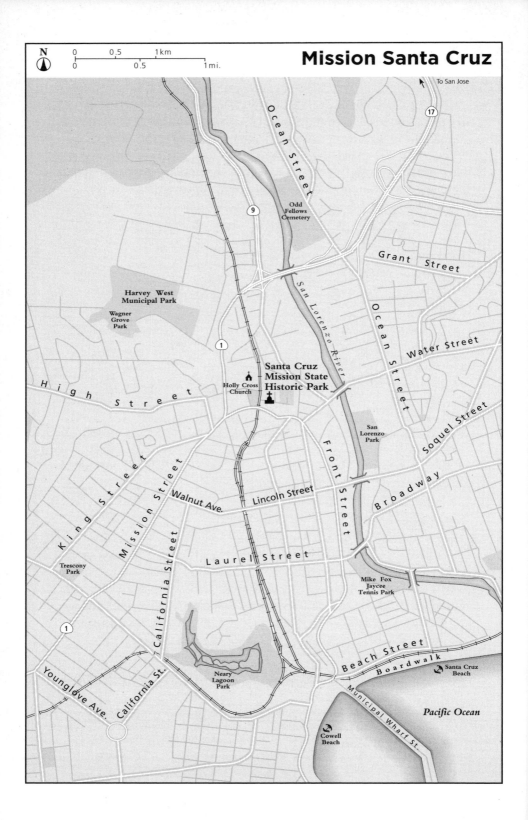

N

0   0.5   1km
0   0.5   1mi.

To San Jose

17

9

Ocean Street

Odd
Fellows
Cemetery

Grant Street

San Lorenzo River

Harvey West
Municipal Park

Wagner
Grove
Park

Ocean Street

Water Street

1

Santa Cruz
Mission State
Historic Park

Holly Cross
Church

San
Lorenzo
Park

Soquel Street

High Street

King Street

Mission Street

Walnut Ave.

Lincoln Street

Front Street

Broadway

California Street

Trescony
Park

Laurel Street

Mike Fox
Jaycee
Tennis Park

1

Neary
Lagoon
Park

Beach Street

Boardwalk

Santa Cruz
Beach

Younglove Ave.

California St.

Municipal Wharf St.

Pacific Ocean

Cowell
Beach

Mission Santa Cruz

The Patron Saint: Like other missions along El Camino Real, the Santa Cruz Mission has a much grander formal appellation: Mission La Exaltation de la Santa Cruz. The name refers to the Holy Cross upon which Christ was crucified, one of the most potent symbols in Catholicism.

FOUNDING DATE: September 25, 1791

ADDRESS: 126 High Street, Santa Cruz, 95060 (mission replica); Santa Cruz Mission State Historic Park, 144 School Street, Santa Cruz, 95060

TELEPHONE NUMBER: Mission Galeria (831) 426–5686; Santa Cruz Mission State Historic Park (831) 425–5849

WEB SITES: www.geocities.com/athens/aegean/7151 (mission); www.parks.ca.gov (state park—follow the links); www.santacruz stateparks.com

HOURS: The mission and its galeria are open Tuesday through Saturday from 10:00 A.M. to 4:00 P.M., and on Sunday from 10:00 A.M. to 2:00 P.M. The galeria is closed on Monday. Santa Cruz Mission State Historic Park is open Thursday through Sunday from 10:00 A.M. to 4:00 P.M. A moderate donation is requested at the galeria; no fee is charged at the state park.

DIRECTIONS: To reach Mission Santa Cruz from the south or east (via California Highway 17), follow California Highway 1 north to its intersection with Mission Street. Turn left onto Mission Street, then left again onto Emmet Street.

To reach the mission from southbound CA 1 (Mission Street within Santa Cruz proper), follow the highway to its intersection with Mission Street (CA 1 veers left to San Jose and Watsonville). Stay on Mission Street for two blocks to Emmet Street. Turn left onto Emmet Street to the mission.

The state historic park is located on School Street to the right (east and behind) the mission. California Historic Landmark No. 342.

PARKING: Parking for the mission is available along the streets surrounding Plaza Park, or in parking lots for both the state historic park and Holy Cross Church.

SERVICES AND EVENTS: Mass is celebrated daily at 8:00 A.M. and 12:10 P.M. in the mission chapel. The chapel is also available for weddings and funerals; call (831) 423–4182 for information. The state park hosts an annual Mission Adobe Day in September; contact the park for more information.

The Mission Santa Cruz that padres and neophytes knew was gone by 1857. A half-size replica now squats next to a sycamore-shaded square near downtown Santa Cruz, overshadowed by the steepled Holy Cross Church that occupies the spot on which the original mission church stood.

Still, the new mission's plain, whitewashed facade, its dome-capped bell tower, and the covered veranda fronting its reliquary adequately recall the history and magic of the mission era—a history more vividly rendered by the old adobe that anchors the neighboring state park. Together chapel and adobe relate the tale of a troubled mission with appropriate brevity.

The Mission Yesterday

The history of Mission Santa Cruz is short and sad. Situated on the northern shores of Monterey Bay, its site had been scouted and named by Gaspar de Portolá in 1769, a natural complement to Spanish settlements at Monterey to the south. The large resident population of friendly Ohlone Indians seemed a good omen—their conversion to Catholicism being the ultimate goal of the missionary movement—as did the seemingly fertile soils and a limitless supply of fresh water.

Though Padre Fermín Francisco de Lasuén raised a cross for the twelfth mission in the chain on the banks of the San Lorenzo River in August 1791, the settlement was not dedicated for another month, which is why a founding date of September 25, 1797, is sometimes cited in historical sources. That first rough compound was destroyed by flood twice, in 1791 and 1792, prompting the mission's relocation to its present hilltop site.

Relations between the missionaries and the Indians who had lived on the land for centuries were relatively harmonious during the first years of the mission's existence. State park literature describes the fruits of their labors: In 1796 the more than 500 neophytes living at Santa Cruz reaped a harvest that included 1,200 bushels of grain, 600 of corn, and 60 of beans. The quadrangle was completed in 1797, testament to the industry of the Native builders. No doubt other domestic and agricultural tasks were peaceably performed as well—chores such as weaving, candle making, wine making, metalworking, and the making of pottery and baskets.

But the Santa Cruz Indians were not content. One source notes that the Natives practiced both their own religion and that of the Spaniards in tandem, a sign that peaceful coexistence was tenuous at best. And relations couldn't have improved when mission priests and Spanish soldiers traveled over the Santa Cruz Mountains and brought members of the Yokut tribe to buttress an Ohlone workforce that had been decimated by disease.

But the establishment of Villa de Branciforte, a civilian settlement named for the viceroy of New Spain, is generally heralded as the beginning of a torturous end to Mission Santa Cruz. The pueblo was established across the river from the mission—too close for comfort, as far as the protective padres were concerned—and peopled by soldiers and reprobates who battled both Indians and missionaries for land and resources while securing a reputation for lawlessness, drunkenness, and rowdiness. The discontent of some Mission Indians found an outlet in Branciforte, which either drew them in or incited them to run away. The priests, in turn, imposed severe punishments on both neophyte revelers and runaways.

Like the proverbial vicious circle, mistreatment of the Indians by the missionaries incited retaliation in kind. Padre Andrés Quintana, who was, by one account, particularly dreadful to wayward neophytes, was ambushed by a group of disgruntled Indians who killed and mutilated him. Lorenzo Asisaro, whose father was one of the conspirators in Quintana's death, justified the violence by telling a historian, "The Spanish Fathers were very cruel toward the Indians. They abused them very much. They had bad food, bad clothing, and they made them work like slaves. . . . The Fathers did not practice what they preached in the pulpit."

And then there was the pillaging of the mission by residents of Branciforte in the wake of the pirate Hippolyte Bouchard's attack on the Presidio of Monterey in 1818. When the padres and neophytes fled the mission, one of the fathers asked the mayor to protect the mission. Instead, the villagers threw a party, drinking the mission's wine and looting the church.

When Mexico got around to secularizing the missions in 1834, troubled Santa Cruz found itself at the front of the queue. It was put up for sale and sold in pieces, and eventually became part of Roman Rodriguez's Rancho Agua Pueria y Las Trancas. Rodriguez, who would survive the title fights that ensued in the wake of the Mexican-American War with his holdings mostly intact, proved a godsend for the adobe residence building in which he and his family made their home for a time; the adobe was destined to stay in the Rodriguez family until the death of the last heiress, Cornelia Lunes Hopcroft, at 104, and thus was maintained in relatively pristine condition.

But no one came to rescue the Santa Cruz Mission church, and Mother Nature wasn't much help, either. An earthquake in 1840 toppled the bell tower; a temblor that struck in early 1857, in tandem with adobe-eating winter rains, further damaged the original church, which stood until 1883 (though it wasn't used as a church). A wooden parish church was erected next to it the following year. In 1859, unclaimed parcels of the mission land holdings were returned to the Catholic Church by the Americans, who had acquired California from the Mexicans in 1848.

The original adobe church would be replaced by the majestic Holy Cross Church, which still stands on the site, in 1889. The chapel that stands in the shadow of Holy Cross is a small replica of the original mission, a project spearheaded and financed by Gladys Sullivan Doyle, who is interred within the chapel. Both the replicated mission and the original adobe survived the Loma Prieta quake in 1989, perhaps an omen of better luck in modern times.

The Mission Today

The Santa Cruz Mission is, quite simply, dwarfed by Holy Cross Church. The tiny chapel and its attached reliquary, which stretches half a block from its left side, is a Cinderella before the ball, all ornamentation lavished on its bigger sister.

Still, the mission has its charm. Its facade, bell tower, and arcade are modest and appropriate. Votive candles burn just inside the doors, filling the intimate nave with a warm, worshipful scent. The baptismal font is at the rear of the chapel behind a grille, as is a lovely statue of the Blessed Mother. Stations of the Cross, accented by wooden crosses, are the only decoration on the white walls. The pews are simple and plain, the windows are simple and plain, the ceiling above and the red tile floor below are simple and plain, and even the altar, with its three statues—Our Lady of Sorrows on the left, San José in the center, and San Miguel on the right—is subdued. The gaudiest decoration in the chapel is the Latin prayer that decorates the arch between nave and sanctuary, which, according to a translation provided by a mission volunteer, reads, "We adore you O Christ, and we bless you, because by your Holy Cross you have redeemed the world."

A door near the back of the nave leads into the reliquary, which houses the Mision Galeria and those few items from the mission's early days that survived its trials. Bibles, statuary, prayer books, and vestments; an original statue of the Blessed Mother and a small Lamb of God; handmade square nails and a piece of the original mission's tile floor; a painting of the mission by Leon Trousset and a chalice once used by Padre Serra share space with the modern memorabilia for sale in the gift shop.

The back door of the galeria opens onto a tiny court paved in flagstones and blessed by a statue of Padre Serra. Goldfish and purple fish swim beneath the lily pads that cover the surface of the water in the small fountain at the center of the court; palm trees and olive trees shade the original baptismal font that has been placed in a corner of the garden.

A half-size replica of the original Mission Santa Cruz keeps the mission's heritage alive.

A statue of the Virgin Mary watches over the quiet courtyard behind Mission Santa Cruz.

Santa Cruz's colonial heritage is more vivid in Santa Cruz Mission State Historic Park, located around the corner on School Street. The park's museum is housed in the former neophyte residence building, built between 1822 and 1824 by Ohlone and Yokut Indians and preserved by its various residents over the ensuing years.

A tour of the adobe begins in the courtyard, which is shaded by a cluster of massive redwood trees. The old adobe, once made up of seventeen rooms and now composed of seven, runs along the street side of the modern courtyard. The other side is open to the city of Santa Cruz and the bay—wonderful vistas, if they are not obscured by fog.

Inside the adobe, the modest chambers are dedicated to various aspects of the mission's history. Displays in one room describe the legacy of the Rodriguez family: The old adobe was in their hands, or the hands of their descendants, for 144 years, according to museum literature.

In other rooms you can view an excavation of the building's foundations and see how the adobe was constructed, its layers peeled away like those of an onion. Looking up into the rafters of the covered veranda outside, you can see the slender boughs, bound with leather straps and topped with curved red tiles, that form the underpinnings of a roof that protected the adobe from the weather. A scale model of the mission and its quadrangle is also on exhibit, along with historical pictures, floor plans of the adobe's various incarnations, and displays explaining the lives of the indigenous people before and after the missionaries arrived. Other rooms hold artifacts of mission life, including re-creations of Mission Indian and *Californio* living quarters, and workshops out-fitted with the pottery, basketry, and tools used in different domestic tasks.

The adobe's layers of occupation are revealed in the final room, from wall-paper and wainscot to plain adobe. Though Indians and *Californios* had occupied the building as well, two Irish American families, the Nolans and the Nearys, are the focus here.

The broken walls and aborted ceiling of another chamber frame the final doorway of the adobe, which opens into the redwood-shaded patio. The court-yard holds an arbor supporting scraggly grapevines at each of its corners, pic-nic tables, a beehive oven (*horno*), a fire pit encircled by sawed-log seats, barbecues (*comals*), an olive tree, and a persimmon tree. A low whitewashed wall encloses a second, paved patio, this one perfumed by roses, lemon trees, and lavender. Restrooms and the gift shop are located off this patio.

Plaza Park, which fronts both chapel and Holy Cross Church, was the cen-ter of the mission's original quadrangle. Sycamores shade park visitors, who can enjoy its fountain and relax on the verdant lawns spread beneath the broken canopy. Holy Cross Church, on the north side of the square, is an architectural party, its arches and towers reminiscent of churches you might see in Europe. But its mission-era underpinnings are abundantly evident: An archway com-memorating the hundred-year anniversary of Santa Cruz Mission's founding rises at the foot of the church's stairs.

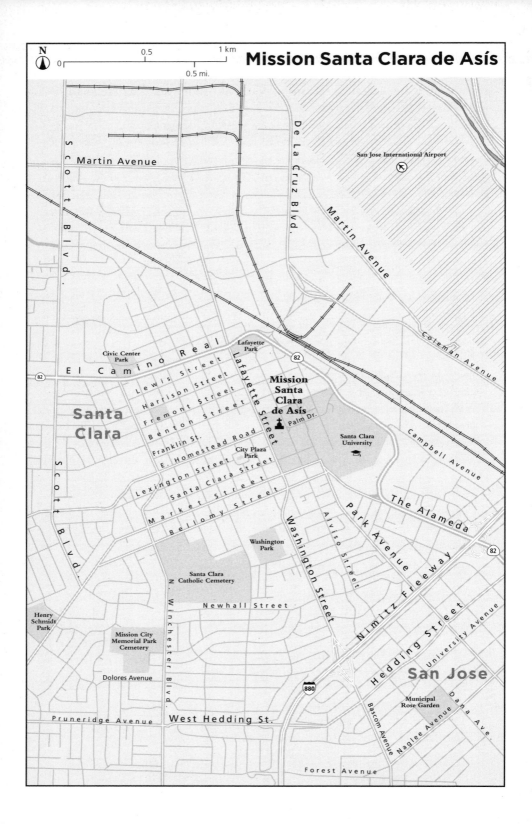

Mission Santa Clara de Asís

N

0   0.5   1 km

0.5 mi.

Martin Avenue

Scott Blvd.

De La Cruz Blvd.

San Jose International Airport

Martin Avenue

Coleman Avenue

Civic Center Park

Lafayette Park

82

El Camino Real

82

Lewis Street

Harrison Street

Fremont Street

Benton Street

Lafayette Street

Mission Santa Clara de Asís

Palm Dr.

Santa Clara University

Campbell Avenue

Santa Clara

Franklin St.

E. Homestead Road

City Plaza Park

Lexington Street

Santa Clara Street

Market Street

Bellomy Street

The Alameda

Scott Blvd.

Washington Park

Washington Street

Alviso Street

Park Avenue

Nimitz Freeway

82

Santa Clara Catholic Cemetery

N. Winchester Blvd.

Newhall Street

Henry Schmidt Park

Mission City Memorial Park Cemetery

Hedding Street

University Avenue

San Jose

Dolores Avenue

880

Municipal Rose Garden

Bascom Avenue

Naglee Avenue

Dana Ave.

Pruneridge Avenue

West Hedding St.

Forest Avenue

Mission Santa Clara de Asís

The Patron Saint: *Mission Santa Clara de Asís is the first California mission named for a woman—one of the few holy women so honored in Alta California. Clare was born in 1194 in Assisi, and would die there in 1253 after founding the Order of Poor Clares and living within the order's cloister for most of her life. She was inspired to embrace a religious life as a young girl after hearing Francis of Assisi preach, and strove to emulate his devotion to piety and poverty. She was canonized in 1255.*

FOUNDING DATE: January 12, 1777

ADDRESS: The mission is located on the campus of Santa Clara University. The address is 500 El Camino Real, Santa Clara, 95053-0025

TELEPHONE NUMBER: (408) 554–4023

WEB SITE: www.scu.edu/mission

HOURS: The mission church is open every day of the year from sunrise to sunset. The mission office is open Monday through Friday from 1:00 to 5:00 P.M.

DIRECTIONS: To reach Mission Santa Clara de Asís from U.S. Highway 101 in San Jose, take Interstate 880 south toward Santa Cruz. Travel about 4 miles to the exit for The Alameda/California Highway 82. Follow The Alameda north for about 0.5 mile until it veers left; stay right on El Camino Real. Remain on El Camino Real for about 1 mile to the Santa Clara University entrance, which is on the left (west). Turn left onto Palm Drive; the mission is at the end of this short access drive.

From Interstate 280 in San Jose, take I–880 north to the exit for The Alameda/CA 82, and follow the directions above. California Historic Landmark No. 338.

PARKING: Parking is available along Palm Drive, within a short walking distance of the mission.

SERVICES AND EVENTS: Masses are celebrated on Sunday at 10:00 A.M., 7:00 P.M., and 10:00 P.M. during the school year (from about mid-September to mid-June), and at 10:00 A.M. during the summer months. Masses are scheduled Monday through Friday at 12:05 P.M. year-round. The mission also hosts weddings for affiliates of Santa Clara University.

The Guadalupana Celebration, an annual event honoring Our Lady of Guadalupe, is held in early December. Contact the mission for more information.

When Mission Santa Clara de Asís was founded in 1777, it stood alone and exposed in a broad valley at the southern tip of San Francisco Bay. These days it's surrounded by the suburban sprawl of the Silicon Valley, a metropolis of glass, asphalt, and steel as far removed from its rough frontier roots as acorn mush is from foie gras.

Fortunately, the mission church, a reconstruction of what was erected on the site in the 1820s, is beautifully buffered by the perfectly coiffed palm trees, close-cropped lawns, and flowering gardens of Santa Clara University. The setting is so well manicured, in fact, that it's hard to picture the chaotic history of the mission, to imagine it the repeated victim of fire, flood, and earthquake. The elegant mission that stands today is evidence that adversity breeds resilience, that persistence and faith can enable even the most afflicted to endure.

The Mission Yesterday

Most of the California missions have been destroyed and rebuilt in their histories, but Santa Clara is arguably the champion, with six incarnations at five different sites. You might question the wisdom of rebuilding given the scanty odds that it would be long lived, but the Franciscans who colonized California were never quitters.

The fact that the Santa Clara Valley was an ideal location for a mission may explain the padres' persistence. The population of the local Ohlone Indians was generous—one source notes that there were as many as forty *rancherias* in the area—the land was fertile, water was ample and ran year-round, and the site was strategically situated at the south end of San Francisco Bay, a short day's ride from Mission Dolores near the Golden Gate and relatively close to the Carmel Mission to the south. It had been scouted and praised by well-respected members of earlier expeditions to the region, including Juan Bautista de Anza and Padres Juan Crespí and Francisco Palóu.

The Ohlone Indians, members of a rich hunting and gathering culture sustained by bay and woodland harvests of seafood, wild game, and the staple acorn, were deemed friendly and willing converts by the Franciscans. Wooed with gifts and mystery, Indians were drawn to the eighth mission and ensnared, converted to a religion and lifestyle from which they would be hard pressed to free themselves. Together with fathers Tomas de la Peña and José Murguía, the new neophytes would erect a church, residences, and corrals—rudely constructed of logs and brush—on the banks of the Guadalupe River by the winter following the mission's founding.

The first settlement survived a scant two years before it was destroyed by flood. A temporary mission was erected nearby, this one serving from 1779 to 1781, until a third mission was started across the street from the present mission (the site is now marked by a towering cross). Constructed of adobe and completed in 1784, the new church and the establishment that grew up around it were to flourish for thirty-four years. Guided by competent padres, the mission would become one of the most prosperous in the system, noted by several historians as having the largest neophyte population (1,247 in 1800, according to one source) and boasting more baptisms and burials than any of its brethren. Santa Clara also husbanded great numbers of livestock—by one account, the mission's cattle and sheep totaled more than 30,000 head—and produced prodigious amounts of wheat and other crops.

This success came despite the establishment of a pueblo—the third prong in the Spanish colonizing strategy—near the mission in 1777. There would be conflict between El Pueblo de San José de Guadalupe and both Missions Santa Clara and San José (a series of letters published in *Lands of Promise and Despair* focuses on disputes surrounding boundaries and pasturage for livestock), but the relationship was not one of crippling antagonism.

Problems with the Mission Indians also arose. Many would succumb to disease as the mission era progressed, depleting Santa Clara's population of laborers. Tales of conflict are few, though one is repeated several times in mission histories and is indicative of tumultuous undercurrents: Padre José Viadér's leadership apparently aggravated a small group of neophytes, who then attacked him. The reportedly burly padre turned the tables on the Indian gang during the attack, however, trouncing them and thus winning the friendship of their ringleader.

In 1818 an earthquake toppled the third mission church. Yet another temporary chapel served padres and neophytes between 1819 and 1825; in the latter year, a fifth "permanent" mission, built where the present church now stands, was completed. The new mission was substantial, its roof supported by beefy redwood beams, its thick adobe walls decorated with the artistic creations of Augustín Davila, its facade anchored by a stately bell tower.

Mission Santa Clara was one of the last missions to be secularized. But once the order was carried out in 1836, it suffered the same hardships as other missions in the chain: Civil administrators sold off its land, its neophytes scattered (though it still functioned as a parish church), and its buildings fell into disrepair, some of them occupied by squatters. The mission was rescued before the neglect became terminal with the establishment of a Jesuit college on the site in 1851. That college would grow into Santa Clara University, and in the process the mission would be remodeled on one occasion (outfitted with a wooden facade and a second bell tower) and enlarged on a second.

However permanent that fifth mission appeared in its one hundred years of service, it, too, would fall, brought down by fire in 1926. The church erected in its stead is a replica of the 1825 church, and hopefully it will remain unsullied for a long time to come.

The Mission Today

Mission Santa Clara's chapel is perfectly coordinated with the rest of the Santa Clara University campus (or the campus is perfectly matched to the mission), painted in the same gentle apricot tones, the architecture classically, immaculately Spanish. Bronze replicas of the original pearwood statues of San Juan Bautista, Santa Clara, and San Francisco de Asís stand serene and protective around the entrance to the mission church; pilasters, ornamental scrollwork, and a representation of the Holy Trinity in the angle of the peaked roof decorate the facade; and a bell tower rises on its left side, housing four mission bells including one that dates back to 1789, a gift to the mission from King Carlos IV of Spain. The tall wooden cross that rises across the road from the mission doors recollects the third mission; a portion of the original cross is preserved inside the new.

Passage through the heavy wooden doors leads into a lofty and spacious nave. The vestibule, relatively plain by comparison to the rest of the church, is hung with bronze plaques memorializing servicemen who fought in World War II and other military conflicts. The choir loft above holds the mission's pipe organ.

The nave is elegantly painted in soft yellows, reds, greens, and blues, the tile floor shiny, comfortable straw-seated chairs placed in orderly rows. Confessionals of heavy, dark wood hung with equally heavy blue curtains are set into shallow alcoves in the walls of the nave. The Stations of the Cross, hung on the arches between the alcoves, are rendered in bas-relief. In an alcove midway up the main aisle is the altar of Saint Ignatius, founder of the Society of Jesus (Jesuits); in the alcove opposite is the altar of Saint Joseph, ornamented with a lovely depiction of foster father and infant son. The faces of cherubs surround the chandelier that hangs from the ceiling and gently lights the chancel and pews closest to it.

The gilded reredos behind the high altar, created by master of mission restoration Harry Downie, holds within its niches San Miguel (at the top), and Santa Clara (in the center), with the Virgin Mary and Saint Joseph on either side. Beautifully rendered paintings commissioned by the Jesuits in 1928 to honor the Franciscan padres who established the mission grace the walls on either side of the reredos, one showing San Francisco de Asís at the foot of the cross, the other depicting San Antonio de Padua with the Christ child. The roof above the chancel is fantastically painted in a re-creation of Augustín Davila's

The facade of Mission Santa Clara recalls the church that was erected on the site in 1825. That church was destroyed by fire in 1926.

Heavenly Court. Smaller altars outside the sanctuary on either side of the nave are dedicated to Christ, to the life-sized crucifix dating back 200 years, and to the Virgin of Guadalupe (the smaller picture of Our Lady of Sorrows above the Virgin is a historic painting that was salvaged from the church after the fire of 1926).

Outside the church, walkways lined with roses lead to the Santa Clara Mission Historical Area, which is on the left as you face the mission entrance. A map guides you to the various sites within what was once the mission's quadrangle. A long wooden arbor hung with wisteria (the trunk of which measures 6 feet around) flows the length of the church into the heart of the quad; along the back and left borders of the plaza stand the only extant historic mission structures. The Adobe Lodge, once a two-story building in which Mission Indians made candles, baked breads, and carried out other domestic tasks, is now a single story high and used for receptions and other events. The free-standing adobe wall, whitewashed and protected by an authentic-looking overhang, is broken by thick windows and doorways that frame picture-perfect views of the fragrant and well-kept gardens. At one end of the wall, portholes and breaks let you touch the original adobe inside. The rest of the quadrangle is sprinkled with grinding stones, religious statuary, including the Sacred Heart, and students sunning themselves (and their textbooks) on the soft lawns.

The mission graveyard is the burial ground for 6,000 Natives and is also noted for its beautiful rose garden.

The mission graveyard and rose garden is to the right as you face the mission, the final resting place for 6,000 Natives, Spaniards, *Californios*, and Americans who died between 1777 and 1851. A statue of Junípero Serra is tucked behind the cemetery, peaceful and secluded like California itself before it was "discovered" by Europeans. The roses, when in bloom, are breathtaking.

Nearby Points of Interest

In the de Saisset Museum, the mission's next-door neighbor, a variety of rotating exhibits explore the art and history of the region and beyond. The museum is open Tuesday through Sunday from 11:00 A.M. to 4:00 P.M.; admission is free. For more information, call the museum at (408) 554–4528 or visit the Web site at www.scu.edu/deSaisset.

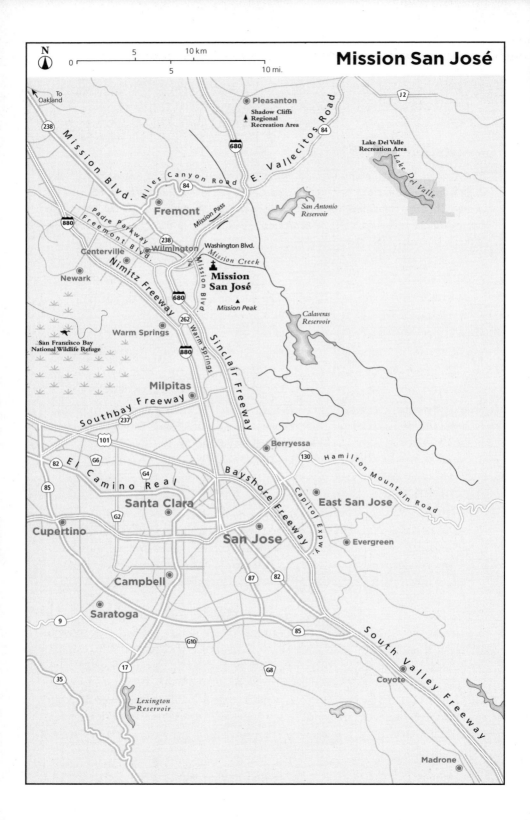

Mission San José

The Patron Saint: *Saint Joseph was a carpenter, the husband of Mary, and the foster father of Jesus Christ. He was twice counseled by an angel, who informed him of the identity of Mary's child and later warned him to flee to Egypt to escape the dire pledge of King Herod, who would kill all male children in an effort to destroy the infant King of the Jews.*

FOUNDING DATE: June 11, 1797

ADDRESS: 43300 Mission Boulevard/P.O. Box 3159, Fremont, 94539

TELEPHONE NUMBER: (510) 657–1797

WEB SITE: There is no official Web site for Mission San José.

HOURS: The mission is open from 10:00 A.M. to 5:00 P.M. daily. It is closed on New Year's Day, Easter, Thanksgiving, and Christmas. Self-guided tours of the mission and its museum are free, but donations are welcome.

DIRECTIONS: To reach the mission from Interstate 680 northbound or southbound, take the Washington Boulevard exit in the town of Mission San José. Head east on Washington Boulevard for 1 mile; the road dead-ends on Mission Boulevard at the mission. California Historic Landmark No. 334.

PARKING: Parking is available along the road fronting the mission.

SERVICES AND EVENTS: Masses are celebrated in the mission church at 8:00 A.M. Monday through Friday. The mission hosts an annual Fiesta in early June to commemorate its founding, and hosts performances of Las Posadas each December right before Christmas.

Mission San José is yet another example of Franciscan missionaries' remarkable ability to select lovely sites for their settlements. The mission sits at the base of folded hills at the eastern edge of Fremont's sprawling suburbs—if houses and trees hadn't sprung up on the plain before it, the mission would have priceless views of San Francisco Bay. Perhaps, in the early nineteenth century when Mission Santa Clara, Mission San José, and the pueblo of San José were thriving, the smoke of domestic fires could have been seen across the flatlands that separated them.

Confusion may spring from the fact that Mission San José is located in Fremont, not in the nearby city of the same name. It made sense, however, in the days of Spanish empire building, when mission and pueblo were distinct entities. The pueblo of San José, now the heart of the modern city of the same name, was established at about the same time as Mission Santa Clara, and the padres struggled to keep mission resources from intermingling with pueblo resources. The same conflicts would arise following the founding of Mission San José, which bounded the pueblo on the east. But the mission's mandate was clear—it served religious interests, not secular, as the pueblo did. Fortunately the bounty of the valley and the abundance of Native labor allowed both to thrive.

The Mission Yesterday

Mission San José lies well off the El Camino Real so familiar to Californians, on a branch of the royal road that led from the Bay Area to the San Joaquin Valley. The interior valley was the obvious next frontier for Spanish colonialists, who by the turn of the nineteenth century were well on their way to securing the coastline for king and Crown. Established by Padre Fermín Francisco de Lasuén, the fourteenth mission in the chain was intended to fill a gap between existing missions, and to Christianize the Ohlone Indians who lived in the area.

But hostile Indians, some Ohlone, some from other tribes, would trouble San José for most of its existence. Indeed, it seems almost prescient that military men—Sergeant Pedro Amador and his soldiers—would be integral to the mission's founding, in light of the fact that it would be the focal point of several violent military campaigns.

The mission was established close to an Ohlone village, on a site with good water and soil, and was fortified by immediate donations of cattle and supplies from nearby missions, which ensured its short-term success. But members of the local tribelets were loath to join the mission—they were no longer "stupefied" or fearful of the Spaniards, as they had been when encountered by Padre Pedro Font of the Anza Expedition twenty years before, nor were they bewitched by gifts of glass beads and clothing. Though mission buildings went up swiftly in the first year, only thirty-three neophytes entered the fold.

This unpromising start didn't prove prophetic, however: Converts at San José would eventually rival those at other successful missions, according to historians. At its height, in 1831, the neophyte population at San José would include nearly 2,000 souls, a remarkable accomplishment given that the mission was plagued both by disease—including an 1805 smallpox epidemic that, according to one account, wiped out 150 Natives in eighteen months—and runaways. Another account relates that a measles outbreak killed nearly 800 Mission Indians.

Buenaventura Fortuni and Narciso Duran, two dedicated padres who arrived at the mission in the early 1800s, would guide San José for more than twenty years. They would oversee the construction of a stodgy and utilitarian adobe church (erected between 1805 and 1809), an enormous quadrangle, and mission buildings that would include a *convento*, a dormitory for unmarried Indian girls, barracks, a mill, a tannery, and a soap factory. The mission would become a prodigious producer of trade goods that Padre Duran would ferry across the bay to exchange for supplies the mission couldn't produce itself. Its livestock herds were enormous, totaling more than 30,000 head of cattle, pigs, and sheep by the early 1830s, and its croplands and orchards were also fruitful, providing the mission population with pears, peaches, a variety of grains, grapes, figs, olives, pomegranates, apples, prickly pears, tobacco, limes, and onions.

Padre Duran was an inspired musician who taught the neophytes in his care to read music and play classical instruments, and then conducted them in legendary Indian orchestras and choirs. He would also serve as padre presidente of the mission chain before retiring to Santa Bárbara in 1833. His partner, Padre Fortuni, was also an able administrator, according to mission histories. But the successes of both Duran and Fortuni were clouded by neophyte discontent, and the story of the rebellion of Estanislao informs this conundrum.

Estanislao was, according to historical accounts, a favorite of Padre Duran's, but that position didn't stop him from fleeing the mission in 1826 and organizing a revolt of more than 1,000 Natives, some of them escapees from both San José and Mission Santa Clara. Spanish authorities twice dispatched military forces to corral the renegades. The first attempt was repulsed, though not without loss of life on both sides; the second, led by General Mariano Guadalupe Vallejo, was a bloody success. Though many of his compatriots were murdered, Estanislao was brought back to Mission San José, and was protected from reprisals by the padre whom he had betrayed.

Secularization was not carried out at Mission San José until 1836. A Mexican missionary was put in charge of the church and its ministry, while the rest of the mission was placed under the civilian oversight of José de Jesús Vallejo, a member of one of the most powerful political and military families in Alta California at that time. As was the case elsewhere, mission lands intended for Indian ownership were instead sold by Mexican governor Pio Pico to wealthy *Californios* like the Vallejos.

Mission buildings languished in the wake of secularization. San José passed from Mexican to American hands following the Mexican-American War, and was returned to the Catholic Church in 1859. Though the mission church would endure as the locus of a parish, the *convento* would be put to other uses, including service as a general store during the Gold Rush.

After an 1868 earthquake irreparably damaged the 1809 adobe church, a wooden church was erected on its foundations, its rectory filling the void between church and *convento*. In 1982 restoration of the original mission structure was initiated, which involved moving the old wooden church to a site across the bay and excavating and rebuilding the 1809 church. In this remarkably successful undertaking, adobe bricks were assembled into walls 4 to 5 feet thick, timbers were shaped by hand, and hazelwood branches were tied with rawhide and used in the construction of the roof, just as had been done nearly two centuries before. The result is an impressive monument to California's mission heritage.

The Mission Today

Bulky and stolid, Mission San José backs up against open spaces that roll upward almost 1,000 feet. A semicircle of red tile stairs leads from a quiet street lined with shops and restaurants to its closed front doors. The facade is imposingly blank, whitewashed, and broken only by a couple of windows and the bell tower, which rises from the left corner and houses the mission's four original bells.

The museum entrance is reached via the covered corridor of the original cloister, once the padres' living quarters. You can pick up an interpretive guide as you pass through the gift shop; the museum is housed in *convento* rooms to the right.

The first room of the museum is dedicated to the Ohlone, the hunting and gathering culture that thrived on the southern and eastern shores of San Francisco Bay prior to the arrival of Europeans; here you'll find examples of the basketry, stone tools, and other items fashioned and used by the indigenous people. The neighboring room focuses on the padres, and houses religious relics including spectacular vestments and artifacts of San José's musical legacy, including a page from a choir book used by Narciso Duran, celebrated music teacher to the neophytes.

Another chamber is dedicated to the story of Rancho San Ramon, and encompasses historical paraphernalia from the Amador, Vallejo, and Bernal families. An adjacent pair of rooms focuses on the mission's restoration, using pictures, words, and a model to tell the story of its evolution from original adobe to wooden church to reconstructed adobe. An audiovisual theater is housed in what was once the mission chapel. As much as the artifacts in the rooms evoke mission days, the rooms themselves are just as powerful—square, spare, clean, and separated by thick walls broken by doorways capped with low, heavy lintels.

To reach the church, pass through the gift shop and cross an open patch of earth upon which lie the exposed and broken foundations of mission-era

A simple cross rises from the cemetery at Mission San José.

buildings. Original roof beams lie amid the stonework, all of which is dwarfed by the exterior wall of the church and the three broken buttresses that support it.

Unlike its exterior, the interior of the church isn't ponderous at all. The nave is spacious, with a simple tile floor and functional pews, its white walls decorated with columns, ribbons, and balconies that are re-creations of original designs created by artist Augustín Davila. Paintings of the Stations of the Cross also line the walls.

An altar to Christ's martyrdom is opposite the entrance, above the grave of Robert Livermore, the only one of ten people buried in the church whose marker was uncovered in the restoration. The original baptismal font of hammered copper is set against the buttressed wall. Closer to the sanctuary, an altar dedicated to San Buenaventura, featuring a poly-

With its variety of headstones, the cemetery at Mission San José is one of the best in the mission chain.

chromed wood statue of the saint that dates back to 1808, is on the left; San Joaquin is honored on the right. A painting of Christ, Mary, and Joseph is framed in gilt at the top of the colorful reredos, with an ancient Spanish statue of San José, the mission's patron saint, in the niche below. A rendering of the Holy Trinity includes a dove, symbolic of the Holy Spirit.

Sunbaked or windswept or gloomy with fog, the mission cemetery is one of the best in the chain. Crowded with headstones of enormous variety—broken and new, wooden and marble, barricaded by rusted iron grates or lonely among withered grasses—no beautiful plantings or verdant lawns soften the mystery of death here. The burials date from the 1860s, and immigrants from Spain and France and Ireland are among the dead; the bones of the Ohlones lie in a separate cemetery on Washington Boulevard, according to mission literature. Set against the whitewashed glare of the high mission wall, an image of a skull and crossbones—a cemetery symbol found at a scattering of missions—will doubtless capture your attention as you pass back into the church.

On the other side of the church, in the patio behind the ruins, you can visit still more graves. A plaque honoring the Anza Expedition, which forged an overland route from northern Mexico to San Francisco Bay in 1775 and 1776, also sits in the courtyard, along with a statue of Padre Serra, a fountain, a rose garden outfitted with benches, and olive trees that throw a filtered shade over all.

Mission San Francisco de Asís
(Mission Dolores)

The Patron Saint: *Francis of Assisi is one of the most venerated figures in Christendom. Born in 1181, he abandoned a career as a soldier to devote himself to Christ. His life was circumscribed by poverty, obedience to the church, and chastity, the three vows that members of his religious order, including California's missionaries, would adhere to. Known as a great preacher, as a lover of animals, and for suffering the stigmata of Christ, Francis died in 1226 and was canonized two years later.*

FOUNDING DATE: June 29, 1776

ADDRESS: 3321 Sixteenth Street, San Francisco, 94114

TELEPHONE NUMBER: (415) 621–8203

WEB SITE: www.missiondolores.citysearch.com

HOURS: The mission is open for tours from 9:00 A.M. to 4:00 P.M. daily. Hours are extended until 4:30 P.M. from May 1 through October 31. The mission is closed on Thanksgiving, Christmas, and New Year's Day; it is open from 9:00 A.M. to noon on Good Friday and from 10:00 A.M. to 1:00 P.M. on Easter Sunday. Donations are suggested ($3.00 for an adult, $2.00 for a child, with an audio tour available for $5.00). The parish offices are open from 8:30 A.M. to 4:00 P.M. (closed for the noon hour), closed on Thanksgiving and Christmas, and open for short hours on Good Friday and Easter.

DIRECTIONS: To reach the mission from either northbound U.S. Highway 101 or southbound US 101 (Van Ness Avenue) in San Francisco, exit Van Ness onto westbound Mission Street. Follow Mission Street west for about 0.5 mile to Dolores Street. Turn left (south) onto Dolores Street and travel about 0.3 mile to Sixteenth Street. The mission is next to the basilica that dominates the southeast corner of Sixteenth and Dolores Streets. The mission can be reached via a variety of alternative routes as well—a good street map will help you find your way. California Historic Landmark No. 327.

PARKING: Metered parking is available along city streets; there is a two-hour limit. On weekends, parking is available in the Mission Dolores schoolyard at 445 Church Street.

SERVICES AND EVENTS: Mass is celebrated in the Old Mission weekdays at

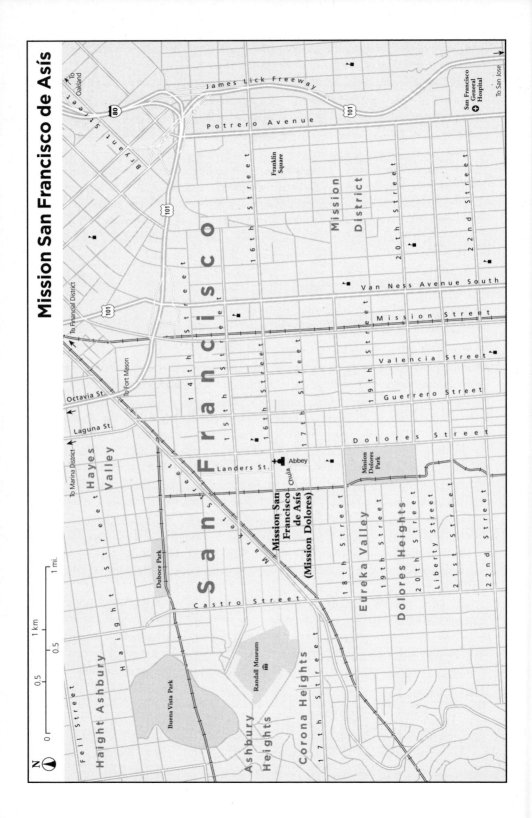

Mission San Francisco de Asís

7:30 A.M., and on Saturday at 5:00 P.M. Mass is held in the neighboring basilica at 9:00 A.M. Monday through Saturday, and on Sunday at 8:00 A.M., 10:00 A.M., and noon (Spanish). Baptisms and marriages are conducted by appointment.

The mission holds an annual Fiesta in early October to celebrate its founding. In addition, docent and school tours are available by appointment.

Arguably the most unusual and moving portraits of Mission Dolores are those showing the mission, the oldest building in San Francisco, squatting untouched amid the rubble of the 1906 San Francisco Earthquake. The image may be from the wrong religion, but it's apt: The mission resembles a sitting Buddha, fat, secure, and serene.

Even today, surrounded by a city that spends more time walking around the mission than contemplating its place in history, a city swept by storms of fashion and finance and fad, Mission Dolores is uniquely steadfast, an island of faith unmoved by the earthly forces that batter it.

The Mission Yesterday

Mission San Francisco de Asís marked the end of El Camino Real in Padre Junípero Serra's time and, indeed, for a good part of the mission period. It was founded by Serra's student and friend Francisco Palóu, a dedicated missionary who would retire after Serra's death to write an enduring biography of his mentor.

The sixth mission was established about 3 miles from the Golden Gate and the Spanish presidio built to defend both harbor and settlement. The bay had been "discovered" by explorer Gaspar de Portolá seven years before, and securing claims to it had been a goal of Spanish colonialists ever since. Juan Bautista de Anza was dispatched with a party of settlers to make an overland trek from Mexico to the bay in 1776, but politics would delay him in Monterey; instead his subordinate, Lieutenant José Joaquin Moraga, led the settlers and padres to the new mission's site, near a lake and stream named for Nuestra Señora de los Dolores.

The new mission would come to bear two names and two founding dates. Though dedicated to San Francisco de Asís, it would become more familiarly known as Dolores, even after both namesake lagoon and stream were buried beneath San Francisco's city streets. The most common date given by writers for the mission's founding is in June, a few days before the signing of the Declaration of Independence, because that was when the first Mass was celebrated, but others cite October 9, when the mission was formally dedicated and a cross was raised.

Regardless, once on the ground, the mission was there to stay. A church of mud and logs was erected that first year (along with attendant structures); the building that stands today—composed of adobe and redwood, 144 feet long and 22 feet wide, with Mexican bells cast in honor of Saint Francis, Saint Martin, and Saint Joseph mounted in its bell wall—was erected between 1782 and 1791. The church stood in the southeast corner of a quadrangle which, when finished in 1828, would encompass a *convento*, a school, a girls' dormitory, workshops, and storerooms, as well as mills, a tannery, and a soap works. The soil and weather at the site never proved conducive to great gardens or pasturage, so crops and livestock were raised on more protected, productive lands to the south.

But the mission's successes are tarnished by tales of discontent and disease, which demoralized and decimated its neophyte population. Mission Dolores was situated near the Ohlone Indian village of Chutchui, one of many around San Francisco Bay that the padres would harvest for souls and laborers with questionable success. Indians from the more distant *rancherias* of the Coast Miwok, the Wappo, the Patwin, and the Yokut would find themselves living at one time or another at the mission, where they would work at becoming good Christians as well as good builders, farmers, weavers, and tanners, and, from many accounts, long to return to their native homes and lifestyles. They would also find themselves plagued by whippings, hunger, and disease.

The future neophytes were variously described by early explorers as "poor and miserable," "quick-witted," and "docile," and were almost immediately put off by the behavior of the *soldados* who accompanied the first missionaries. One history describes an early encounter in which Indians who had "disgraced themselves" by stealing from the settlers were hunted down by soldiers and flogged. Needless to say, those Indians, and doubtless their fellow villagers, never returned to the mission to be converted.

But eventually some Indians did convert, swelling the mission's population to nearly 1,000 by 1794. Runaways and disease kept the numbers in check, however: A measles epidemic struck in 1795, killing a huge number of neophytes, and more than 200 fled the mission in its aftermath. The disease couldn't be helped—it was an inadvertent plague imposed by the Europeans, no doubt exacerbated by the cold and fog that blanket San Francisco even in summer. The tendency of neophytes to run away might have been assuaged, however, if the missionaries had been less strict. Two priests are described in histories as particularly unkind, prompting rebuke from within their own order. The neophytes fled, reported Padre José Maria Fernandez, because of the "terrible suffering they experienced from punishments and work" imposed by these two friars.

The mission's troubles were alleviated by the establishment of a hospital *asistencia* in San Rafael on the north side of the bay in 1817, but it fell into a decline that quickened after Mexican independence was won in 1821 and secularization was ordered in 1834. Mission records note that by 1842, only 196 people were left in the settlement, including 37 Indians. The mission church was placed in the care of a secular priest, and attempts to sell mission properties (instigated by Mexican governor Pio Pico) weren't successful.

The coming of the Americans—more specifically, forty-niners seeking their fortunes in the Sierra Nevada—boosted the mission along with the rest of San Francisco. Swallowed by the exponential growth of the city, the mission was used for private businesses; for a time it was surrounded by lascivious entertainments that no doubt would have curled the tonsures of its founding padres. The parish that grew up around it eventually warranted the construction of a bigger church—the neighboring basilica—and the mission's future was secure.

Even a devastating earthquake couldn't bring the stalwart mission down. The basilica was demolished by the temblor, but Mission Dolores stood unscathed, needing little more than the reinforcement of its redwood ceiling beams. The rest of San Francisco should be so strong . . .

The Mission Today

Save for the sturdy columns and the cross that juts skyward from its peaked roof, the architecture of Mission Dolores is unremarkable, outflashed by the neighboring basilica, no taller or wider than some of the homes that crowd the San Francisco neighborhood in which it stands. There is no bell tower or *campanario*—the mission bells are housed in three arches above the balcony that splits its facade. A high, whitewashed wall stretches south, backed by a beckoning tower of greenery. A small mission bell and two historical plaques (one recognizing the mission, the other commemorating the end of Serra's El Camino Real) are the only other clues to the magic that abides within.

A self-guided tour of the mission begins in the gift shop. The first stop is the church itself, high and bright and grand, its ceiling painted in a geometric pattern of Indian design in gold and red, silver and white. A golden light filters through the high windows, illuminating the red tile floor, the wooden pews, and the artwork along the walls of the nave: a statue of San Francisco de Asís, a portrait of the Madonna, and an extraordinary mural painting of the Last Supper that also depicts the virtues of Faith, Hope, and Charity, and priests holding offerings of wine and bread.

The gilded reredos, which was brought to the mission from Mexico in 1796, wraps around the altar in the church's sanctuary. Lovely polychromed wood statues gaze out from high niches—the Blessed Mother, San Francisco de Asís, San Joaquin, San Miguel, Santa Ana, Santa Clara. The two side altars also are decorated in gold leaf, their wooden columns painted to look like marble. The grave of Lieutenant José Joaquin Moraga rests in the floor of the mission, along with the graves of several Americans who died after the mission era.

Tiny Mission Dolores, with its sturdy columns, is dwarfed by an adjoining basilica.

The Frank J. Portman Memorial diorama of historic Mission Dolores, created for the 1939 World's Fair, sits in the narrow courtyard that separates the church from the basilica. Heavy doors offer access into the grander building, a cavernous place heavy with Gothic arches and anchored by an army of pews. Intricate stained-glass windows depicting the twenty-one missions and their patron saints run down both sides of the nave, allowing a colorful if muted light to fill the high, dark spaces. An enormous turquoise vault arcs over the sanctuary and altar, simply adorned with candelabra and a fine crucifix. Shrines dedicated to Christ, Our Lady of Guadalupe, and other saints are housed in alcoves along the nave, more intimate sanctuaries for the prayerful.

Back in the courtyard, a path leads from the diorama to a fascinating hall of pictures. The images reveal mission life through the 1800s and into modern times, including a photograph of the mission after the 1906 earthquake, with the bigger church in ruins beside it. Photographs also commemorate the 1987 visit of Pope John Paul II.

A beautiful mosaic representation of the arrival of the Spanish in Alta California by sea and by land, including Juan Bautista de Ayala's *San Carlos*, the first European ship to sail into San Francisco Bay, and pioneers Junípero Serra and Juan Bautista de Anza, marks the entry to a small patio in which you can find amenities such as restrooms and a drinking fountain. Beyond, the gardens of the mission's cemetery beckon.

A plan of the *camposanto* interprets what you'll see in the lovely churchyard. Among the worn and leaning gravestones rest a number of noteworthy Californians, including Don Francisco de Haro, the first *alcalde* of San Francisco, and Don Luis Antonio Arguello, the first governor of Alta California. Of the more than 5,000 individuals buried here, only 200 are not Indian, according to mission literature. These many graves lie unmarked amid redwoods and roses, poppies and sedges, cacti and fragrant sage. Narrow paths wind through the plantings and the gravestones, and small stone benches offer respite in the shade. Native plants and a tule hut settled in a corner of the garden near the mission wall remember the many neophytes who lived and died at the mission.

A small museum that was once the church's sacristy holds a number of interesting artifacts. A plaque above a section of exposed adobe notes that approximately 36,000 bricks were used to build the chapel alone. Other items include relics of Indian cultures that flourished in the area for thousands of years, and relics of the early mission days, including original altarpieces and slates from the mission school. Among the interesting documents are a record of the first baptism at Mission Dolores in April 1778 (bearing the signature of Padre Palóu), and the *Law of the Kingdoms of the Indies*, a book used by missionaries and soldiers as a guide to the rights of the Native peoples. Pictures document the mission through time; there is also an interesting 1903 retrospective of historical

The stained-glass windows of Mission Dolores Basilica spotlight all the missions as well as their patron saints.

mission prints on display. The art of Father John Giuliani, who depicted holy men as Natives, including Christ as an Apache, is also on display in the museum.

Nearby Points of Interest

The most obvious nearby point of interest is the adjoining basilica—that is, if you haven't already made it part of your mission tour. There is also the Presidio of San Francisco. A walk through North Beach, down by Fisherman's Wharf, will place you back in Yerba Buena, the Spanish pueblo from which San Francisco grew. The city's historical fabric is intricate, its Spanish heritage a significant fiber, but not the only one. You might begin your exploration of its convoluted and fascinating story by contacting the San Francisco Museum and Historical Society at (415) 775–1111 or www.sfhistory.org.

Mission San Rafael Arcángel

The Patron Saint: One of the three angels mentioned in the Bible, Raphael's very name means "God has healed" or "God's remedy." He is said to have cured Tobit of blindness and to have expelled a devil that killed anyone betrothed to Sara, the future wife of Tobit's son, thereby allowing her to marry.

FOUNDING DATE: December 14, 1817

ADDRESS: 1104 Fifth Street, San Rafael, 94901

TELEPHONE NUMBER: (415) 454–8141

WEB SITE: The mission has no specific Web site, but the parish site is www.saintraphael.com.

HOURS: The mission is open from 11:00 A.M. to 4:00 P.M. daily.

DIRECTIONS: From southbound U.S. Highway 101, take the central San Rafael exit, which deposits you on Hetherton Street. Follow Hetherton Street south for one block to Mission Avenue. Turn right (west) onto Mission Avenue for 0.2 mile to Court Street. Turn left (southwest) onto Court Street for one block to Fifth Street. Turn right onto Fifth Street; the mission and Saint Raphael's Church and School are on the right (north).

From northbound US 101, take the central San Rafael exit, which deposits you on Irwin Street. Follow Irwin Street north for about 0.3 mile to Mission Avenue. Turn right onto Mission Avenue and follow the directions above to reach the mission. California Historic Landmark No. 220.

PARKING: Parking is available along Fifth Street and on surrounding city streets. Most is metered. Parking may be difficult on busy weekends.

SERVICES AND EVENTS: Masses are celebrated weekdays in the mission chapel at 6:30 A.M. and 8:30 A.M. Additional services are held in the church on Saturday at 8:30 A.M. and 5:00 P.M., and on Sunday at 7:30 A.M, 9:00 A.M., and 10:30 A.M. Spanish Masses are conducted in the church on Sunday at noon and 7:00 P.M. The mission chapel is used for Masses celebrated in Vietnamese on Sunday at 9:00 A.M. and in Haitian on the fourth Sunday of each month at 6:30 P.M.

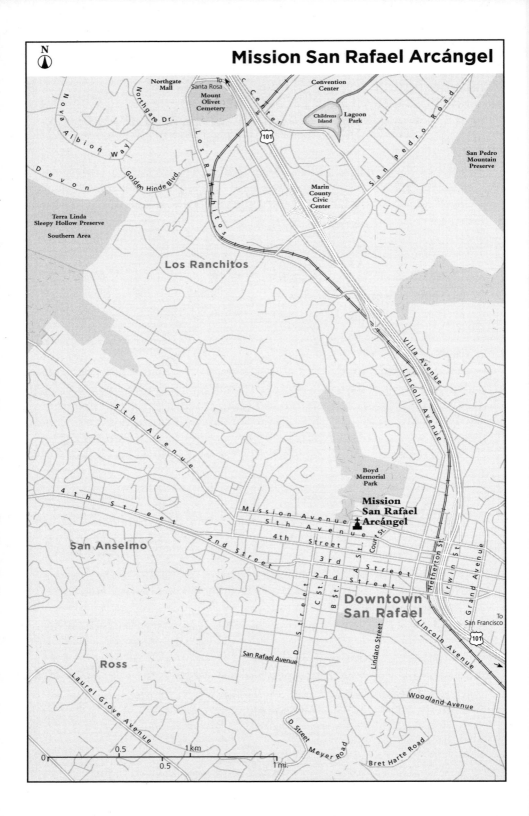

Marin County is blessed with sunshine—a heavenly blanket of healing and warmth that inspired padres at foggy Mission San Francisco de Asís to establish a hospital mission for ailing neophytes in the North Bay.

Mission San Rafael would be short lived, its success compressed into the thirteen-year tenure of a single padre, and was destined for all but complete obliteration. A modern replica now commemorates the lost mission, though it scarcely recalls its pastoral progenitor, obscured as it is in the tony downtown district of modern-day San Rafael. But with its bells, its welcoming chapel, and a pair of star windows reminiscent of those at the mother church at the Carmel Mission, Mission San Rafael serves as a touchstone for contemplation of what came before.

The Mission Yesterday

The wildlands of Marin County, shaded by acorn-bearing oaks, roamed by game both large and small, and surrounded by the maritime bounty of San Francisco Bay and the Pacific Ocean, had long sustained the Coast Miwok Indians and their ancestors. This ancient hunting and gathering society, in addition to harvesting sustenance from a generous land, maintained a rich oral tradition, developed a remarkable basketweaving technology, conducted trade with surrounding Native cultures, and developed a lifestyle that meshed harmoniously with their natural world.

These Natives may have had contact with white men before the coming of the Spanish missionaries—there's a good chance that Francis Drake, the English privateer who circumnavigated the globe in 1579, landed in Drakes Bay on the Point Reyes peninsula and claimed the land for his queen—but it was with the coming of the padres and the military forces that supported them that the Coast Miwok world changed significantly and forever.

Originally an *asistencia* to Mission Dolores, Mission San Rafael began as a sanatorium. Indian converts who grew ill in the dense fogs and moist winds of San Francisco were taken across the bay to the small outpost—built on a site with a southern exposure and a buffer of wooded hills between it and the vapors of the seas—with the hope that the warmer climate would heal them. Dedicating the *asistencia* for Saint Raphael, performer of miraculous acts of healing, was the obvious choice given its intention.

And though the well-being of the Mission Indians was perhaps foremost in the minds of the mission's founders, politics also played into the genesis of what was then Spain's northernmost settlement. The Russians, foraying south from Alaskan strongholds in search of sea otter pelts and expansion of their North American empire, had established Fort Ross north of Bodega Bay in 1812, and the Spanish, seeking to cement their claim to all of Alta California, hoped their mission settlements would prove an effective deterrent.

The hospital mission's cross was raised late in the mission era by Frays Ramon Abella, Narciso Duran, Luis Gil, and Padre Presidente Vicente de Sarria. A plaque on the face of the mission notes that the fathers conducted twenty-six baptisms and enlisted nearly 200 neophytes for instruction in the Catholic faith on that first day. Padre Gil, who had some medical expertise, was put in charge of an *asistencia* that showed promise from the outset.

Construction of the chapel and hospital wing, as well as the other structures that typically supported a mission, began in 1818 and continued for about fifteen years. What stands today reflects neither the original mission's size nor its orientation, though it is built on roughly the same ground. Historical sketches show an L-shaped configuration with the church perpendicular to the hospital wing and cloister.

During the reign of the Franciscans, the land that had so generously sustained the Coast Miwok continued to prove fruitful. The neophytes, who numbered 1,140 in 1828, grew a variety of crops (peas, corn, fruit trees, grapes) and husbanded livestock (cattle, pigs, sheep, and more). Women were taught to weave and prepare flours from corn and grain. The successes prompted the elevation of the *asistencia* to a mission in October 1822. A sole padre, Juan Amorós, oversaw the mission in those years: He is remembered by writers as an inventive man who taught the neophytes to build Spanish-style boats and who constructed a working water clock. Amorós died in 1832 and was buried at the mission.

Yet despite the bounty and the fact that friendlier weather did indeed bolster the health of ailing Natives, Mission San Rafael saw its share of turmoil and death. A tiny marble gravestone behind the present mission chapel memorializes the 835 Indians interred on mission grounds (a sister gravestone is dedicated to the memory of those "executed . . . awaiting birthdays"). By the time the mission was secularized in the early 1830s, no viable Coast Miwok culture remained, though those with Coast Miwok blood have since joined with the Pomo Indians of southern Sonoma County to form the Federated Indians of Graton Rancheria.

The tiny marker behind the chapel also memorializes two Coast Miwok leaders, Chief Marin and Chief Quintin, both of whom fought the mission during their tenures. Chief Marin was captured while resisting the Spanish authorities in 1815 or 1816, lived at the mission for a time, then escaped and set about harassing soldiers and other Spaniards living in the area. He was recaptured in 1824 and sent back to the mission, where he spent the rest of his life.

The Indians weren't the only troublemakers for the mission—turmoil also came from within. Padre Amorós was followed by a priest universally reviled by mission historians: Fray José Mercado, a Franciscan from Mexico remembered as "strict" and a man of "violent temperament," clashed with both Mission

Indians and his political and military contemporaries. After he orchestrated a confrontation between neophytes and visiting Indians that resulted in the deaths of more than twenty people, he was, essentially, fired.

The mission never recovered from the double blows of Mercado's mismanagement and secularization, which removed control of California's mission property from the purview of religious authorities and handed it over to civilians. In Mission San Rafael's case, secularization resulted in both the mission's lands and its Indian population falling under the oversight of General Mariano Vallejo, onetime *comandante* of the Presidio of San Francisco and owner of vast ranchos surrounding both Mission San Rafael and Mission San Francisco Solano (the Sonoma Mission).

After secularization, the neophytes melted back into the wilderness, mission lands were absorbed into Vallejo's holdings, and the mission church and hospital wing fell quickly into disrepair (though it was intact enough to offer shelter to Captain John Frémont as he fought to bring California into the United States in 1846). In 1855, with California now part of the Union, Uncle Sam returned what was left of the mission buildings and some surrounding acreage to the Catholic Church.

But by 1870 most of the original mission structures had returned to the earth, and the city of San Rafael, more mindful of how the land could be used in modern times than of the historical import of the mission that had once occupied that land, grew vigorously on ground fertilized by its remains.

In 1909, under the auspices of the Native Sons of the Golden West, the mission did enjoy a renaissance of sorts. A replica of the chapel and hospital wing, erected near the original site, was finished in 1949. The cost of that replication—$85,000, according to materials in the gift shop/museum—is a paltry sum given the price of real estate these days in Marin County, and given the value of the heritage it recalls.

The Mission Today

Mission San Rafael's surroundings are most definitely *not* evocative of the mission era. The small church is awash in the busyness of downtown San Rafael, situated as it is one street north of the main drag, and wedged between glass-walled office buildings and the much more imposing Saint Raphael's Catholic Church. It takes a healthy imagination to re-create the relatively pristine Marin County—one of rolling oak woodlands and free-flowing waterways—that the mission was established in.

The doors of the mission open onto a small plaza that also serves Saint Raphael's Church. On the facade of the chapel, a plaque commemorates the mission's founding. No bell tower was ever built for the mission, but the original bells remain, three mounted on a rough wooden frame to one side of the

The original mission bells of tiny Mission San Rafael were never housed in a tower; instead they hang on a simple wooden frame.

chapel doors. A simple wooden cross, along with a statue of Padre Junípero Serra, stands sentinel on the narrow strip of lawn and garden that separates the chapel from the sidewalk and busy Fifth Street.

The mission's interior is plain, practical, and, while architecturally true to the mission style, obviously modern. The only ornamentation on the walls of the nave are Stations of the Cross and the six flags under which the mission has operated—those of Spain, Mexico, California, the United States, the Vatican, and the city of San Rafael. The floor is paved with red tiles, the pews are of a pale wood, and electric chandeliers in the Spanish style are suspended from the beamed ceiling.

The altar is decorated with gold candelabra; statues of the Holy Mother and Saint Raphael flank the crucifix that is its centerpiece. High, narrow windows allow afternoon sunshine to bathe the chapel in a soft infusion of gold— a subtle light special to many of California's missions. In the vestibule a separate altar has been set up in honor of Our Lady of Lavang, an incarnation of the Blessed Mother that appeared to persecuted Vietnamese believers in the late eighteenth and nineteenth centuries. The entryway also holds a plaque honoring Junípero Serra that includes his oft-quoted motto: "Always to go forward and never to look back."

The gift shop and the restrooms are found in the mission annex, a replica of the wing that would have served as the hospital and priests' quarters during the mission's heyday. The shop sells an abundance of mission and religious memorabilia, and also houses a modest museum. Beautiful religious paintings are crowded on the walls, and glass cases house fragments of pottery and roof tiles from the original mission, as well as old Bibles, priestly garments, and historical and religious artifacts. Sketches by General Mariano Vallejo, who would come to control much of the mission's lands, are among the drawings and models that depict Mission San Rafael as it once was.

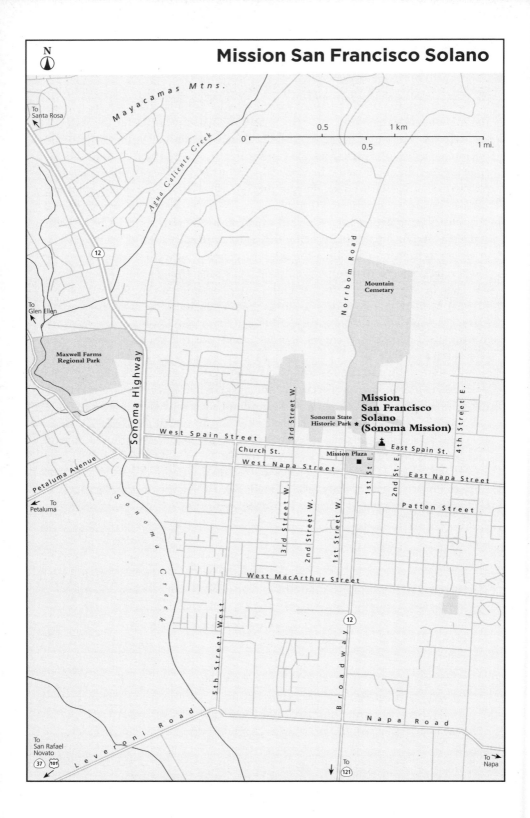

Mission San Francisco Solano

N

To
Santa Rosa

Mayacamas Mtns.

Agua Caliente Creek

0.5   1 km

0   0.5   1 mi.

12

Norrbom Road

Mountain
Cemetary

To
Glen Ellen

Maxwell Farms
Regional Park

Sonoma Highway

3rd Street W.

Sonoma State
Historic Park ★

**Mission
San Francisco
Solano
(Sonoma Mission)**

4th Street E.

West Spain Street

Church St.

East Spain St.

West Napa Street

Mission Plaza ■

1st St. E.

2nd St. E.

East Napa Street

Petaluma Avenue

3rd Street W.

2nd Street W.

1st Street W.

Patten Street

To
Petaluma

Sonoma Creek

West MacArthur Street

5th Street West

12

Broadway

Leveroni Road

To
San Rafael
Novato

37   101

To
121

Napa Road

To
Napa

Mission San Francisco Solano
(Sonoma Mission)

The Patron Saint: Francis Solano, called the Apostle of South America and the patron saint of Peru, was born in Spain in 1549 and ordained a Franciscan priest in 1576. After earning praise as a healer, a musician, and a preacher, he embarked on a mission to South America, where he worked for twenty years. A favorite of Padre Junípero Serra's, Francis died in 1610 and was canonized in 1726.

FOUNDING DATE: July 4, 1823

ADDRESS: The mission is located at the corner of First Street East and East Spain Street in downtown Sonoma; Sonoma State Historic Park is located at 363 Third Street West, Sonoma, 95476-5632.

TELEPHONE NUMBER: (707) 938–9560

WEB SITES: www.parks.ca.gov (follow the links); www.parks.sonoma.net/sonoma.html

HOURS: No Masses are celebrated at this mission. However, the mission is open for tours from 10:00 A.M. to 5:00 P.M. daily. It is closed on Thanksgiving, Christmas, and New Year's Day. A small fee is charged, which is good for admittance to the mission, the neighboring Sonoma Barracks, General Vallejo's Home, and the Petaluma Adobe.

DIRECTIONS: To reach the mission from U.S. Highway 101 in Novato, take the California Highway 37/Sonoma/Vallejo exit. Head east on CA 37 for 7.5 miles to its intersection with California Highway 121, the turnoff for Sonoma. Turn left (north) onto CA 121, and go 6.6 miles to where it intersects California Highways 12 and 116. Stay right on CA 121/12 for 0.8 mile; CA 12 breaks off to the left (north) at this point. Follow CA 12 north for 3.8 miles to Napa Street, which forms the south boundary of the Sonoma Plaza. The mission is located on the northeast corner of the plaza. California Historic Landmark No. 3.

PARKING: Plenty of parking is available around the plaza and in the parking lot behind the Sonoma Barracks. Parking can be difficult, however, during special events and on weekends.

SERVICES AND EVENTS: Docent-led tours of the mission are offered on Friday, Saturday, and Sunday. Group tours and school tours are also available. The mission hosts weddings and private parties. Annual events include a Patron's Tasting during the Valley of the Moon Vintage Festival, held in late September, and two events held early in December: the Blessing of the Olives and Christmas at the Mission, which includes candlelit caroling inside the chapel.

The end of the mission trail. The northernmost mission. The last mission established in California. The only mission founded during Mexican rule. Though significant for all these reasons and more, Mission San Francisco Solano (the Sonoma Mission) is more an afterthought than part of the grand plan, and its short history tosses in the restless currents of California history in the early 1800s.

Though the mission was technically separate from the *cuartel* in Sonoma and the pueblo that blossomed around both, its proximity to the impressive bulk of the Sonoma Barracks and the splendid home of General Mariano Guadalupe Vallejo testifies to its links with both. It blossomed at the tail end of mission glory, was stymied by secularization, and suffered ruin and decline, all at an accelerated pace. Yet it has endured, a stodgy fixture on the landscape and an important voice in the chorus of history that rings out from Sonoma's plaza.

The Mission Yesterday

In the immediate wake of Mexican independence from Spain, won in 1821, an ambitious priest from Mission Dolores raised a cross at the foot of the Mayacamas Mountains in the Sonoma Valley. The establishment of Padre José Altimira—the northernmost of Franciscan religious outposts, and the only mission founded under the Mexican flag—looked south across oak-shaded flatlands toward San Pablo Bay, which stretched fingers of fog into the fertile valley and fostered the salmon that swam in its clear streams.

With the intent of replacing both Missions Dolores and San Rafael, the controversial Altimira skirted established religious channels to establish San Francisco Solano, capitalizing on Mexican fears of Russian encroachment from the north to secure the approval of the secular governor rather than his own padre presidente. This maneuver provoked a lack of goodwill among his fellow priests, who would, after some wrangling, allow Altimira to establish his mission but would keep the other two missions open as well.

Altimira's conceit forever changed the lives of the Coast Miwok, Wappo, and Pomo Indians who had shared the bounty of the Sonoma Valley for centuries. Cattle and horses introduced by the Spaniards consumed the same forage as the native elk and deer, their numbers declined, and the big game the Natives had long hunted was suddenly in short supply. The introduction of pigs was an even bigger blow to the fortunes of the indigenous people, because the swine consumed the acorns that were the Natives' staple food. The Indians began to starve.

But the new mission offered food, and some Indians were attracted by that; others may have come because they were curious. Whatever the reason, once they entered the mission, the Natives were not allowed to leave. They were baptized and schooled in the Catholic religion. They were denied the use of sweat lodges, in which they had traditionally cleansed both body and soul, and were forced to work long and hard at tasks that were unfamiliar and sometimes dangerous. They found themselves unable to fight off European diseases, and epidemics decimated their numbers. In the words of a Sonoma Mission docent, "Their ways were lost."

Still, under the strict supervision of Altimira, San Francisco Solano's neophytes were industrious, erecting a wooden chapel and other structures, planting and harvesting numerous crops, and tending to growing herds of livestock. They became adept in the traditional tasks of Mission Indians, from the making of adobe bricks to the weaving of cloth and the making of candles.

The neophytes were not content, however, and their dissatisfaction with Altimira's management of the mission spawned a revolt in 1826, in which the Indians burned the chapel and raided the food supplies. In the aftermath of the rebellion, Padre Altimira left the mission, having lasted only three years in the post he'd created. A more experienced padre, Buenaventura Fortuni, took his place.

Fortuni, who had been a priest at Mission San José for twenty years, was the only priest assigned to the mission for six and a half years, but those years proved prosperous: More than 7,000 animals were raised on its lands in 1829, according to one historian; more than 1,500 bushels of wheat, barley, beans, peas, corn, and garbanzos were harvested in 1830; and a hefty (but fluctuating) population of neophytes—more than 900 in the early 1830s—lived in mission *rancherias*. Fortuni was able to keep the Indians content, but that was probably not through the ritual of worship: According to a mission docent, Fortuni delivered homilies that lasted nearly an hour, stretching Masses to more than two hours, during which the congregation, standing on a dirt floor that had been spread with ox blood and manure to quell the dust, swatted at the vermin that thrived in the pungent mixture.

Fortuni also oversaw the construction of a grand adobe church and the completion of a large mission quadrangle that housed workshops, a laundry, a blacksmith's shop, a *convento*, and a dormitory for unmarried Indian girls. The mission also encompassed a number of ranchos and *rancherias* throughout the valley and beyond.

In 1834 San Francisco Solano was secularized, its administration turned over to General Mariano Vallejo, who commanded the neighboring Sonoma Barracks. Mission lands, originally to be returned to the Natives, were eventually absorbed into Vallejo's vast holdings, and the church, now headquarters of a parish, served the newly established pueblo of Sonoma. When the larger adobe church fell into disrepair in the early 1840s, Vallejo built an adobe chapel on the site of the original wooden chapel.

Then came the Mexican-American War, and California's transfer to the United States. Sonoma was caught up in those changes in a big way—it was the home of the Bear Flag Revolt, in which the short-lived independent republic of California was born—but the mission languished. In 1862 the chapel and some surrounding lands were deeded back to the Catholic Church, but that did nothing to stop its descent into ruin.

The bounty of Sonoma's fields and streams came to be part of the vast social and economic net cast by San Francisco, and a railroad line was built to transport goods and people between the metropolis and the country town. Completed in the late 1870s, this proved fortuitous for Sonoma, but not for the mission, because the rail line ran right in front of the church doors. The clamor of trains proved too disturbing for both priests and congregations, and led to the sale of the mission in 1881 to a local businessman who would build a saloon in front of the chapel and use the chapel itself for storage.

Mission San Francisco Solano's revival is linked to the renewed interest in California's heritage that developed at the turn of the twentieth century. The California Historic Landmarks League, with the help of newspaper magnate William Randolph Hearst, acquired the chapel in 1903, and it underwent restoration at that time. The mission eventually was incorporated into Sonoma State Historic Park, which also encompasses the Sonoma Barracks and General Vallejo's Home.

The Mission Today

The Sonoma Mission is part of a complex of historic structures that forms the backdrop of the Sonoma Plaza. It sits on a tree-shaded plaza, across the street from the Sonoma Barracks, kitty-corner to the Bear Flag Monument, and surrounded by other structures, such as the Blue Wing Inn and the Toscano Hotel, that simply exude history.

The chapel is a simple building, its facade a wash of white broken by the deep brown of its wooden doors and the slender lintels that top both door and a window above. An original mission bell is suspended from a frame of hewn wood, and another mission bell marks the end of El Camino Real, which spanned three centuries and stretched south from Sonoma into Central America and east to Florida.

A red tile walkway through a xeriscape garden leads to the closed chapel doors and on to the cool veranda of the former padres' quarters, now a visitor center.

The first room of the former *convento* is stocked with books and other mission memorabilia. Artifacts from the mission days are on display in the next

Mission San Francisco Solano is a model of architectural simplicity. The only orna-
mentations are the thin wooden lintels above the door and window.

room, including a bit of original adobe, a Spanish *fanega* (measurement box), and a mission bell.

The walls of the second chamber are lined with original watercolor paintings of each of the California missions. The Virgil Jorgensen Collection, painted by Christopher Jorgensen and named for his son, captures the missions in ruins, melded harmoniously into landscapes of green and gold. A long, heavy dining table stretches the length of the chamber.

The third room holds a number of displays that describe various facets of what was once Alta California: pueblos and presidios, the Spanish and Mexican legacy, the collision of Native American and European cultures. The doorway at the end of this room leads into the chapel.

Bereft of pews, confessionals, Stations of the Cross, and other invitations to worship, the Sonoma Mission chapel is hollow and museum-like. Voices, even hushed, ring off the naked walls and floor, a hard ricochet that discourages even a prayer delivered standing up. The walls are painted with Indian designs representing mountains, valleys, flowers, and the river of life, a flowing image in blue that depicts the highs and lows of earthly existence.

The altar, a rather simple affair hosting a statue of Christ and a painting of the mission's patron saint, Francis Solano, is a still life of Catholicism, all its pieces suspended in place and time. Many of the religious accoutrements with which the chapel was outfitted—altar cloths, chalices—were gifts from the Russian Orthodox Church—a generous enemy, as it turns out. The padre's chair on the chancel dates back to the days of the original mission, as does the sacramental lamp. The reredos also holds a statue of Mary in a red dress, an unusual depiction that took advantage of a Native belief that the color red possessed healing powers.

The single burial that was made in the chapel, that of Maria Ygnacia Lopez Carrillo, mother-in-law of Mariano Vallejo, lies near the back of the church. This amazing woman, who walked with her nine children north from San Diego to be closer to her daughter and son-in-law, wanted to be buried near the holy water stoup so that when worshipers blessed themselves, some of the sacred water might fall upon her grave—or so the story goes.

A door in the artifact room of the museum opens onto the mission quadrangle. Shade thrown by olive trees drapes the enclosure, which contains a fountain occasionally sprinkled with vibrant flowers left by a wedding party, a wall of tall cacti laden with red prickly pears in season, a covered cauldron in which Native boys once stirred beef fat as it was rendered into valuable tallow, and an adobe oven, along with more modern conveniences including restrooms and barbecue pits.

A memorial to Mission Indians unlike any other in the California mission system runs along the west side of the mission—a memorial that recognizes by name those who died at San Francisco Solano and were buried in a mass grave now lost under the adjacent roadway. Etched in polished black granite, only the Christian names are remembered, but you can run your fingers over them, much as you can the names chiseled on gravestones in other mission cemeteries. Their Native names may be forever lost, but the lives of the 896 Mission Indians who died here have been given, in hard stone, a legitimacy and an immediacy unique to the mission system.

Sonoma Barracks

The Sonoma Barracks, across the street from the Sonoma Mission, are evidence of Sonoma's military and political past, the tangible evidence of an ephemeral presidio that played a significant role in the development of the California psyche.

The barracks were founded in 1834 by General Mariano Vallejo, then *comandante* of the Presidio of San Francisco, on the orders of the Mexican governor José Figueroa, who wanted to deter the Russians from penetrating farther into Alta California, and to keep an eye on their existing settlement at Fort Ross. Vallejo brought his San Francisco garrison north to the Valley of the Moon and set up shop on the Sonoma Plaza, next to the thriving Mission San Francisco Solano. Because secularization had also been ordered in that year, Vallejo was named civilian administrator of the mission, and shouldered the task of establishing the pueblo of Sonoma.

Construction of the barracks, a boxy two-story building of adobe and heavy wood, was completed in 1841, but the soldiers housed within never faced a serious threat from the Russians, who retreated from California to their strongholds in Alaska in the same year. Instead they were employed in the not-so-easy task of keeping local Indian tribes in check.

But these are not the historic events for which Sonoma would earn renown. Before victory in the Mexican-American War consolidated American power from sea to shining sea in 1848, the tiny northern outpost would host a prescient event. For a time—just a short time—California would declare its independence with the raising of a homemade flag emblazoned with a golden bear. The flag flew for less than one month over the Sonoma Plaza before the American flag was raised in its stead, but you could say that California's penchant for bucking the norm saw its genesis under that ragtag banner.

Of course, the Bear Flag Revolt of 1846 was not a widespread movement—indeed, it was the brainchild of a small band of "frontiersmen" who, spurred by the upheaval of the times, saw an opportunity to establish a state free of Mexican tyranny. The spoils were the bounty of trade goods—tallow and hides, primarily—generated by both Mission San Francisco Solano and Vallejo's vast ranchos. Vallejo had released the presidial soldiers in the wake of the Russian withdrawal, so there was no violence in the revolt—the renegades easily

The Sonoma Barracks was originally established to deter the Russians from pushing farther south into Alta California.

captured the *comandante* and shipped him off to Sacramento, established their headquarters in the barracks, and settled in.

Once Monterey, capital of Mexican California, acquiesced to American forces, so too did the Bear Flaggers. Vallejo returned to oversee the slow decay of his empire, and the barracks were occupied for nearly a decade by Americans, first by members of Captain John C. Frémont's California Battalion, then by the First New York Volunteers (many of whom, according to museum literature, deserted to take part in the Gold Rush), then by U.S. Army dragoons. After military occupation ceased, the barracks were used as a winery, a printing office, a mercantile, and a private residence. The site was acquired by the state in 1958, and restored between 1976 and 1980.

Today the barracks are part of the Sonoma State Historic Park and house a gift shop; a theater in which an excellent video explains the history of the mission and barracks and explores the legacy of Mariano Vallejo; and a couple of exhibit rooms. In the first you'll find a re-creation of soliders' quarters, with neatly made cots pushed up against the walls and rifles balanced against the adobes. In the second room exhibits describe California as both the Mexican and American frontier, covering the Bear Flag Revolt, the escapades of John C. Frémont, the establishment of ranchos (and vineyards) in the area, and preservation of the barracks and other historical resources around Sonoma's historic plaza.

Nearby Points of Interest

Sonoma State Historic Park also encompasses Lachryma Montis, the home of General Mariano Guadalupe Vallejo, the Toscano Hotel, the Blue Wing Hotel, and, farther afield, the Petaluma Adobe. It is a great resource for more information on the history of Sonoma, and can be reached by writing 20 Spain Street, Sonoma, 95476; by calling the Barracks gift shop at (707) 939–9420; or by visiting http://members.napanet.net/~sshpa/.

The Presidios

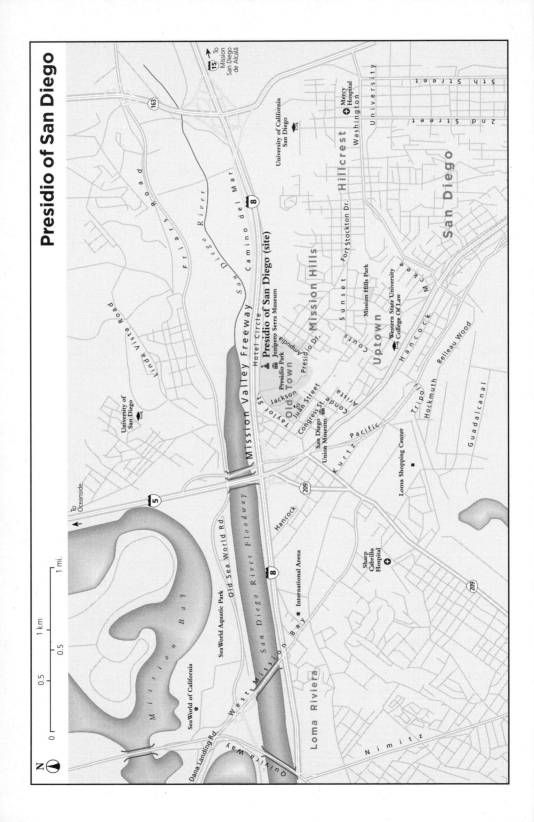

Presidio of San Diego

The Presidio of San Diego

FOUNDING DATE: 1769

ADDRESS: The remnants of the Presidio of San Diego lie within Presidio Park, which is also the site of the Junípero Serra Museum, repository of presidio artifacts and history. The museum address is 2727 Presidio Drive, San Diego, 92103-1053.

TELEPHONE NUMBER: (619) 297–3258

WEB SITE: www.sandiegohistory.org

HOURS: The presidio site itself, being a park, is open all day, every day. The Junípero Serra Museum is open Tuesday through Sunday in summer, from 10:00 A.M. to 4:30 P.M., and on Friday, Saturday, and Sunday in winter, also from 10:00 A.M. to 4:30 P.M. Museum admission fees are moderate ($5.00 for adults; seniors, students, and military personnel are $4.00; children six through seventeen are $2.00).

DIRECTIONS: To reach Presidio Park from northbound or southbound Interstate 5, take the Interstate 8 exit. Follow I–8 east for 0.6 mile to the exit for Taylor Street and Airport Circle. Go right (west) on Taylor Street for 0.6 mile to Presidio Drive. Go left on Presidio Drive, which climbs to the museum. California Historic Landmark No. 59.

PARKING: There is plenty of parking in paved lots both below the Junípero Serra Museum and above, near the picnic grounds.

Presidio Park commands the southern buttress of tablelands that rise above the San Diego River, a strategic point near the river's outlet that offers commanding views of the once pristine Mission Bay and the narrowing valley that reaches inland to Mission San Diego de Alcalá. These extensive views were an obvious boon to Spanish colonialists seeking to establish the first presidio in Alta California. Where better to set up fortifications than on an overlook that offered unobstructed views of enemies approaching by land or by sea?

And where better to get a bird's-eye view of modern San Diego. These days, the hill rises above freeways, shopping centers, and residential areas, but the vistas are still engaging, and the setting remains lovely. Homes pock the brushy slopes of the San Diego River Valley, but from on high the valley walls still evoke a gentle wildness. The estuary at the river's mouth is a silvery shadow of what it once was, its braids now defined by the dull gray of concrete, but on a clear day the blue waters of Mission Bay float in the distance, dotted with the white sails of ships that now are commonplace, but once were scarce.

The Presidio Yesterday

Founding a colonial outpost at San Diego was a twofold proposition, and one that had decidedly shaky beginnings. The rudiments of a presidio were established in the spring of 1769 with the arrival of two beleaguered ships, the *San Antonio* and the *San Carlos*, the seafaring prongs of an expeditionary force charged by authorities in New Spain with securing Alta California for the Spanish Crown. A mission was established two months later on the site, after the arrival of Alta California's missionary leader, Junípero Serra, and the region's new governor, Gaspar de Portolá.

Both mission and presidio were troubled from the outset, hamstrung first by scurvy, which killed or disabled the bulk of sailors on the *San Carlos* and *San Antonio*, and then by a chronic shortage of supplies—including food—expected to be sent from home ports in Baja California. The soldiers who had arrived both by land and by sea found themselves struggling to survive in a foreign and hostile landscape, working as healers, explorers, farmers, builders, and ranch hands as well as military men.

The colonists built rough constructions of wood and brush—a chapel, residential quarters, and workshops surrounded by a palisade—near a large Kumeyaay Indian village, the inhabitants of which would be exploited by soldiers and missionaries as a source of labor and of Catholic converts. This didn't endear the newcomers to the Natives, whose natural suspicion flowered into animosity when the *soldados* began raping their women and stealing their food, and zealous priests began exacting harsh punishments on newly recruited neophytes. The skirmishes that peppered the presidio's first years grew into open rebellion in 1775, when hundreds of Indians descended upon San Diego's mission and destroyed it.

Historical accounts of that rebellion describe first its seed: a friction between the religious arm of the conquest and the military that would plague Spanish California for most of its existence. San Diego's padres moved the mission, which had been located within the presidio at its founding, 6 miles up the San Diego River in 1774, placing distance between those who considered themselves saviors of the heathen souls and those who saw the heathen as a force to be conquered. There were other reasons, of course—better farmland, a better water supply—but the decision to relocate proved calamitous for the mission, which witnessed the martyrdom of its priest and the torching of its chapel. Survivors of the attack fled back to the presidio, which remained unaware of the disaster until after it was over.

Life in San Diego, both for missionaries and soldiers, settled after the rebellion. Maps, models, and drawings of the military complex, which was officially declared a Royal Presidio on January 1, 1774, depict a well-fortified *castillo* (fortress), its wooden structures replaced by more formidable constructions of adobe arranged in a quadrangle. The high walls of the quad surrounded barracks for single and married *soldados*, more elaborate homes for commanders, a chapel and quarters for the padres who ministered to the garrison, warehouses, granaries, and gun batteries. By one account, as many as 400 people lived in or around the presidio in its heyday.

Though both presidio and mission conducted surreptitious trade with foreign visitors while under Spain's rule—in some cases, this was the only way the colony could acquire needed supplies—this activity became sanctioned once Mexican independence was won in 1821. Though this was a boon for occupants of the presidio, secularization was not. Handed down by Mexican authorities in 1834, the secularization order ultimately resulted in the redistribution of mission lands into civilian hands, where they were incorporated into ranchos that enriched the *Californios* who owned them. Trade was essential to that enrichment process, and traffic in hides—California's greatest export at the time—took on special importance. To facilitate the sale and transport of the commodity, a pueblo was established at the base of Presidio Hill—the origins of what is now called Old Town—and focus shifted from the presidio on the hill to the port and pueblo at its feet.

The *castillo* was abandoned by the Mexicans in 1837, but was briefly used by the Americans following their victory in the Mexican-American War. When the Americans left, the structures were scavenged for tiles, boards, and other building materials; after that it was utterly neglected, and its adobe fortifications disintegrated into the earth.

Though the presidio, unlike the mission, would never be resurrected, it would enjoy a renaissance of sorts. The early 1900s saw a resurgence of interest in California's mission-era heritage, which inspired George Marston, a wealthy San Diego businessman, to preserve what was left of the presidio site. He purchased the land for Presidio Park and built a Spanish-style museum to tell the story of the presidio in artifacts and displays. In 1929 the Junípero Serra Museum was dedicated with a grand ceremony that employed modern-day neophytes, *soldados*, and padres in historical reenactments.

Archaeological examination of the presidio began in 1965, and has continued periodically as techniques have improved. Low mounds cover the remains, buffering them from disturbance with earth and grass.

The Presidio Today

These days San Diego's presidio is little more than a big lawn. A lovely, sloping lawn, shaded by the occasional evergreen, that wraps up and around the Junípero Serra Museum, around picnic tables and a playground, around the tall brick cross erected in honor of Junípero Serra, and down to a statue of a brawny half-naked Indian. A lawn that protects the elongated mounds marking the foundations of the former presidio buildings.

It doesn't sound like much, but the presidio site is more than worth a visit, if only for the views. The premier vistas are offered by the Junípero Serra Museum, which crowns the hilltop and looks north across the San Diego River and Mission Valley to Linda Vista and beyond, as well as west to Mission Bay and the Pacific Ocean.

And then there is the museum, a gorgeous building with such well-rendered Spanish architecture that it is sometimes mistaken for Mission San Diego de Alcalá. A huge wine vat from Mallorca, Spain, reminiscent of those used in the missions, sits on the red tiles of the museum's arcade; inside, exhibits describe the research and excavations that have uncovered the story of the presidio from the time of the Kumeyaay to its occupation by Americans in the mid-1800s, and beyond.

The main gallery of the museum is light and airy, with exhibits generously spaced and well presented. Native artifacts include baskets and hunting tools, as well as a re-creation of a Kumeyaay tule hut. Other display cases hold relics of the mission era, including a polychromed wood statue of San Diego de Alcalá. Both a map and a model of the presidio illustrate physical components of the establishment that are now lost to time—chapel and barracks and workshops and protective adobe walls. The rancho era is described with maps and artifacts, including stirrups, spurs, and a massive old rawhide trunk. American occupation through the Gold Rush is described, as is the founding of New Town in 1871 by Alonzo Horton.

And finally, a symbol of war—an old cannon, perfectly preserved and the only large weapon displayed on lands that once supported a fortress.

In the small theater at the rear of the main gallery, videos describe the history of the presidio and San Diego from founding to modern times. A flight of stairs leads up into a mock bell tower that holds smaller galleries; the wall alongside the narrow staircase is vividly painted with a map tracing the Spanish missionary journey in both Alta and Baja California.

The gallery on the first landing showcases life in San Diego in the late 1920s, with a focus on the dedication of the Junípero Serra Museum in 1929. A plentitude of pictures, toys, and media offer a glimpse into the pleasures of the era. More stairs lead up into a glass-walled cupola, where historical pictures and panoramic views illustrate changes on the landscape and seascape over time.

The museum at the Presidio of San Diego sports a beautiful red tile patio and arcade.

Outside the museum, remnants of the presidio and memorials to significant figures of the mission era are scattered under the San Diego sunshine. In a small grove of trees, a statue of Padre Serra watches over a time capsule. A redbrick cross, also commemorating the missionary, towers above another row of trees. In an overlook on a rise below the museum, a bronze statue of an Indian by Arthur Putnam watches all who approach from the road below; behind him a small tule hut has been constructed. Elsewhere, a plaque honors the memory of Sylvester Pattie, the first American who traveled to Alta California over southland trails. And of course, there are the mounds, long and low, that mark the boundaries of the former presidio itself.

Nearby Points of Interest

The myriad San Diego attractions, including Mission San Diego de Alcalá, are available to visitors to Presidio Park. But the most obvious choice for those who spend time exploring the presidio site and the Junípero Serra Museum is Old Town. Tucked against the foot of the hill facing the water, what once was a tiny pueblo is now a charming business district with a cozy, hometown feel. Boutiques offer great selections for shoppers, and a bevy of restaurants offer gastronomic delights for every palate. Taylor Street forms one of the former pueblo's main drags; follow this from Presidio Drive to reach the heart of Old Town.

More information on historical sites around San Diego (of which there are plenty) can be found by visiting the San Diego Historical Society Web site at www.sandiegohistory.org.

The Presidio of Santa Barbara

FOUNDING DATE: April 21, 1782

ADDRESS: El Presidio de Santa Barbara State Historic Park 123 East Canon Perdido Street, Santa Barbara, 93101

TELEPHONE NUMBER: (805) 965–0093

WEB SITE: www.parks.ca.gov (follow the links). The site for the Santa Barbara Trust for Historic Preservation is www.sbthp.org.

HOURS: El Presidio de Santa Barbara State Historic Park, home to the Presidio of Santa Barbara, is open from 10:30 A.M. to 4:30 P.M. daily. A small fee ($3.00) is levied.

DIRECTIONS: To reach the presidio from northbound or southbound U.S. Highway 101, take the Carrillo Street exit. Go northeast on Carrillo Street (toward downtown) for 0.5 mile to Anacapa Street (a one-way street heading southeast). The presidio is located one block south of Carrillo Street on East Canon Perdido Street, between Anacapa and Santa Barbara Streets. California Historic Landmark No. 636.

PARKING: Metered parking is available along the streets around the presidio and in city lots scattered around the downtown area. Moderate parking fees are levied in the lots.

EVENTS: The Presidio Chapel can be rented for weddings. The Santa Barbara Trust for Historic Preservation, in association with the state park, sponsors a number of cultural and educational programs at the presidio, including guided tours for students and community members, living history demonstrations (adobe brick making, archaeology), family days, lectures, and a holiday reenactment of Las Posadas. Contact the trust for more information.

The rebirth of the Presidio of Santa Barbara has been controversial, but nowhere else in the state does the military aspect of California's Spanish heritage come this close to physical revelation. The Presidio of San Francisco still stands, but it has been so thoroughly overbuilt that remnants of its Spanish roots are as rare as galleons on the bay. The barracks at Sonoma help flesh out the military presence in Mexico's northernmost outpost, but are only a nugget of the legacy, a bullet as compared to a cannonball. The presidios at both San Diego and Monterey are now more museum pieces than reality.

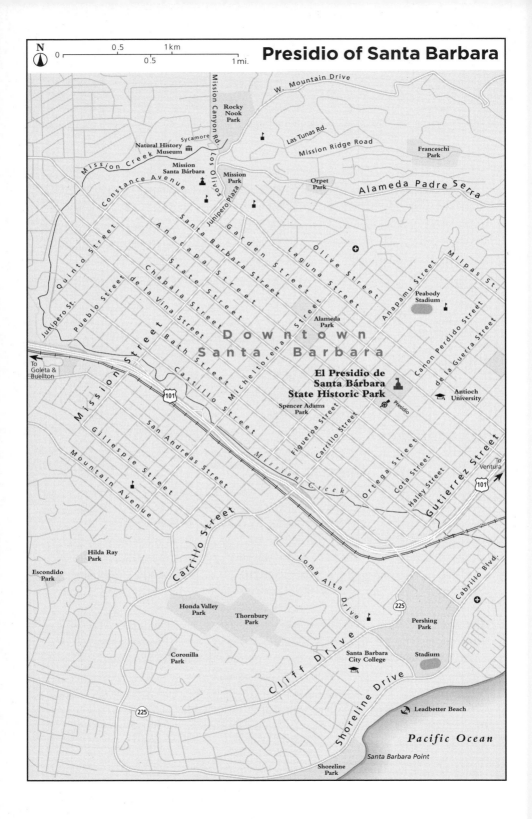

Santa Barbara's revived presidio is substantial, however, and is presented with a flourish. Its buildings were reconstructed using the methods employed by *soldados* and Indians in the mission era, and its artifacts are thoroughly documented and artfully displayed. Located in the heart of downtown Santa Barbara, its setting in no way resembles that of the late eighteenth and early nineteenth centuries, but inside its chapel, or inside one of its residences, you can, for the moment, feel yourself transported back to mission times.

The Presidio Yesterday

A presidio on the Santa Barbara Channel was deemed necessary by Spanish authorities for the same reasons that a mission was planned for the area—the protection of Spanish imperial claims to Alta California and the subjugation (and conversion) of the Chumash Indians.

Established by Lieutenant José Francisco Ortega and blessed by Padre Junípero Serra in 1782, Santa Barbara's presidio would battle for both during its history, dispatching soldiers to protect Spanish holdings from Hippolyte Bouchard, the privateer who sacked the Presidio at Monterey in 1818, and assisting in the defeat of the Chumash Indians, who organized a revolt in 1824, seizing (for a brief time) missions Santa Bárbara, Santa Inés, and La Purísima Concepción.

The presidio was originally a complex of wooden structures surrounded by a palisade, but within a few short years (1784–88) those buildings and walls were replaced by ones made of sturdy adobe bricks. Residences, a chapel, guardhouses, storerooms, and armories were built in a square around the *plaza de armas* (parade grounds), with a first wall of defense constructed around the interior quadrangle. Only two of those original adobe structures have survived into modern times—the Cañedo Adobe, named for the soldier to whom it was deeded in the 1830s, and El Cuartel (soldiers' quarters), the oldest building in Santa Barbara and the second oldest in California, according to presidio literature. A second wall of defense was erected in 1792 to accommodate a remodel of the chapel, which had to be enlarged as the presidio's population grew.

Presidial soldiers performed a number of tasks, not all of them military. The sphere of protection provided by the Santa Barbara Presidio extended from San Luis Obispo south to Los Angeles, and within that range soldiers provided protection for missions, quashed Indian uprisings, and provided military escorts for missionaries and other travelers. They also worked to build the adobe structures at both the presidio and its surrounding missions, delivered mail and dispatches, and maintained their military gear, which included the typical accoutrements of a *soldado de cuera*, from leather jackets to lances, muskets, and swords. Some were also family men, and their wives and children kept house, cooked meals, and performed other domestic chores, much as they might in a mission or pueblo.

The presidio's demise began with earthquake damage sustained in 1806 and 1812. After Mexican independence was won in 1821, it was no longer charged with staving off foreign traders (a Spanish policy sometimes heeded, sometimes not). The presidio also suffered from the Mexican government's inability to financially support its Alta California holdings, much as the missions did. By the 1840s the presidio was in ruins, according to park literature. Its occupation by Colonel John C. Frémont during the Mexican-American War essentially ended its military mandate.

Aspects of the presidio remained intact after the coming of the Americans, and some lingered into modern times. The chapel served as a parish church into the 1850s, and the Cañedo Adobe and El Cuartel passed into private hands, both used as private residences, and the latter, for a time, as a "Boy Scout headquarters." But the bulk of the presidio melted away, leaving only traces buried under the streets and buildings of downtown Santa Barbara, which grew up beautifully on top of it.

The presidio's distant past is interesting, but its recent history is also provocative. The reconstructed presidio occupies valuable real estate in downtown Santa Barbara, and was erected at the expense of businesses that had been established on the site in modern times. Those enterprises were moved to other locations, but not without forcing the question: What's more important—the past or the present?

The answer took years to sort out, and pitted the Santa Barbara Trust for Historic Preservation (SBTHP) against business and political interests. The trust, founded in 1963, had purchased El Cuartel in 1966 as the "nucleus of El

This painting shows Santa Barbara's presidio as it appeared during the colonial era.

Presidio de Santa Barbara State Historic Park," and is dedicated to the preservation of the site. It eventually won the endorsements needed to begin that preservation, and broke ground on the reconstruction of the padres' quarters in 1977.

Reconstruction of the presidio has been guided by extensive research of maps, letters, and pictures from the historical record. Five phases of rebuilding are planned; as of this writing, only the northeast corner of the original quadrangle had been completed. The California Conservation Corps, the state park, and the SBTHP have all provided critical support, staffing, and funding for the presidio restoration project.

The Presidio Today

Archaeology and reconstruction are central to the modern experience of the Presidio of Santa Barbara. Sure, there are buildings on the site to be explored, but there are also grids on the ground, sectioned off with taut pieces of string, enabling excavators to document and log each artifact unearthed on the site.

Adobe bricks are part of the experience, lined up on the grounds in front of the reconstructed chapel and administrative buildings in neat military rows. The bricks are made the same way they were in the mission era—mud and straw meshed by local laborers (these days, volunteers and schoolchildren), set into molds, and allowed to bake under the Santa Barbara sun.

Passing both grids and adobes, a tour of the presidio begins in the visitor center—housed in the Cañedo Adobe—where fees are paid and merchandise can be purchased. Items for sale in the gift shop are interspersed with historical relics and information—the family trees of the presidio's founding families, displays of military artifacts—and a video room offers the opportunity to view a film about the post's history and reconstruction.

Outside the adobe, ongoing excavations of the northwest corner of the quadrangle border the tour route, which leads to a dirt patio planted with fruit trees and roses; the presidio's Research Center is located at the rear of the patio. Another courtyard sits behind the visitor center, this one dominated by a statue of King Carlos III of Spain—the ultimate force behind the Spanish conquest of Alta California—and the tools and rewards of ongoing excavations: the trowels and screens of archaeologists mingled with half-buried foundations and cracked adobe bricks.

An open door leads into the padres' quarters, a room simply furnished with a narrow cot, a chair, a trunk, and a crucifix. The adobe walls are whitewashed and aged, the roof composed of beams slung with strips of hide and topped with curved red tiles.

The presidio chapel is a powerful and accurate reconstruction of a mission-era church. The long walls of its nave are painted a brick red below, and white

Bricks made of mud and straw bake in the sun in front of the chapel at the Presidio of Santa Barbara.

with accents of blue, gold, and red above, with the Stations of the Cross hung below the high windows, along with a portrait of Our Lady of Guadalupe and other works of religious art. Niches for holy water are carved into the walls, and a choir loft hangs above the door that opens onto Canon Perdido Street, shadowing a tile plaque that lists the names of those buried at the presidio long ago.

A flyer on a small table near the street door lists the identity and provenance of the chapel's marvelous paintings and statuary. Santa Bárbara occupies the top niche in the authentic Spanish reredos, with San Francisco de Asís and San Antonio de Padua on either side of the Madonna and Child in the niches below. An eighteenth-century silver cross, and a tabernacle that dates back to the 1500s, alight on the altar. Paintings on either side of the chancel depict "El Buen Pastor" and Our Lady of Solitude. Tiles in the chapel floor near the sanctuary commemorate the burial of Antonio Miranda Rodriguez in 1784. Everything about the chapel evokes authenticity.

The religious gives way to the secular as you head around the back side of the chapel and encounter a reconstruction of the presidio's first wall of defense. Passage through a thick, narrow break in the wall leads into the backyard of the *comandancia* (living quarters for the presidio's *comandante*). The aqueduct that lies exposed here dates back to 1783 and once carried water from Pedregosa

Creek (now known as Mission Creek) to the presidio. The *comandancia* was built in 1787 for Felipe de Goicoechea and his successors, according to historical literature provided by the presidio, and consists of an entrance hall (with cannon), a living room (with wax dripping from the candelabra), an office (with books on the shelves), and a bedroom. Quarters in this location were used until 1812, when damage caused by earthquakes forced the *comandante* to move into apartments located across Santa Barbara Street. Of course, the street wasn't there in those days; a map shows how modern thoroughfares now crisscross the old presidio grounds.

In buildings located on the other side of Santa Barbara Street, a display lists the supplies needed by the presidio in 1793. Written in both English and Spanish, the list includes the expected: chocolate, saffron and cinnamon, rosaries and catechisms, lead and a bullet mold, dye, tablecloths and beads, one barrel of wine for Mass and two for the soldiers . . . and the unexpected, such as four dozen silk stockings for girls and 8,000 sewing needles.

In a separate room, a mural depicts the presidio and the nearby Santa Barbara Mission, and descriptive panels describe the lives of the vaqueros, the importance of music and chocolate to the Spanish colonialists, how health problems were dealt with, and how trade was conducted. Display cases hold artifacts found on the site: cannonballs and candle molds, ointments and liniments used in the healing arts, coins and trade items. A description of the Yuma Campaign, an Indian revolt that took the lives of ninety-five Spaniards and two priests in the high desert east of San Diego, is described in detail in the words of onetime Alta California governor Felipe de Neve on a wall's worth of placards in a separate chamber.

Other rooms are set up as living quarters for the families of soldiers, complete with kitchen gardens grown in small courtyards outside the apartments. The *cocina* includes ceramic water filters, ovens, grinding stones, and flat irons upon which tortillas could be cooked—if they weren't cooked outdoors. Another chamber boasts an original tile floor (it is thought to have belonged to an officer); a loom faithfully reproduced using plans from the nearby mission dominates yet another. In the small courtyard outside the loom room, native plants from the medicinal lore of the Chumash Indians thrive—salvia, yerba buena, and others, fragrant and colorful, maintained in part by students from a local school.

El Cuartel—the guardhouse and the oldest structure in Santa Barbara—sits across the street from the presidio chapel and visitor center, a humble little adobe that was once part of a row of soldiers' quarters on the west side of the presidio. A tile plaque in its patio was presented to Santa Barbara by Spain in commemoration of the presidio's restoration, as "testimony of the common historic past shared by the Spanish and American peoples."

Nearby Points of Interest

The sprawling adobe residence of the fifth *comandante* of the Santa Barbara Presidio, José de la Guerra, is located a short distance from the presidio and is open for tours. The Casa de la Guerra was built over ten years starting in about 1820, and the de la Guerra family lived there under three flags—the Spanish, the Mexican, and the American. The grand and spacious rooms of the adobe now house historical displays of maps, pictures, and models that hark back to mission times, as well as art galleries and re-creations of living quarters. The adobe is located at 15 East de la Guerra Street and is managed by the Santa Barbara Trust for Historic Preservation. For information, call (805) 965–0093 or visit the Web site at www.sbthp.org.

The Presidio of Monterey

FOUNDING DATE: June 3, 1770

ADDRESS: Active military installations at the Presidio of Monterey are located on Presidio Hill overlooking downtown Monterey. The public is not permitted in the Defense Language Institute, but the lower twenty-six acres are open to the public. The contact information provided is for the Presidio of Monterey Museum, which is located on Corporal Ewing Road, Building 113, Presidio of Monterey, 93944.

TELEPHONE NUMBER: (831) 646–3456

WEB SITES: www.monterey.org/museum/pom; http://users.dedot.com/mchs/presidio.html

HOURS: The museum is open Monday from 10:00 A.M. to 1:00 P.M., Thursday through Saturday from 10:00 A.M. to 4:00 P.M., and Sunday from 1:00 to 4:00 P.M. It is closed on Thanksgiving, Christmas, and New Year's Day.

DIRECTIONS: To reach the Presidio of Monterey Museum from California Highway 1, take the Munras Avenue exit and head north on Munras (toward the waterfront) to its intersection with Abrego Street. Stay right (north) on Abrego Street for 0.4 mile to its intersection with Washington Street. Stay straight (north) on Washington Street to its intersection with Lighthouse Avenue. Turn left (northwest) onto Lighthouse Avenue and pass through the tunnel to where the road forks, staying right (northwest) on Foam Street. A series of quick turns now: Go left (east) onto Reeside Avenue, left again onto Lighthouse Avenue, and then right (east) onto Private Bolio Road. Corporal Ewing Road breaks to the left (south) off Private Bolio Road before you reach the presidio guardhouse. The museum is about 0.2 mile down Corporal Ewing Road, on the right (east).

PARKING: Free parking is available in the large lot in front of the museum.

Named for the Count de Monterrey, viceroy of New Spain at the time of Sebastian Vizcaino's 1602 explorations, Monterey was once the capital of Alta and Baja California, the heart and brains of Spain's northern frontier. A presidio and

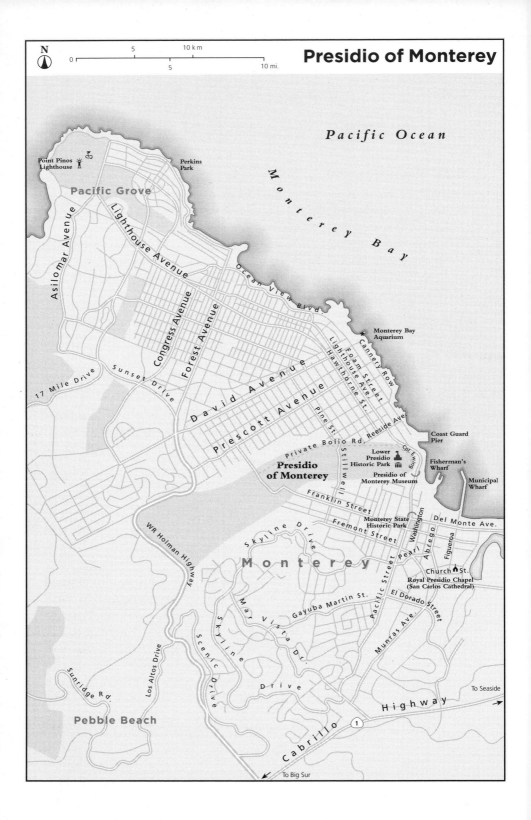

a mission were established on the shores of Monterey Bay in 1770, and though the mission was later moved to the mouth of the Carmel River in what is today Carmel-by-the-Sea, the presidio remained, serving first as a Spanish, then as a Mexican, and finally as an American military outpost.

The military installations now located on the presidio are off-limits to the public (they were off-limits prior to September 11, 2001). However, you can see why the high spot on the southeast margin of Monterey Bay was chosen for a defensive position—even the lower portions of the presidio that are open to the public boast commanding views of the harbor. Once the domain of the great sailing ships of European explorers, the harbor is now dotted with colorful fishing boats and rimmed with busy wharves and tourist attractions.

Remnants of the presidio outpost are scattered about the base of Presidio Hill, revealed on a delightful walking tour through Monterey's Spanish heritage. The story of the presidio from inception to its most recent incarnation is beautifully documented in the Presidio of Monterey Museum.

The Presidio Yesterday

Monterey Bay was, from the beginning of Spanish exploration of the Pacific coast of North America, a coveted site. It was "discovered" by Juan Rodriguez Cabrillo in 1542, and both named and praised by explorer Sebastian Vizcaino in 1602—in fact, Vizcaino's description of the harbor was so full of hyperbole that the Portolá Expedition marched past it in 1769, according to historians. Overshooting Monterey proved fortuitous, however, because Portolá went on to "discover" San Francisco Bay, another grand addition to Spain's North American empire, before he turned around to reconnoiter.

Portolá led a second expedition to Monterey—a successful one—in 1770, and, along with Franciscan missionary extraordinaire Junípero Serra, cemented Spain's claim to California on June 3 of that year by establishing both a mission and a presidio at the same site where Carmelite missionaries had celebrated Mass during the Vizcaino journey.

The original presidio fortifications were built on an estuary (El Estero) near the beach in what is now downtown Monterey. Primitive constructions of wood and mud—soldiers' barracks, a church, a warehouse—were erected by a small contingent of soldiers, missionaries, and neophytes. The mission would later be moved to a few miles south of Monterey, but a chapel, also dedicated to San Carlos Borromeo, remained part of the presidio and stands near the estuary to this day.

The first years were difficult, given the post's isolation and the irregularity with which supply ships arrived. Food grew so scarce that famine threatened the colony, and was only alleviated with help from the native Rumsien Indians and when hunters returned from San Luis Obispo with thousands of pounds of

This image of the Presidio of Monterey as it appeared in 1791 or 1792 was created by José Cardero.

bear meat. Support from New Spain, and later Mexico, would never be plentiful for any presidio in Alta California, a neglect that all four posts struggled to overcome with varying degrees of success.

In 1777 the burgeoning settlement at Monterey, boosted by the selection of the Carmel Mission as home base for Junípero Serra and his missionaries, supplanted Loreto as capital of both Alta and Baja California. This added to the presidio's cachet: It was now not only headquarters for military operations in Alta California, but also the region's political center.

It remained a crude frontier establishment, however, even though by that time its wooden buildings had been replaced by constructions of adobe. Staffed by an astonishingly small force—thirty-two soldiers and officers, plus a carpenter, a surgeon, and two blacksmiths, according to writer and military historian Kibbey M. Horne—the post conformed to a standard plan, with a tall outer wall enclosing a smaller quadrangle bounded by quarters for officers, soldiers, and the presidio's chaplain, warehouses, shops, an infirmary, and a kitchen. Cannon were mounted in embrasures at the four corners of the outer wall. The first *castillo*, a fort located on a hill overlooking the bay and harbor, wasn't built until around 1792; it housed cannon that could be trained on hostile parties entering the harbor, though diarists of the era disparaged it as inadequate.

The presidio began its slow decline in the 1790s with the expansion of the pueblo of Monterey, which competed for already slender resources. The battle for Mexican independence, which began in 1810, resulted in even less support for the post. That the Presidio of Monterey holds the dubious distinction of being the only installation along California's coast ever to have been overrun by a hostile force is no doubt a result of this neglect. The Frenchman Hippolyte Bouchard, a privateer flying the flag of Argentina (which was also shedding the reins of Spanish empire), brought the revolution to Monterey in 1818. With two ships grandly called "La Armada Argentina," Bouchard stormed El Castillo, the presidio, and the town. The Spanish garrison, outnumbered by the invaders, fled inland to take refuge at the presidio's rancho near Salinas. The Frenchman and his crew went on to burn and loot the settlement, then packed up what booty they could find and sailed south, terrorizing a rancho outside Santa Barbara before returning to home ports.

The Mexican flag was raised over the presidio after independence was won in 1821. The new government relaxed restrictions on trade, which resulted in an influx of entrepreneurs from overseas and the United States into Monterey's harbor and a corresponding rise in the material and political fortunes of the pueblo. The presidio didn't see the same benefits, however, and though soldiers remained in town and cannon remained at El Castillo, the presidial structures were slowly incorporated into the village, or into the ground.

Mexican control of Alta California would give way in the mid-1840s to the United States, which was driven inexorably westward by its credo of Manifest Destiny. The taking of California by the Americans came in fits and starts: In 1842 Thomas Catesby Jones, a naval commodore who mistakenly thought Mexico and the United States were at war, seized Monterey and raised the American flag over post and pueblo. Outmanned and outgunned, the garrison offered no resistance. When the commodore was informed that hostilities had not been declared, he apologized, and the Mexican flag was raised over pueblo and presidio once more.

In 1846, with war now formally declared, Commodore John Drake Sloat seized Monterey, again without a battle. By then the presidio proper had essentially disappeared, but El Castillo was taken and transformed into an American military installation. It became Fort Mervine, named for the navy captain who had raised the American flag over the fortification, and was occupied for a time by Lieutenants Edward Ord and William Tecumseh Sherman, both destined to become generals in the American Civil War.

Monterey's mission-era military fortifications were dealt a final blow by the Gold Rush, when men abandoned post and presidio to seek their fortunes in the Sierra Nevada. Now fully Americanized, installations at Monterey enjoyed a brief and stingy renaissance during the Civil War; then interest died away. The Spanish-American War, waged at the turn of the twentieth century, again revived the post—upkeep and rebuilding became a priority when the Fifteenth Infantry was stationed at the present presidio site in the autumn of 1902. The men lived in tents until 1904, when permanent buildings were completed and the post was renamed the Presidio of Monterey "in honor of the 1770 Royal Spanish Presidio" that had stood in its place a century before.

Infantry, artillery, and cavalry units stationed at the presidio in the early 1900s became known for peacetime engagements, taking part in movies and parades, providing aid in the aftermath of the 1906 San Francisco Earthquake, and battling an oil fire ignited by lightning that consumed Cannery Row and threatened to destroy Monterey and Pacific Grove. During World War I, signal corps and medical corps trained at the presidio; by 1919 that training had shifted a few miles north to the military reservation at Fort Ord. In World War II the presidio, like its counterpart on the shores of San Francisco Bay, served as a "reception center," or processing post, for soldiers shipping out to distant battlefields in the Pacific Theater.

In the wake of World War II, the presidio became home to the Military Intelligence Service Language School, and has continued to the present day in that role. Now called the Defense Language Institute, soldiers, sailors, and marines at the Presidio of Monterey are learning foreign languages—Spanish undoubtedly among them.

The Presidio Today

To experience the Presidio of Monterey today, you can either join the army or visit the Presidio of Monterey Museum. Housed in a former magazine bunker built of corrugated metal and refurbished to look like a typical Monterey adobe, the museum and neighboring historic sites sit on twenty-six acres known as Lower Presidio Historic Park.

The museum entrance is guarded by a French-made iron cannon dating back to the early 1700s, and its rear flank is watched by the great stone eagle of the Sloat Memorial, which commands views that spread over downtown Monterey to the blue bay beyond.

Inside the small rectangular structure, a number of displays illustrate the evolution of the presidio from its origins as a Rumsian Ohlone Indian village to a component of Spanish empire building to its role today in preparing military personnel for duty in foreign countries.

Among the many interesting and enlightening displays are pictures of the Plaza del Presidio de Monte Rey created by José Cardero in 1791. Other exhibits describe the role of the presidio in major conflicts over the years, the famous people who have been part of presidio life—from Civil War generals to Ronald Reagan—and the role the cavalry played in presidio history.

Outside the museum, on the lawn that slopes down from Corporal Ewing Road to Lighthouse Avenue, you can explore the site of El Castillo (the foundations of which have been excavated and then buried again to preserve them).

El Castillo I is marked by a plaque under the boughs of a Monterey cypress; El Castillo II, built after the aborted American takeover in 1842, is unmarked. Elsewhere on the lawn you will find the 1770 grave of Alexis Niño and the burial of a "black freeman," a large statue of Junípero Serra that dates back to 1891, and a monument commemorating the Bouchard incident.

Reminders of Monterey's Spanish and Mexican history—military, secular, and religious—are scattered throughout the busy tourist and business district that has grown up at the base of Presidio Hill. There's a lot to do in Monterey—visiting the Monterey Bay Aquarium, strolling Cannery Row and Fisherman's Wharf, playing golf on world-class links—but the chance to experience the rich heritage of this onetime capital of California shouldn't be neglected. Several publications (at least one of them free) document a self-guided walking tour of historic buildings and sites that date back to the days of Spanish and Mexican rule. This 2-mile Path of History is overseen by the Monterey State Historic Park, which has placed markers in the sidewalks and on signposts to show the way. The maps can be picked up at the state park offices at 20 Custom House Plaza or by contacting the park at (831) 649–7118; the Web site is www.mbay .net/~mshp/.

A tour of the town will take you through the Customs House, the oldest part of which dates back to 1827. Central to the operations of Puerto de Monterey during the Mexican period, the Customs House these days brims with artifacts relating to shipping and commerce in the port in the 1830s. Other sites along the path include the Stanton Center, the Maritime Museum and History Center, El Estero Park, and an abundance of adobes and casas, some private and some that fall under the auspices of the state park and are open for tours. Colton Hall, site of California's 1849 constitutional convention, is in Monterey's City Hall.

But arguably most significant—at least in terms of a book focused on missions and presidios—are the Royal Presidio site and the Royal Presidio Chapel of San Carlos Borromeo (California Historic Landmark No. 105). The presidio site—roughly bounded by Webster, Abrego, and Fremont Streets, and Camino El Estero—is as historically evocative as a doughnut, having been essentially obliterated by residences, businesses, and parking lots. But the chapel, now known as San Carlos Cathedral and located on the southern border of the presidio site, is marvelously preserved, a sanctuary of history and faith amid the plain-faced and utilitarian structures that surround it.

The chapel is the fourth built within the original presidio, the first two having been constructed of wood and mud, the third of adobe. This edition, built between 1791 and 1795, features a facade as grand as or grander than those of other mission-era churches, with a tall campanile and scrollwork draped above and around the doors. An active parish church, the interior of the cathedral is

The facade of San Carlos Cathedral, located in the business district at the base of the presidio hill, has a tall campanile and intricate scrollwork.

simple and classy, with a long, narrow, high-ceilinged nave and an altar as elegant as the rest, all lit by the tenuous light of high recessed windows. A cross section of the oak tree under which Carmelite friars traveling with Sebastian Vizcaino, and then Fray Junípero Serra, conducted Masses on the shores of Monterey Bay is preserved in the vestibule, along with pictures of the living tree. The grounds include a grotto, a shrine to Our Lady of Bethlehem, and a small, colorful, urban garden dotted with other shrines that invite prayer and contemplation.

The cathedral—the smallest in the country—is located on Church Street between Figueroa and Fremont Streets. The rectory, gift shop, and San Carlos School, along with other parish offices, surround the historic structure.

Nearby Points of Interest

Monterey is home to a plenitude of historic, educational, culinary, and scenic delights. The Monterey Bay Aquarium, located just north of Presidio Hill on historic Cannery Row, is a spectacular showcase of aquatic life and marine geography. Fisherman's Wharf is located at the base of Presidio Hill, and Monterey State Beach is southeast of that. The Monterey Peninsula Recreational Trail, a former railroad line that has been transformed into a mostly paved path for walkers, cyclists, and other recreationalists, traces the bayshore from Monterey north to Pacfic Grove, offering pedestrian access to all the sites.

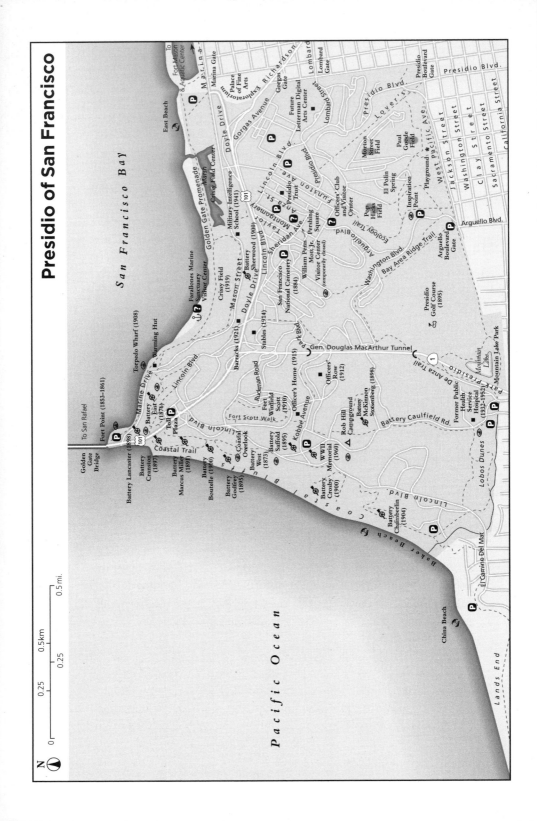

Presidio of San Francisco

N

0.25   0.5km
0   0.25   0.5 mi.

San Francisco Bay

Pacific Ocean

Golden Gate Bridge
To San Rafael
Fort Point (1853–1861)
Battery Lancaster (1898)
Battery Cranston (1897)
Battery East
Toll Plaza
Marcus Miller (1891)
Battery West
Boutelle (1900)
Battery Godfrey (1895)
Coastal Overlook
Coastal Trail
Battery Saffold (1895)
WWII Memorial
Battery Crosby (1900)
Battery Chamberlin (1904)
El Camino Del Mar
China Beach
Lands End

Warming Hut
Torpedo Wharf (1908)
Marine Drive
Lincoln Blvd
Fort Scott Walk
Fort Winfield Scott (1910)
Ruckman Road
Kobbe Avenue
Officer's Home (1915)
Rob Hill Campground
Battery McKinnon Stotsenberg (1898)
Battery Caulfield Rd.

Farallones Marine Sanctuary Visitor Center
Crissy Field (1919)
Mason Street
Doyle Drive
Barracks (1921)
Stables (1914)
Battery Sherwood (1900)
Officers' Row (1912)
Gen. Douglas MacArthur Tunnel
Former Public Health Service Hospital (1932–1952)
Lobos Dunes
Mountain Lake Park
Mountain Lake

East Beach
Golden Gate Promenade
Crissy Field Center
Military Intelligence School (1941)
Doyle Drive
Taylor Street
Lincoln Blvd
Sheridan Ave.
San Francisco National Cemetery (1884)
William Penn Mott Jr. Visitor Center (temporarily closed)
Pershing Square
Park Blvd
De Anza Trail
Presidio Golf Course (1895)

To Fort Mason & Aquatic Center
Marina Gate
Palace of Fine Arts
Exploratorium
Gorgas Avenue
Gorgas Gate
Montgomery St.
Presidio Trust
Funston Ave.
Officers' Club and Visitor Center
Presidio Blvd
Arguello Blvd
Washington Blvd
Bay Area Ridge Trail

Lombard Street
Lombard Gate
Future Letterman Digital Arts Center
Morton Street Field
Paul Goode Field
El Polin Spring
Pop Hicks Field
Inspiration Point
Ecology Trail
Playground
Arguello Boulevard Gate

Presidio Blvd.
Presidio Boulevard Gate
Lover's Lane
West Pacific Ave.
Jackson Street
Washington Street
Clay Street
Sacramento Street
California Street
Arguello Blvd.

The Presidio of San Francisco

FOUNDING DATE: September 17, 1776

ADDRESS: Golden Gate National Recreation Area, Building 201, Fort Mason, San Francisco, 94123; or William Penn Mott Jr. Visitor Center, Building 102, Montgomery Street, San Francisco, 94129. The Presidio Visitor Center is temporarily housed in the Officers' Club, Building 50, Moraga Avenue, while the permanent building undergoes earthquake retrofitting.

TELEPHONE NUMBER: (415) 561–4323

WEB SITES: www.nps.gov/prsf; www.nps.gov/goga

HOURS: The presidio's visitor center is open daily from 9:00 A.M. to 5:00 P.M.

DIRECTIONS: Several major highways bisect the presidio, and webs of city streets offer access to various sites and trailheads. The main thoroughfare along the San Francisco Bay coastline, U.S. Highway 101, offers easy access to Fort Point and the Main Post. California Highway 1, also known as Park Presidio, runs north to south through the park, but offers no access to its amenities. Lincoln Boulevard skirts the coastal bluffs overlooking the Pacific Ocean, offering access to Baker and China Beach, various coastal fortifications, and the Coastal Trail.

I advise anyone traveling to the presidio to pick up a good street map. The park has also produced an excellent map that shows trails, points of interest, and, most important, parking and access roads. The maps are available at any visitor center. PresidiGo, the free shuttle service offered by the Presidio Trust, stops regularly at many of the presidio's premier destinations. California Historic Landmark No. 79.

PARKING: The parade ground on the Main Post is the mother of all parking lots. Adequate parking is available at most presidio recreational and historic sites.

EVENTS: The Golden Gate National Parks Conservancy (415–561–3000; www.parksconservancy.org), the Presidio Trust (415–561–5300; www.presidio.gov), and the Crissy Field Center (415–561–7690; www.crissyfield.org) sponsor a number of special events—lectures, tours, classes—at the presidio throughout the year. These events are printed in seasonal publications and are available online. Contact the Presidio Visitor Center for more information.

It's come a long way from a few mud huts.

Once a rough-hewn outpost of Spanish imperialism isolated in the wilderness of northern California, the Presidio of San Francisco is now a fascinating conglomerate of open spaces and historic structures occupying nearly 1,500 acres of lovely real estate at the tip of the San Francisco peninsula. Its frontier roots have long been buried beneath constructs of the American military, but with the post's designation as a national park has come a revival of that heritage, in spirit if not on the ground.

The Presidio Yesterday

For centuries before the arrival of Europeans, the landscapes and seascapes of San Francisco Bay—marsh and bluff and beach and open water—were the domain of the Ohlone Indians, a confederation of hunters and gatherers nurtured by their environment, and bound to it in custom, technology, and spirit. They were hidden for a time from European explorers charting California's coastal waters by the very nature of the bay—the Golden Gate is a narrow strait that renders the bay a desirable and defensible port—and by an unpredictable but nearly ubiquitous veil of fog.

It's assumed that fog hid the Golden Gate from the scouting eyes of Juan Rodriguez Cabrillo in 1542, from Sir Francis Drake in 1579, and from Sebastian Vizcaino in 1602. But Gaspar de Portolá, gazing down on a promising expanse of shimmering blue from a ridgetop in 1769, was not blinded in any way to the beauty and potential of the geography spread before him.

The importance of Portolá's "discovery" was immediately clear to Spanish authorities worried about Russian invasion from the north, and plans to colonize the area were set in motion as soon as possible. Juan Manuel de Ayala sailed the *San Carlos* through the gate to survey the bay in 1775. Juan Bautista de Anza selected settlement sites during his overland exploration of California in 1775; his lieutenant, José Joaquin Moraga, would return the following year with a group of settlers to establish both a presidio and a mission near the bay shore.

The Presidio of San Francisco started out much as other Spanish settlements—a cluster of brush and tule huts surrounded by a palisade that housed, according to one historian, about forty *soldados* and nearly 150 settlers. Adobe would replace wood and mud within a few years, with a chapel, a guardhouse, officers' residences, barracks, warehouses, and other buildings forming a square protected by a defensive wall—the quadrangle-within-a-quadrangle configuration universal among California's presidios.

In 1794 the Spanish built El Castillo de San Joaquin on a promontory of white cliffs at the mouth of the gate. This *castillo*, armed with cannon set in

The Presidio of San Francisco as it appeared to an unknown artist in 1849.

embrasures, was so strategically located that Americans would later build Fort Point on the same spot. Another fortification, Bateria de Yerba Buena, was built overlooking Yerba Buena Cove, site of today's Fort Mason.

But the presidio was plagued by lack of support, lack of personnel, and the vagaries of nature. Historians transcribe account after account of visitors to the bay—Russian, American, and English—who describe the presidio as derelict, one remarking that it looked like a cattle pen. It was hit by earthquake, fire, and rainstorms, and its *comandantes* were constantly in need of more men and supplies, which were seldom forthcoming.

Despite weather conditions that were more conducive to the propagation of newts and slugs than of empire, presidial soldiers carried out their duties with some success. They went on repeated sorties to retrieve runaway neophytes from Missions Dolores, San José, and Santa Clara; they reinforced their comrades at Monterey after the 1818 attack by the privateer Bouchard; and they put down the revolt of Estanislao in 1824.

The presidio's situation did not improve when the Mexican government took over in the early 1820s. The mid-1830s proved pivotal for the dilapidated post: The pueblo of Yerba Buena was established, drawing off more resources, and Mariano Guadalupe Vallejo, then *comandante* of the presidio, moved most of the garrison north to Sonoma so he could keep closer tabs on the Russian settlement at Fort Ross. By 1846, when Captain John Montgomery raised the Stars and Stripes over the pueblo, much of the presidio had disintegrated into lumps of adobe.

But the Americans proved a lifesaver for the beleaguered post. After gold was discovered at Sutters Fort, the presidio became the locus of efforts to protect the wealth flowing out of the Sierra Nevada, and a period of expansion and improvement of fortifications that would last into the twentieth century was under way.

Layers of construction at San Francisco's presidio date to nearly every war fought by the United States, each layer representing an enormous investment in technology that ultimately became obsolete. Massive Third System forts such as Fort Point were all the rage before the Civil War, but fell out of favor shortly thereafter. The presidio was outfitted for the modern battlefield of the late 1800s and early 1900s with the construction of coastal defensive batteries—first earthwork dugouts, then concrete bunkers, both mounted with cannon of increasing firepower—which were carved into the headlands on both the north and south sides of the Golden Gate. The presidio's exposed landscape was also "improved" during the late 1800s, when hundreds of thousands of trees were planted, a massive beautification project spanning ten years that resulted in a majestic and orderly windbreak known today as the Presidio Forest.

The stately redbrick barracks that line Montgomery Street on the Main Post were also built in the latter part of the nineteenth century. During the Spanish-American War, the presidio served as a staging area for troops sent to battle in the Philippines; the Letterman Hospital complex was built in these years. The aforementioned batteries, the lattermost built during the tenures of the Secretaries of War William Endicott and William Taft, fell under the purview of Fort Winfield Scott, established in 1912. Meanwhile, presidial troops went off to Mexico in search of the rebel Pancho Villa, and fought on the battlefields of World War I. In 1920 Crissy Field was activated, supplementing already impressive coastal defenses with air power.

During World War II the presidio served as headquarters for the Western Defense Command. During the Cold War, installations of the Nike missile system were built along the San Francisco coastline from the Marin Headlands south to Milagra Ridge, and the presidio served as headquarters. When more sophisticated weapons rendered Nike missiles obsolete, the age of coastal defense also ended, as did the presidio's 200-year history as a military post.

Though the presidio was incorporated into the Golden Gate National Recreation Area when the park was established in 1972, the army didn't close the base

These stately redbrick barracks line Montgomery Street within the Presidio of San Francisco.

until 1989, and the transfer of jurisdiction wasn't completed until late in 1994. The presidio was placed under the joint oversight of the National Park Service and the newly created Presidio Trust, which is charged with making the park self-sufficient by 2013 through the leasing of presidio buildings. That process, the subject of much research and debate, is still evolving, but has been thus far successful. To learn more about the Presidio Trust, write to P.O. Box 29052, San Francisco, 94129, or call (415) 561–5300. The Web site is www.presidio trust.gov.

Today the park complex includes 870 buildings, many of which are historically and architecturally intriguing, and approximately 800 acres of open space, including beaches and restored natural areas. Not a bad legacy for an entity drawn up from mud and reeds.

The Presidio Today

In a remarkably short time, the Presidio of San Francisco has been transformed from a military post into a first-rate urban park. To explore the park thoroughly would take weeks—and to describe it thoroughly would take more pages than you'd want to read—but there are certain sites, some related to the post's Spanish and Mexican occupations and some not, that should be part of every tour.

The Spanish and Mexican Military Legacy

Well, there ain't much left, and what remains of the post's first hundred years is scattered among modern relics that generally overwhelm them. A cannon here, a monument there . . . understated remnants of a heritage obscured by time.

A plaque mounted on a boulder in Pershing Square marks the northwest corner of the original presidio quadrangle, and a pair of cannon once mounted in embrasures at El Castillo de San Joaquin guard the square's flagpole. Cast in Peru at the end of the seventeenth century, these cannon—called San Francisco and Virgen de Barbaneda—are among a handful scattered around the presidio; their compatriots can be found by the doors to the Officers' Club, and at Fort Point.

The old stone powder magazine on the corner of Anza Avenue and Sheridan Street—a squat, whitewashed structure capped by a tile roof—was built between 1847 and 1863 using materials salvaged from the old adobe fort. Adobe from the original presidio is also part of the walls within the Officers' Club.

The tail end of the overland route from Mexico to San Francisco that was blazed in 1775 and in 1776 by de Anza and his entourage of settlers is part of the presidio's growing trail network. You can tread the path of the pioneers—now overlaid by roadways and pavement—for about 3 miles from Mountain Lake (where the Anza Expedition camped) in the southern reaches of the park north to the Golden Gate Bridge.

Fort Point, in the shadow of the bridge, is built on the promontory once occupied by El Castillo de San Joaquin. Exhibits in the imposing Civil War–era bastion recall the adobe structure well, but the old brick fort has much more to offer—a tour of its spiraling tiers, corridor-like living quarters, and cavernous casements leads to the exposed barbette tier at the top of the fort, from which you can enjoy fabulous views of the entire Bay Area. Fort Point is open Friday, Saturday, and Sunday from 10:00 A.M. to 5:00 P.M.; it is closed Monday through Thursday, and on Thanksgiving, Christmas, and New Year's Day. An audio tour and a printed interpretive guide are available. For more information, call (415) 561–4395 or visit the Web site at www.nps.gov/fopo.

Education and Outdoor Recreation

The Presidio of San Francisco and the surrounding Golden Gate National Recreation Area overflow with opportunities for recreation and education. Historic sites include the San Francisco National Cemetery, an absolutely incredible place to wander; the many turn-of-the-twentieth-century batteries that line the Coastal Trail south of the Golden Gate Bridge; the bridge itself, completed in 1937 and now an integral feature of the landscape; Crissy Field, the domain of military aviators in the 1920s and 1930s; and Fort Winfield Scott, with its impressive Spanish-revival style architecture and sloping parade ground.

Natural history is a major facet of the modern presidial experience. About 15 miles of developed trails wander through the park, including the 3.4-mile-long Golden Gate Promenade, which traces the bayshore along Crissy Field, and a stunning 3.6-mile segment of the Coastal Trail, which links the end of the promenade with a portion of the Anza Trail and offers access to the Golden Gate Bridge, a number of batteries, fabulous views of Lands End and the Marin Headlands, and Baker Beach. Restored natural areas including Lobos Creek, Inspiration Point, and the marsh at Crissy Field are also open to exploration. And then there are the beaches—Baker, China, and East, which front on the bay or the strait, and Ocean, an incredible stretch of sand along San Francisco's Pacific front, and one of the best places on the planet to enjoy a sunset.

Visitor Centers

Stashed in a redbrick barracks built in the 1890s, the William Penn Mott Jr. Visitor Center is an excellent starting point for any journey through the presidio—a hub of historical displays, books, and park information. The visitor center is housed in Building 102 on Montgomery Street, the fourth building from the right (second from the left) as you face the barracks row. It is open from 9:00 A.M. to 5:00 P.M. daily, with the exception of Thanksgiving, Christmas, and New Year's Day, when it is closed. For more information, call (415) 561–4323. Note that the Montgomery Street site was undergoing renovations as of this printing; the visitor center is temporarily housed in the Officers' Club on Moraga Avenue.

The Crissy Field Center, which overlooks a restored tidal marsh and offers easy access to the Golden Gate Promenade, is located in a Mason Street building that once served as an army commissary and a photo lab. The center hosts a variety of programs for the environmentally curious of all ages; check out the center's expansive Web site or call for more information. The center is open Wednesday through Sunday from 9:00 A.M. to 5:00 P.M.

The Warming Hut, located on the Golden Gate Promenade at West Crissy Field, houses an information kiosk, gifts, and a small cafe. It is open seven days a week from 9:00 A.M. to 5:00 P.M.

The focus of the Gulf of the Farallones National Marine Sanctuary Visitor Center, also located on West Crissy Field, is more than 1,200 square miles of protected coastline and open ocean west of San Francisco Bay and the Point Reyes National Seashore. The compact center, housed in the historic Coast Guard Station, is stuffed with fascinating exhibits, information, books, and gifts. Managed by the Farallones Marine Sanctuary Association, the center is open Wednesday through Sunday from 10:00 A.M. to 4:00 P.M. For more information, call the Farallones Marine Sanctuary Association at (415) 561–6625 or visit www.farallones.org.

Nearby Points of Interest

San Francisco takes great pride in its past, and showcases that diverse history whenever possible. From Chinatown to the Embarcadero, North Beach to Potrero Hill, Alcatraz Island to Union Square, there is plenty to see and learn. The Exploratorium and Palace of Fine Arts, which are adjacent to the presidio on the east, are great places to start your explorations.

The definitions below are specific to California's missions and presidios, and do not necessarily reflect modern usage.

Alcalde: A mayor or magistrate. A title also bestowed on the Native leaders of Indian *rancherias*.

Alta California: The frontier of New Spain roughly encompassed within the boundaries of today's modern state of California was known as Alta (or Upper) California, and was thus differentiated from Baja (or Lower) California, which is currently part of Mexico.

Asistencia (*estancia*): An auxiliary or "helper" mission established secondary to an existing mission.

Calderon: Cauldron or large pot.

Californio: The name by which California ranch owners and politicians of Mexican descent were known after about 1820.

Campanario: A wall, most often attached to a mission church, in which bells are hung.

Campanile: Bell tower.

Camposanto: Churchyard cemetery.

Castillo: Fortress.

Cocina (*pozoleria*): Kitchen.

Comandancia: Headquarters of the comandante, or commander, of a military post.

Comandante: Commander.

Convento: Living quarters for padres; a cloister or monastery.

Corredor: Covered walkways, sometimes incorporating arches; an arcade.

Cuartel: Soldier's quarters; barracks.

Fanega: A unit of measurement for grains and other dry goods used in mission days.

Fray: Brother or friar of a religious order.

Herreria: Blacksmith's shop.

Hornos: Adobe ovens constructed in a beehive shape.

Hospice: An inn.

Ladrillos: Floor tiles.

Las Posadas: A reenactment of Joseph's search for an inn for his wife, the mother of Jesus Christ, traditionally presented at Christmastime.

Lavanderia: A basin in which laundry is cleaned (sometimes used by Mission Indians for bathing).

Mayordomo: Overseer of a mission's domestic and agricultural concerns.

Metate: A stone vessel in which grains such as corn or wheat were ground into flour. Used in association with mano, or pestle.

Monjerio: A dormitory for unmarried women.

Neophyte: A Mission Indian who has been indoctrinated in the Catholic religion.

New Spain: The Spanish colonial term for Mexico.

Plaza de Armas: Presidial parade ground.

Quince Anos: A celebration held on or near a girl's fifteenth birthday.

Rancheria: A Native village. Missions were often established near populations of Indians clustered in *rancherias*, giving the missions an ample population of future neophytes.

Rancho: A ranch, associated with a mission during the Spanish era, held privately in the Mexican era.

Reredos: An ornamental backdrop for an altar, sometimes gilded, featuring niches in which religious statuary is installed.

Sala: A living room or sitting room.

Soldados: Soldiers.

Soldados de cuera: Leatherjackets, so named for the buckskin armor they wore; soldiers of the Alta California frontier.

Tejas: Curved roof tiles.

Vaqueros: Cowboys.

The list that follows is by no means inclusive. Many of the books, papers, and pamphlets mentioned here are available for purchase at the various missions and presidios, which also offer free materials (and often Web resources) that include good information.

A Companion to California, James D. Hart, Oxford University Press. 1978.

A Hiker's Guide to California Native Places, Nancy Salcedo, Wilderness Press. 1999.

A History of the Presidio of Monterey, Kibbey M. Horne/Defense Language Institute Foreign Language Center, Presidio of Monterey. 1970.

A World Transformed: Firsthand Accounts of California Before the Gold Rush, edited by Joshua Paddison, Heyday Books. 1999.

The Burning of Monterey: The 1818 Attack on California by the Privateer Bouchard, Peter Uhrowczik, CYRIL Books. 2001.

California Missions: A Guide to the State's Spanish Heritage (California Traveler Guidebooks), Gregory Lee, Renaissance House Publishers. 1992.

The California Missions: A Pictorial History, Sunset Editors, Sunset Books. 1979.

California's El Camino Real and Its Historic Bells, Max Kurillo and Erline Tuttle, Sunbelt Publications. 2000.

California's Missions, edited by Ralph B. Wright, Lowman Publishing Co. 1950, 1999.

California: The Golden Shore by the Sundown Sea, W. H. Hutchinson, Star Publishing Company. 1980.

The Carmel Mission, Sydney Temple, Western Tanager Press. 1980.

El Castillo de San Francisco: A History Under Spain and Mexico 1776–1846, John Phillip Langelier and Daniel Bernard Rosen, U.S. Department of the Interior. 1992.

Exploring Point Reyes National Seashore and Golden Gate National Recreation Area, Tracy Salcedo-Chourré, Globe Pequot Press. 2003.

Fort Point: Sentry at the Golden Gate, John A Martini, Golden Gate National Park Association. 1991.

The History of Alta California, Antonio María Osio, translated, edited, and annotated by Rose Marie Beebe and Robert M. Senkewicz, University of Wisconsin Press. 1996.

Indian Life at Mission San Luis Rey, Pablo Tac, translated by Minna and Gordon Hewes, Old Mission San Luis Rey and San Luis Rey Mission Indian Foundation. 1952, 1998.

The Indians of Mission Santa Barbara in Paganism and Christianity, Maynard Geiger, OFM, Ph.D., Franciscan Fathers of Old Mission Santa Barbara. 1986.

Junípero Serra: The Illustrated Story of the Franciscan Founder of California's Missions, Don DeNevi and Noel Francis Moholy, Harper and Row. 1985.

Lands of Promise and Despair: Chronicles of Early California, 1535–1846, edited by Rose Marie Beebe and Robert M. Senkewicz, University of Santa Clara and Heyday Books. 2001.

The Life and Times of Fray Junípero Serra, Msgr. Francis J. Weber, EX Nature Books. 1988.

Little Chapters About San Juan Capistrano, St. John O'Sullivan. 1928.

Mission La Concepción Purísima, Fr. Zephyrin Engelhardt, OFM, McNally & Loftin, Publishers. 1986.

Mission San Buenaventura (The Mission by the Sea), pamphlet from Mission San Buenaventura. No date.

Mission San Juan Capistrano Map and Guide, Mission San Juan Capistrano Docent Society. 2000, 2003.

Mission San Luis Rey, A Pocket History, Harry Kelsey, Mission San Luis Rey. No date.

Mission San Rafael: A Historical Guide, Katherine Coddington, Northern California Shopper. 1996.

Mission Santa Barbara: Queen of the Missions, Maynard Geiger, OFM, Ph.D., Franciscan Friars of California. 1986, 2001.

Mission Santa Inés: The Hidden Gem, Cresencia and Dal Olmstead, Capuchin Franciscans/Mission Santa Inés. 1995.

Mission Santa Inés Virgen Y Martir, Fr. Zephyrin Engelhardt, OFM, McNally & Loftin, Publishers. 1986.

The Missions: California's Heritage (series of twenty-one books describing individual missions), Mary Null Boulé, Merryant Publishers, Inc. 1988.

The Missions of California, Melba Levick, text by Stanley Young, Chronicle Books. 1988.

The Missions of California: A Legacy of Genocide, edited by Rupert Costo and Jeannett Henry Costo, Indian Historian Press. 1987.

The Ohlone Way, Malcolm Margolin, Heyday Books. 1978.

Old Mission San Juan Capistrano, Raymond C. Kammerer, KM Communications. 1980.

Oxford Dictionary of Saints, David Farmer, Oxford University Press. 1978, 1997.

Post and Park: A Brief Illustrated History of the Presidio of San Francisco, Stephen A. Haller, Golden Gate National Park Association. 1997.

Ramona, Helen Hunt Jackson. 1884.

Saints of the California Missions, Norman Neuerburg, Bellerophon Books. 2001.

San Diego de Alcalá: California's First Mission, I. Brent Eagen, brochure available at Mission San Diego de Alcalá. No date.

San Francisco Solano de Sonoma (The Sonoma Mission), Robert S. Smilie, Valley Publishing. 1975.

Santa Barbara: Her Story, Capistran J. Haas, OFM, Old Mission Santa Barbara. 1988.

Santa Cruz County History Journal 3 (1997), Art and History Museum of Santa Cruz County.

The Spanish Frontier in North America, David J. Weber, Yale University Press. 1992.

The Story of Mission San Antonio de Pala, Fr. J. M. Carrillo MCCJ. 1959.

The Swallows of Capistrano, Lydian Bruton, Paragon Agency/Old Mission San Juan Capistrano. 1975.

Webster's New World Spanish Dictionary, edited by Mike Gonzalez, William Collins & Sons Co. Ltd. 1985.

Web Sites

California Mission History: www.californiamissions.com

California Missions: http://missions.bgmm.com

California Mission Studies Association: www.ca-missions.org

California State Historical Landmarks: http://ohp.parks.ca.gov

Catholic Community Forum: www.catholicforum.com/saints

Monterey County Historical Society: http//:users.dedot.com/mchs

Monterey State Historic Park: www.mbay.net/mshp

Press Any Key.com: www.pressanykey.com/missions/index.html

San Diego Historical Society: www.sandiegohistory.org

San Francisco Museum and Historical Society: www.sfhistory.org

Photo Credits

PAGE 7: Mission San Luis Rey de Francia, exterior, by Bertrand Muller Arthus; Banc Pic 1963.002:0993—C; digital HN00115a; courtesy of the Bancroft Library, University of California, Berkeley.

PAGE 8: Mission San Luis Rey de Francia, floor plan, by Charles Avril; Banc Pic 1963.002:0993a—C; digital HN002578a; courtesy of the Bancroft Library, University of California, Berkeley.

PAGE 10: Presidio of San Francisco (1815) by Louis Choris; fG420.K84C6 1822x Part 3 Plate II; digital brk00000370_24a; courtesy of the Bancroft Library, University of California, Berkeley.

PAGE 14: Padre Narciso Duran and Indian child by Duflot de Monfras; book illustration xF851.D85 v.1 Fol. p. 199; brk00002940_24a; courtesy of the Bancroft Library, University of California, Berkeley.

PAGE 16: Mission Indians dancing, by Wilhelm Tilesius von Tilenau; Banc Pic 1963.002:1023—FR; digital HN000490a; courtesy of the Bancroft Library, University of California, Berkeley.

PAGE 80: Mission Santa Bárbara, rear view, by Henry Chapman Ford; Banc Pic 1963.002:0917:08—ffALB; digital HN002655a; courtesy of the Bancroft Library, University of California, Berkeley.

PAGE 108: Mission San Miguel (late 1800s), by Henry Chapman Ford; Banc Pic 1963.002:0918:11—ffALB; digital HN002660a; courtesy of the Bancroft Library, University of California, Berkeley.

PAGE 114: Mission San Antonio de Padua (late 1800s), by Henry Chapman Ford; Banc Pic 1963.002:0918:14—ffALB; digital HN002664a; courtesy of the Bancroft Library, University of California, Berkeley.

PAGE 136: Mission San Juan Bautista, by Henry Chapman Ford; Banc Pic 1963.002:0918:16—ffALB; digital HN002666a; courtesy of the Bancroft Library, University of California, Berkeley.

PAGE 210: The Presidio of Monterey (1791 or 1792), by José Cardero; Banc Pic 1963.002:1310—FR; digital HN000971a; courtesy of the Bancroft Library, University of California, Berkeley.

PAGE 219: The Presidio of San Francisco (1849), by unknown artist; Banc Pic 1963.002:0625:01—A; digital HN002009c; courtesy of the Bancroft Library, University of California, Berkeley.

All other photos are by the author, Tracy Salcedo-Chourré.

About the Author

Tracy Salcedo-Chourré has authored more than twenty hiking and exploring guidebooks to locales in California and Colorado, including *Hiking Lassen Volcanic National Park*, *Best Easy Day Hikes Lake Tahoe*, and *Exploring Point Reyes National Seashore and Golden Gate National Recreation Area*. She lives with her husband, three sons, and a small menagerie of pets in California's Wine Country.